Asia's naval expansion:
an arms race in the making?

Geoffrey Till

Asia's naval expansion: an arms race in the making?

Geoffrey Till

IISS The International Institute for Strategic Studies

The International Institute for Strategic Studies

Arundel House | 13–15 Arundel Street | Temple Place | London | WC2R 3DX | UK

First published December 2012 by **Routledge**
4 Park Square, Milton Park, Abingdon, Oxon, OX14 4RN

for **The International Institute for Strategic Studies**
Arundel House, 13–15 Arundel Street, Temple Place, London, WC2R 3DX, UK
www.iiss.org

Simultaneously published in the USA and Canada by **Routledge**
711 Third Ave., New York, NY 10017

Routledge is an imprint of Taylor & Francis, an Informa Business

© 2012 The International Institute for Strategic Studies

DIRECTOR-GENERAL AND CHIEF EXECUTIVE Dr John Chipman
EDITOR Dr Nicholas Redman
ASSISTANT EDITOR Janis Lee, Alexa van Sickle
EDITORIAL Dr Jeffrey Mazo, Sarah Johnstone, Dr Ayse Abdullah
COVER/PRODUCTION John Buck, Kelly Verity
COVER IMAGE U.S. Navy/Julia A. Casper

The International Institute for Strategic Studies is an independent centre for research, information and debate on the problems of conflict, however caused, that have, or potentially have, an important military content. The Council and Staff of the Institute are international and its membership is drawn from almost 100 countries. The Institute is independent and it alone decides what activities to conduct. It owes no allegiance to any government, any group of governments or any political or other organisation. The IISS stresses rigorous research with a forward-looking policy orientation and places particular emphasis on bringing new perspectives to the strategic debate.

The Institute's publications are designed to meet the needs of a wider audience than its own membership and are available on subscription, by mail order and in good book-shops. Further details at www.iiss.org.

British Library Cataloguing in Publication Data
A catalogue record for this book is available from the British Library

Library of Congress Cataloging in Publication Data

ADELPHI series
ISSN 1944-5571

ADELPHI 432–433
ISBN 978-0-415-69638-8

Contents

ACKNOWLEDGEMENTS

The research for this book owes much to countless scholars and sailors around the world too numerous to list. But they know who they are and that I am grateful for their help. But I would like to single out the last-minute assistance provided by Peter Swartz of the Center for Naval Analysis in Washington and by the splendid team at the IISS led by Nick Redman, namely Alexa van Sickle, Janis Lee, John Buck, Christian Le Mière and Henry Boyd, who provided tremendous underway support. Of course responsibility for any errors of omission or commission remains mine.

Map 1 **Southeast Asia**

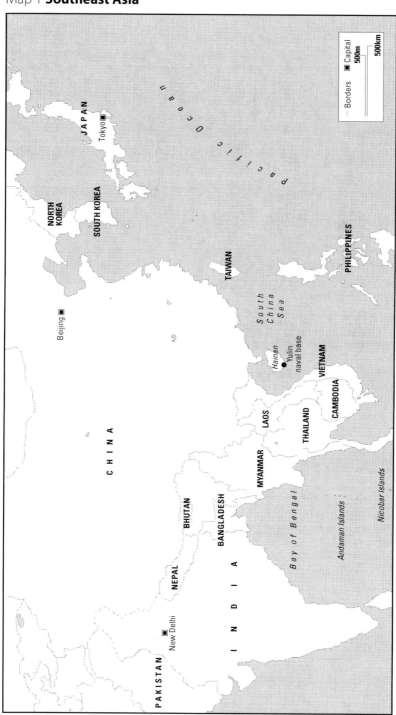

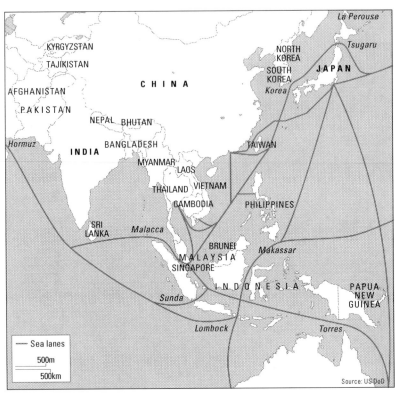

Map 2 **Asia sea lanes**

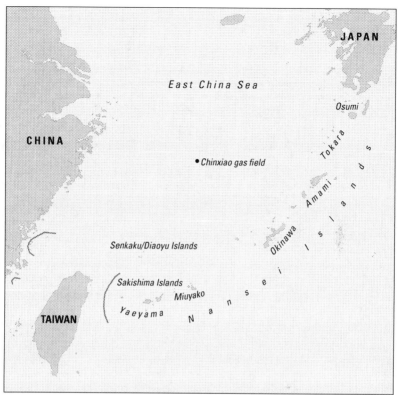

Map 3 **East China Sea**

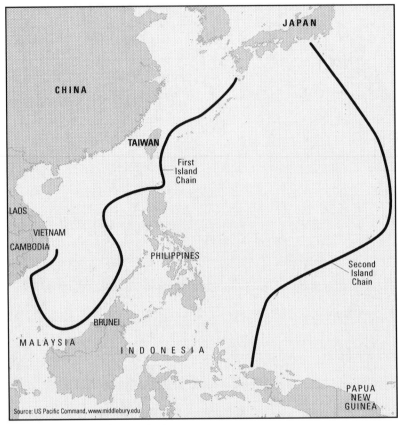

Map 4 **Chinese island chains**

INTRODUCTION

We can all look at the types of ships and the types of
airplanes and the numbers of airplanes – that's interesting and worthy of note. But it is how countries elect
to use those capabilities, and what the purposes are
that they see, and how they will use them and how
they will interact with other navies. That's important
and that's why this dialogue is under way.

Admiral Gary Roughead,
US Chief of Naval Operations, in China for talks
and an international fleet review in 2009[1]

The strength of navies in the Asia-Pacific region has increased
in an unprecedented fashion in the first decade of the twentieth
century. Economic growth has swelled defence budgets and
navies have claimed a growing share of national expenditure to
acquire new vessels and capabilities. This increase in focus and
effort is especially evident in Northeast Asia, an area primarily
engaged in what looks like as typical arms-racing behaviour:
the acquisition of platforms, weapons and sensors such as anti-
ship or land-attack cruise missiles, submarines, anti-submarine

capabilities (ASW), sea-based air- and missile-defence capabilities, electronic warfare capabilities, and so on, which only really make sense for operations against peer competitors.[2] With its acquisition of submarines and modern frigates, something of the same behaviour may be seen in Southeast Asia too.

We may also be seeing a substantial shift in the relative balance between US naval power and other countries in the Asia-Pacific region. Depending on the reaction of other states to this phenomenon, such a development, if true, may in itself be profoundly destabilising.

If Asia is already involved in an arms race, or is on the brink of one, might this have the destabilising consequences often associated with a naval arms race? Will it exacerbate the 'security dilemma' of countries in the region, by which one country's defensive preparations may make its neighbours feel less secure, sparking countervailing reactions on their part, which may in turn feed the original insecurity of the first country? Even if initiated by the domestic imperatives of the military–industrial complex rather than international concerns, such action–reaction cycles can be both economically wasteful and strategically dangerous.[3]

Scope of the study

In the Asia-Pacific region policymakers worry that naval modernisation, while not necessarily a problem in itself, could develop in ways that would tend to lead to destabilising arms races with all the associated malign consequences. For these purposes, it will be useful to explore the characteristics of an arms race in a little more detail and provide an overview of naval modernisation in the region. The major focus of this analysis will be specifically on the 'big four' – the navies of China, Japan, India and the United States, although there will be many references to the smaller, if often significantly growing lesser navies of the region (since here too the same processes are at work), The aim will be to investigate the missions and capabilities of these four most capable navies of the region in order to discern their likely strategic trajectory, and the extent of their proclivities for arms racing.

One set of naval missions is traditional and essentially competitive between states, and of a kind that would have been generally familiar to such nineteenth- and twentieth- century maritime strategists as Alfred Thayer Mahan and Sir Julian Corbett, notwithstanding the particular technological form such missions now take and the words often used to describe them. These missions include the concepts of sea control, the defence (and attack) of trade and territory and competitive naval diplomacy ('gunboat diplomacy'). These days, by extension, we may add the operation of a country's nuclear deterrent and ballistic-missile defence. The common element is that they are generally aimed at peer competitors: other states, their navies and military forces. The more the four navies being considered here emphasise these competitive missions, the greater the prospect for naval arms racing, although it need not necessarily be of a destabilising kind.

The second category comprises the non-traditional, essentially cooperative, system-based missions which make less obvious appearance in the works of Mahan and Corbett. They are basically to do with the mutual defence of common interests, most of which derive in large measure from the participation of states in the sea-based trading system on which globalisation depends. Mahan was aware of this phenomenon although he did not use the term; he was also aware of the risks it faced:

> This, with the vast increase in rapidity of communication, has multiplied and strengthened the bonds knitting together the interests of nations to one another,

> till the whole now forms an articulated system not
> only of prodigious size and activity, but of excessive
> sensitiveness, unequalled in former ages.[4]

The 'excessive sensitiveness' that Mahan had in mind derived from the fact that interdependence, and indeed dependency of any sort, inevitably produces targets for the malign to attack. His warnings have now acquired particular significance because the extraordinary extent and depth of today's version of globalisation depends on a supply-chain philosophy of 'just enough, just in time' that increases the system's vulnerability to disruption, not least because of the lamentably low stocks of such life essentials as oil and food that many states maintain. Steven M. Carmel, the senior vice-president of Maersk shipping, put it in May 2008:

> The global intermodal transportation system is like
> ... an endless system of conveyor belts; packages are
> always in motion, from where they enter the system to
> their final destination. Everything is always in motion,
> being shunted from one belt to the next. If there is
> one break anywhere, then the whole system stops ...
> Disruptions cascade through the system such that a
> disruption in LA is felt almost immediately in places
> like Singapore, Hong Kong and Yantien.[5]

To quote Mahan again, the 'commercial interest of the sea powers ... [lies] in the preservation of peace',[6] because that is a condition for good order in the system. From the uniquely close association of navies with economic activity derives a set of what might be called system-based naval roles, where the national purpose is served by helping to assure the safety of the international trading system. These include the collaborative protection of the international shipping trade through the maintenance of good order at sea and the conduct of expeditionary operations that are designed to protect the conditions for trade ashore. The Iran–Iraq war of the 1980s showed that state action can also threaten the system and so may need to be deterred or managed. However the most usual adversaries faced by navies largely concerned with the defence of the system are likely to be international terrorists, transnational criminals of various kinds, environmental challenges and the like and, in some cases, rogue states or rogue elements within failing states. The sheer range of the threats, and their global character, requires multilateral cooperation since no one state has the level of resource needed to cope with them all, nor is any one state willing to commit to the endeavour while others stand aside. Accordingly, the emphasis is on using naval forces to help develop, in Mahan's words, a maritime 'community of commercial interests and righteous ideals'.[7] Since such an approach is the very opposite of naval arms-racing behaviour, the more the main navies of the Asia-Pacific region adopt it, the less the chance of naval modernisation causing dangerous levels of instability.

Problems of analysis

A number of factors combine to make analysis difficult. Apart from the vexing problem of the words one uses to describe the two approaches described here,[8] the flexibility and adaptability of navies – one of their main selling points – is also one of the major analytical challenges: the conceptual differences between traditional maritime power projection and non-traditional expeditionary operations, for example, are undoubtedly fuzzy.

It is also difficult to draw hard conclusions from the evidence of naval thinking, the composition of fleets and from the record of their past and present activities. A comparison of the naval thought of the United States and China, for example, suffers from the fact that the former is much more transparent in its articulation of doctrine than is the latter. China's naval strategic thinking has to be inferred from its actions and acquisitions, the bland nature of the naval material in its successive White Papers and the discourse of a greatly expanding but largely unofficial 'commentariat' of retired officers, academics and analysts within China. American doctrine, on the other hand, is freely available if open to interpretation. India veers towards the US approach; Japan for its own very individual reasons, towards the Chinese.[9] Nor should the distinctive cultural and semantic approaches that the countries take as part of their strategic culture be forgotten as a factor that complicates comparison and analysis, particularly of China.[10]

Fleet operations – whether in the shape of routine day-to-day training for both traditional and non-traditional disciplines ranging from ASW to the conduct of boarding operations, exercises with or without other navies, planned deployments and the conduct of contingent operations – are also potentially ambiguous in the sense that they may or may not be regarded as preparation for interstate war. Many such operational deployments after all are intended to convey political messages quite apart from their immediate training or functional value and need to be assessed in that light. Moreover, the level of a navy's operational proficiency is notoriously hard to measure.

There are further ambiguities with regard to fleet composition, which is clearly the hardest of evidence available to the analyst. Fleet construction programmes express, and indeed are intended to make possible, a navy's mission priorities. But, although they provide the most solid expression of those priorities, most naval assets are multifunctional and this makes it difficult to allocate them to this or that mission. The Mk 41

Vertical Launching System currently deployed in increasing numbers of navies can, for example, simultaneously accommodate missiles and systems for anti-aircraft, anti-surface, anti-submarines and land attack, and the larger Strike Modules are capable of launching missiles for long-range strike or BMD. As a result individual warships can be highly versatile, particularly aircraft carriers.[11] Moreover, ships are rarely specifically designed for day-to-day diplomatic tasks. Finally, a platform-centric approach which stresses the numbers or even quality of individual ships is in any case of declining validity in an age in which electronic networks mean that a fleet of connected platforms can add up to something much more, or indeed sometimes less, than a sum of its parts.[12] Operational experience, skills and the manner in which the hardware is used matter too.

Moreover, a country's naval power is not simply a function of the size and effectiveness of its forces; instead these have to be set against the range and the operational demands of its commitments, and the resultant balance between resources and commitments has to be compared with the equivalent balances of other countries. All this makes it difficult to deduce workable metrics of relative power between nations. [13] Hence the sometimes heated discussion in the United States which followed the much quoted paper produced by Robert Work, before he assumed the post of under secretary of the navy, in which the current lead of the US Navy over everyone else was given much prominence.[14]

Admiral Gary Roughead , the US Navy's chief of naval operations, summed it all up quite nicely in Qingdao in 2009, when he was visiting the People's Liberation Army Navy (PLAN's) 60th anniversary fleet review, by noting in the passage – quoted at the outset of this chapter – that the intentions lying behind procurement were much more pertinent than the procurements themselves, as the opening quotation of this chapter shows.

This reflects a further difficulty in defining an arms race in the Asia-Pacific region. Arms races are usually popularly defined by the rapidity of the arms purchases and the action–reaction dynamics in the relationship between two or more countries. However, it is not just the acquisition of arms that defines a competitive arms relationship, but the type of arms procured and the doctrinal thought within a navy that lies behind them.

Rather than just being a general modernisation of naval forces in line with economic development, arms-racing behaviour requires specificity in the procurement of arms being sought, in that they are aimed against other states. It relies on perceptions of threat among participants: no state will race with another if it believes its intentions to be benign. Hence, the reasoning behind arms procurements, both real and perceived, is often more important than the acquisitions themselves.

Arms racing in perspective

Naval arms races such as the ones that preceded the First and Second World Wars are usually regarded as a peculiarly malignant and dangerously destabilising phenomena. They have been described by Professor Joe Maiolo of King's College London as 'an independent, self-perpetuating and often over-riding impersonal force that shape[s] events'. He has pointed out how 'politicians and military men the world over [have] struggled to cope in vain with the arms race as an underlying dynamic, the supreme wrecker of all master plans'.[15]

They are often defined primarily by an action–reaction dynamic among participants, whereby action of one party will create a reaction in another designed to counteract the original action. The resultant interactive competition develops a life of its own, becoming a process in which the efforts that states make to defend themselves sparks a reaction which actually makes them less secure.[16]

Working on the classic case of the Anglo-German naval arms race of 1909–14, analysts have shown arms races to have seven common characteristics. They are:

- driven by international rather than domestic imperatives;
- usually bilateral;
- intense in terms of effort, rapidity and expression;
- associated with high levels of political tension;
- operationally specific;
- indicative of high strategic stakes; and
- regarded as such.

Crucially, naval arms races are usually thought to increase the prospects for conflict. Many of these features were also apparent in the US–Soviet nuclear-arms race in the second half of the twentieth century: that too was externally driven, sometimes intense, accompanied by high levels of political tension, operationally specific and involving high stakes. It was also primarily bilateral, although a complicating factor was the emergence of three other nuclear-armed powers.

Rapidity in arms procurement and action–reaction dynamics may be necessary conditions for an arms race, but they are not sufficient. There needs also to be an intention, real or perceived, to use these increased capabilities against other states. In the Asia-Pacific region, as the 2012 disputes in the South and East China seas clearly show, there is certainly a conflictual edge to the international order, despite the increasingly close economic relations between the major powers of the region. Competition for territory and scarce resources, including minerals and fisheries, could well exacerbate these interstate disputes and tensions, especially when the region's manufacturing industries fully recover from the recent recession. Energy demand in the Asia-Pacific region has been rising at 3–5% annually for nearly 20 – years faster, some say, than new supplies can be located.[17] Resource dependency has become securitised with China, India and Japan engaged in acute competition for oil and gas resources in Russia, Kazakhstan, Myanmar, Iran and Sudan (now South Sudan), and this could easily develop geopolitical consequences.

These issues reflect assumptions that arms races are indeed a bad thing, exhausting societies economically and increasing the prospects of conflict. Arms racing in particular forms of weaponry may be particularly dangerous for their potentially destabilising effect. Others take a contrary view, arguing that although the accumulation of armaments may lead to conflict, it will not inevitably do so, and that in some cases the real problem may arise when countries choose not to accumulate new weaponry, thereby increasing the opportunity for others to engage in aggressive and hegemonic activity.[18]

At the same time, more general trade rivalries present tensions, particularly if such trading patterns are seen as unbalanced either in quantity or quality. The fact that some 60% of the containers going to the United States from China return empty can be seen by Americans as unsustainable in the long run, and may be ascribed to unfair practices. The United States has accordingly taken China to the WTO, as it believes Chinese leaders to be guilty of covert protectionism and the manipulation of the currency for its own benefit.[19] Moreover, many analysts would argue that China derives unfair trading benefit from the fact that it still falls far short of the domestic political standards expected of an open market economy. While trade between India and China has grown substantially in recent years, many Indians point out its structure is very much to their disadvantage.

Accommodating a rising China is also a potentially conflictual issue which sparks tensions and differences as well as agreement in the region in a manner which illustrates the continued impact on current policy of traditional nationalism. As Henry Kissinger has remarked, China, India, Vietnam and others all have a powerful, traditional sense of a 'national interest' for which they are prepared to fight. India, for example, 'has a propensity for strategic analysis ... comparable to early twentieth-century Europe'.[20] China maintains it is bent on a 'peaceful rise' of the sort that does not challenge the global system, but which will re-establish a natural, 'harmonious' and historic hierarchy in the Asia-Pacific that will threaten no-one.[21] However, old-fashioned Chinese nationalism is also apparent when the country's basic concerns are seen to be challenged. Episodes such as the Taiwan Straits crisis of 1995–96, the bombing of its Belgrade Embassy in 1999, the aerial collision off Hainan in 2001, or external interference in its domestic affairs have led to very nationalistic responses. Perhaps because of its continuing concerns with Taiwan and its many unresolved border disputes with its neighbours, China remains acutely sensitive to challenges to its sovereignty and for that reason studiedly resistant to the notion that, for humanitarian or any other reason, the international community has the right to intervene in another country's affairs.

Inevitably, the fear of being contained and so denied its natural and rightful place in the order of things causes resentment in China, particularly in military circles advocating a policy of hedging against the potential animosities of the other main players and the 'strategic encirclement' it might lead to.[22] President Hu Jintao apparently warned that the United States

strengthened its military deployments in the Asia-Pacific region, strengthened the US–Japan military alliance, strengthened strategic cooperation with India, improved relations with Vietnam, inveigled Pakistan, established a pro-American government in Afghanistan, increased arms sales to Taiwan and so on. They have extended outposts and placed pressure points on us from the east, south and west. This makes a great change in our geopolitical environment.[23]

Chinese Defence White Papers have consistently made the same kind of pained observations about the nationalist actions of other powers in the region, pointing to the 'growing complexity in the Asia Pacific security environment' as a result of the United States continuing 'to increase, quantitatively and qualitatively, its arms sales to Taiwan, sending a wrong signal to the Taiwan authorities … The US is realigning and reinforcing its military presence in this region by buttressing military alliances and accelerating deployment of missile defence systems.' At the same time, 'Japan is stepping up its constitutional overhaul, adjusting its military and security policies and developing the missile defence systems for future deployment. It has also markedly increased military activities abroad.'[24]

Such wariness is reciprocated by many of the countries of North and Southeast Asia, as well as by India and the United States, a wariness increased by concerns that Chinese defence expenditure and intentions are firstly far from transparent and, secondly, in worrying excess of what outsiders would consider to be China's legitimate security concerns.[25] Thus Japanese Prime Minister Yoshihiko Noda in August 2011:

China's rapid military build-up and expansion of the range of its military activities, coupled with a lack of transparency of its strategic intentions, are a cause of concern for Japan and the whole region. China's

high-handed attitude toward other countries, when
seen against the backdrop of its military capabilities
and recent behavior in the South China Sea and elsewhere, may destabilise the international order within
the region.[26]

From such perspectives, the 'China threat theory' is not as
facile as Beijing argues.[27] Nonetheless the United States and
Japan see China as 'a vital partner as well as a competitor.
The key is for us to make that competition friendly.'[28] While
the evolving relationship between a resurgent China and the
United States may be the most obvious indicator of residual
and possibly expanding national tensions, other countries have
their concerns with China too.[29] India, for example, is clearly
wary.[30]

And indeed, the simple fact of a changing economic and
military balance between all four of the region's strongest
naval powers, but especially between the United States and
China may in itself be a cause of major tension. Thus the much-
discussed 2009 Australian Defence White Paper suggested that
'As other powers rise, and the primacy of the US is increasingly tested, power relations will inevitably change. When this
happens there will be the possibility of miscalculation. There is
a small ... possibility of growing confrontation.'[31]

Other relationships in the region also attest to continued nationalist feelings, for instance between Thailand and
Cambodia or Japan, Korea and Russia, and to the fact that 'this
... region is home to many of the world's most brittle traditional and non-traditional threats'.[32]

Significantly but perhaps not surprisingly in this very
maritime region, these tensions often have a significant sea
dimension either in the sense that they impact on, or are caused
by, a host of maritime jurisdictional disputes stretching from

the Southeast Asia, through the South China Sea, the Taiwan Strait, the East China Sea and up to the Yellow Sea, the Sea of Japan and indeed to the South Kurile Islands north of Japan.[33] The defence of perceived national maritime sovereignty has, unsurprisingly, become a major determinant of naval development in the Asia-Pacific region, and the manner in which such disputes are handled, given their economic and political significance, will shed much light on the extent to which there really is an 'Asian way' that will largely preclude the possibility of a destabilising naval arms race.

The same point may be made about the nature of the naval modernisation process itself. Critics have pointed to the lack of transparency that applies to the naval construction plans not just of China but of many other countries in the Asia-Pacific region as well. This helps explain the absence of the kind of arms-control arrangements that limited naval arms-racing behaviour between Japan, the United States and the UK in the 1920s. These characteristics tend to make a destabilising naval arms race in the region more likely.

Cooperation not conflict?

Alongside these conflict drivers, there are major constraints on arms-racing behaviour. The 'Asian way' is a widely used term denoting the locals' preference for cooperation and consensus, an approach that owes much to the sense of community that derives from growing economic interdependence.[34] Illustrating the point, trade binds China and Japan together, for all their historic antipathies. The recovery in the Japanese economy from its doldrums in the 1990s until the onset of the 2008 economic crisis, for example, owed much to an expansion in Chinese demand. The same mutual benefits may be seen in the burgeoning sea-based economic links between China and India. Bilateral trade in 1993 was a meagre US$350 million, but by 2008–09, this had risen to US$36bn, two billion more than equivalent trade with the United States. By 2015, it could reach US$50bn. Joint China–India ventures consequently have become common, and together with increased trade levels are expected to help improve bilateral relations.[35] Such mutually advantageous linkages explain the regional importance of multilateral economic organisations such as the Asia Pacific Economic Cooperation [APEC] group.[36]

Trade has not in itself always been a sufficient deterrent to conflict historically. Even in the case of the best-known naval arms race – that between the UK and Germany in the early years of the twentieth century, the fact that these two countries were each other's biggest single trading partner did not stop them going to war. Yet the rhetoric of Asian nations themselves highlights what many East Asian leaders and commentators see as a key difference between them and Western countries: a focus on a consensual approach. Thus Dr Han Seung-Soo, prime minister of the Republic of Korea:

> While not nearly as advanced as Europe's, Asia's growing multilateral institutions and cooperative regimes such as the ASEAN Regional forum, the ASEAN Plus Three, APEC, ASEM and the East Asian Summit, all attest to the building of new norms, prin-ciples and practice in Greater Asia.[37]

Many Asia-Pacific countries, moreover, have suffered from, and so have common interests against, terrorism and other forms of transnational crime both on land and at sea; increas-ingly, they accept the need to collaborate against such threats. The successful cooperation of Singapore, Malaysia, Indonesia and Thailand against the piracy once common in the Malacca and Singapore straits is a particularly good example of this approach. Hence also the policy emphasis on unofficial or semi-official 'track-two' activities such as the holding of conferences and workshops, which are intended to improve general understanding, to build security cooperation and to contain the adverse effects of intractable disputes such as that over the South China Sea and hopefully helping to resolve them.[38]

In the same spirit, both the main and the minor powers of the Asia-Pacific region continue to emphasise the benign nature of their intentions and expectations. China's 'smiling diplomacy' towards Southeast Asia and its partial abandonment of its earlier preference for bilateral rather than multinational forums in which its relative power could be compensated for by a banding together of otherwise weaker players, paid dividends in the early years of this century. Moreover, in facilitating the Six-Party talks with North Korea, China has shown an increased readiness to cooperate with others to everyone's benefit. All concerned have acknowledged the advantages of strategic dialogue, the establishment of confidence-building measures and the development of more cooperative relationships between them. In China for example, there are those who even argue for the constructive presence of the United States, and its Navy, as a means of both assuring the safety of the Sea Lines of Communications (SLOCs) on which China's security depends while at the same time making a dangerous resurgence of Japanese militarism at sea less likely.[39]

Notes

1 Quoted in Tania Branigan, 'China Unveils Fleet of Submarines in Bid to Build Global Trust', *Guardian*, 22 April 2009.

2 Tim Huxley, 'Controlling Asia's Arms Race: Multiple Competitions, Suspicions Breed Instability' *DefenseNews*, 30 May 2011.

3 Mary Kaldor, *The Baroque Arsenal* (London: Andre Deutsch, 1982), pp. 219–30.

4 A.T. Mahan, *Retrospect and Prospect* (London: Sampson, Low, Marston & Co., 1902), p. 144.

5 Stephen M. Carmel (senior vice president, maritime services,

Maersk line), in a keynote address to the USNI/AFCEA Joint War Fighting Conference, San Diego, CA, 14 May 2008, see http://blog.usni.org/?p=3272. Carmel made the point that the fighting services are totally reliant on an enabling supply chain derived from the effective workings of this system as well.

6 A.T. Mahan, *The Problem of Asia and its Effect on International Policies* (London: Sampson, Low, Marston & Co., 1900), p. 99.

7 Mahan, *Retrospect and Prospect*, pp. 177–8.

8 Debate in this area is bedeviled by the lack of an agreed terminology. Robert Cooper, in his book *The Breaking of Nations: Order and Chaos in the Twenty-first Century*, usefully divides states into three categories: pre-modern, modern and post-modern. These in turn help produce the concept of pre-modern, modern and post-modern navies, thereby emphasising the link between the development of navies to globalisation and to the nature of the state they serve; Cooper, *The Breaking of Nations: Order and Chaos in the Twenty-first Century* (London: Atlantic Books, 2004) pp. 37–43. Although this categorisation finds expression in naval analysis (see Geoffrey Till, *Seapower: A Guide for the 21st Century* (London: Routledge, 2009, 2nd ed.) pp. 1–19, the association of the word 'modern' with state-centred and traditional modes of behaviour is undoubtedly awkward. The more widely used traditional/non-traditional concepts of security are not entirely satisfactory either, for navies have engaged in such 'non-traditional' activities as the protection of marine resources for centuries. All the same, this study will generally use the alternate descriptors of traditional and state-based on the one hand and non-traditional and system-based on the other.

9 For an account of American doctrine see General James T. Conway, commandant US Marine Corps, Admiral Gary Roughead, chief of naval operations and Admiral Thad W. Allen, commandant US Coast Guard, *A Cooperative Strategy for 21st Century Seapower* (Washington DC: Department of the Navy, October 2007) and *Naval Operations Concept 2010* (Washington DC: Department of the Navy, July 2010). See also *Indian Maritime Doctrine* (New Delhi: Integrated Headquarters, Ministry of Defence [Navy], 2004 and 2009); and *Freedom to Use the Seas: India's Maritime Military Strategy* (New Delhi: Integrated Headquarters, Ministry of Defence [Navy], 2007). Public expressions of Chinese and Japanese naval doctrine, however, are conspicuous by their absence, but see Toshi Yoshihara and James R. Holmes, *Dragon and Eagle: China's Rise and the US Maritime Strategy* (Annapolis, MD: Naval Institute Press, 2010); Yoshihara and Holmes, *Japanese Maritime Strategy in the 21st Century: Tokyo's Next Fateful Choice* (London: Routledge, forthcoming); and Euan Graham, *Japan's Sea Lane Security, 1940–2004: A Matter of Life and Death?* (London: Routledge, 2006).

10 For an authoritative American view of the impact of strategic culture on Chinese naval thinking see Toshi

Yoshihara and James R. Holmes, *Red Star Over the Pacific: China's Rise and the Challenge to US Maritime Strategy* (Annapolis, MD: Naval Institute press, 2010), pp. 14–43, 154–62. See also the same authors' *Indian Naval Strategy in the Twenty-first Century* (London: Routledge, 2009), pp. 62–78.

11 Terry B Kraft, 'It Takes a Carrier: Naval Aviation and the Hybrid Fight', *Proceedings of the USNI*, September 2009, http://www.usni. org/magazines/proceedings/2009-09/ it-takes-carrier-naval-aviation-and-hybrid-fight.

12 Hence the stress by Admiral Jonathan Greenert, chief of naval operations, and his colleagues on the 'payload-centric' Single Naval Battle approach. See Jonathan Greenert, 'Payloads over Platforms: Charting a New Course', *Proceedings of the US Naval Institute*, July 2012. http://www.usni.org/ magazines/proceedings/2012-07/ payloads-over-platforms-charting-new-course.

13 An interesting debate on the problems of metrics may be found in Ronald O'Rourke, *China Naval Modernization: Implications for US Navy Capabilities – Background and Issues for Congress* (Washington DC: Congressional Research Service, June 2010), pp. 23–4, and the same author's equivalent report for 2009 (Washington DC: Congressional Research Service, 23 November 2009), pp. 19–20.

14 Robert Work, *The US Navy: Charting a Course for Tomorrow's Fleet* (Washington DC: CSBA, 2008). I am grateful to Robert Work for the opportunities to discuss this issue

with him and his staff in August 2010. For an earlier investigation of the problem, see Robert O'Rourke, *Naval 17 Force Planning: Breaking Old Habits of Thought* (Washington DC: Congressional Research Service Report 93-332, 19 March 1993).

15 Joe Maiolo, *Cry Havoc: The Arms Race and the Second World War* (London: John Murray, 2010), p. 2.

16 The standard discussion of arms races and dynamics may be found in Barry Buzan and Eric Herring, *The Arms Dynamic in World Politics* (Boulder, CO and London: Lynne Rienner, 1998), esp pp. 75–9.)

17 Philip Andrews-Speed, Xuanli Liao and Roland Danreuther, *The Strategic Implications of China's Energy Needs*, Adelphi Paper 346 (Oxford: Oxford University Press for the IISS, 2002), p. 78. For the background see Kenneth S. Deffeyes, *Hubbert's Peak: The Impending World Oil Shortage* (Princeton, NJ: Princeton University Press, 2008); '2020 Vision: The IEA Puts a Date on Peak Oil Production', *Economist*, 10 December 2009.

18 See Colin Gray, *Weapons Don't Make War* (Lawrence, KS: University of Kansas Press, 1993), pp. 55–6. Quoting Bernard Brodie's famous description of the naval arms-control regime of the interwar period as one of 'faith, hope and parity', Gray argues that Hitler's aggression in Europe was encouraged by the reluctance of France and Britain to engage in the necessary defence expenditure, casting doubt thereby on the assumption that arms control is necessarily a good thing.

19 Steven R. Weisman, 'China Stand on Imports Upsets US', *New York*

Times, 16 November 2007. See also the discussion of this issue in *South China Morning Post*, 12 February 2007; 'US–China Trade Spats May Cloud Obama Visit', *Straits Times*, 7 November 2009.

20 Henry A. Kissinger, keynote address, 8th IISS Global Strategic Review, Geneva, 10 September 2010, http://www.iiss.org/conferences/global-strategic-review/global-strategic-review-2010/plenary-sessions-and-speeches-2010/keynote-address/henry-kissinger/?locale=en.

21 Wang Jisi, *China's Road to Peaceful Development and the United States*, Documento de Trabajo del Trabajo del real Instituto Elcano 2007–11, provides an excellent short discussion of this point; Amitav Acharya, 'Will Asia's Past Be its Future?', *International Security*, vol. 28, no. 3, Winter 2003–04, pp. 149–64. See also Barry Desker, 'New Security Dimensions in the Asia-Pacific' *Asia-Pacific Review*, vol. 15, no. 1, 2008, pp. 56–75.

22 See Jonathan Holslag, *Trapped Giant: China's Military Rise*, Adelphi 416 (London: IISS, 2011).

23 Cited in Andrew J. Nathan and Bruce Gilley, *China's New Rulers: the Secret Files* (London: Granta, 2003), pp. 207–8.

24 Chinese Defence White Papers for 2006 and 2004; see Robert Karniol, 'China Defends Stance on Taiwan', *Jane's Defence Weekly*, 3 January 2005.

25 See, for example, Office of the [US] Secretary of Defense, *Annual Report to Congress: Military Power of the People's Republic of China* (Washington DC, 2009), executive summary and pp. 31–8.

26 Quoted in 'Japan's New PM Set to Hold Steady on Alliance', *Jane's Defence Weekly*, 7 September 2011.

27 For the China threat theory see John J. Mearsheimer, 'China's Unpeaceful Rise', *Current History*, vol. 105, no. 690, April 2006, pp. 160–2; Hugh White, 'Why War in Asia Remains Thinkable', *Survival*, vol. 50, no. 6, December 2008–January 2009; and 'The Geostrategic Implications of China's Growth', in Ross Garnault and Ligang Song (eds), *China's New Place in a World Crisis* (Canberra: ANU E-press, 2009), pp. 89–102. Interestingly, after Singapore's Minister Mentor Lee Kuan Yew's suggestion that the Asia-Pacific needed the United States to 'balance' a resurgent China, there was a furious response from that country's citizens. 'Why Chinese Netizens are Upset', *Straits Times*, 5 November 2009, and '"Balance" Gets Lost in Translation', *Straits Times*, 6 November 2009. See also Li Daguang, 'US Factor in East Asia: More Pros than Cons', originally in *Global Times*, translated in *Straits Times*, 6 November 2009. Some suggest that China's superior power will ultimately prove acceptable so long as it remains non-threatening. See Acharya, 'Will Asia's Past Be its Future?', pp. 149–64.

28 President Obama, quoted in 'Beijing "a Partner and Competitor"', *Straits Times*, 11 November 2009.

29 For example, the ongoing border dispute continues to plague Indo-Chinese relations and Japan is concerned at China's capacity to out-manoeuvre it for influence in Southeast Asia. See, respectively, 'Clash of the Asian Giants', *Straits*

Times, 7 November 2009, and 'Japan and China Jostle for Influence', *Straits Times*, 6 November 2009.

30 Murray Scot Tanner, Kerry B. Dumbaugh and Ian M. Easton, *Distracted Antagonists, Wary Partners: China and India Assess their Security Relations* (Washington DC: CNA China Studies, September 2011). See also Jonathan Holslag, 'The Persistent Military Security Dilemma Between China and India', *Journal of Strategic Studies*, vol. 32, no. 6, December 2009, pp. 811–40.

31 Department of Defence, *Defending Australia in the Asia Pacific Century: Force 2030* (Canberra: Australian Government, Department of Defence, 2009) p. 33.

32 Address by Dr Han Seung-Soo, prime minister of the ROK, 28 September 2008 to the IISS–Asan Korea Forum 2008, reproduced in *Korea in the Emerging Asian Power Balance* (London: IISS, 2008), p. 22.

33 'Japan's Island Row No. 2 – with Russia', and 'Coast Guard Video Riles Japanese Lawmakers', both in *Straits Times*, 2 November 2010.

34 For examples of this kind of thinking see Kishore Mahbubani, *The New Asian Hemisphere: The Irresistible Shift of Global Power to the East* (New York: Public Affairs, 2008); and Barry Desker, 'Why War is Unlikely in Asia', RSIS Commentary no. 71 (S. Rajaratnam School of International Studies, 27 June 2008).

35 J. Mohan Malik, 'The Dragon Rises, the Elephant Stirs', *Guanxi*, vol. 2, no. 8, 2008; 'Trade "Can Cool" India–China Tensions', *Straits Times*, 21 January 2010.

36 Despite its voluntary non-binding approach, APEC appears to foster and liberalise regional trade and encourage an acceptance of mutual need between its 21 members. 'APEC Gives Trade a Big Boost', *Straits Times*, 10 November 2010. See also Barry Desker, *APEC at 20: Old Promises New Challenges*, RSIS Commentary no. 111 (Singapore: S. Rajaratnam School of International Studies: 11 November 2009).

37 Address by Dr Han Seung-Soo, p. 22. However, the debate about the relative weight of these organisations and their diverse memberships often also reflects a degree of national competitiveness, especially between China, Japan and the United States. See Goh Sui Noi, 'Shaping a New East Asia', *Straits Times*, 11 November 2009.

38 W. Lawrence S. Prabhakar, 'The Regional Dimension of Territorial and Maritime Disputes in Southeast Asia: Actors, Disagreements and Dynamics', and Sam Bateman, 'Building Good Order at Sea in Southeast Asia', both in Kwa Chong Guan and John K Skogan, *Maritime Security in Southeast Asia* (London: Routledge, 2007).

39 E.D. Feigenbaum, 'China's Military Posture and the New Economic Geopolitics', *Survival*, vol. 41, no. 2, Summer 1999; Li Daguang 'US Factor in East Asia: More Pros than Cons', *Watching America*, 5 November 2009, http://watchingamerica.com/News/37066/more-pros-than-cons-to-the-american-factor-in-asia/.

CHAPTER ONE

Naval modernisation, action–reaction dynamics and their drivers

The modernisation of Asian naval forces began in the 1980s as part of a growth in its share of global defence expenditure from 11% in the mid-1980s to 20% in 1995, with a corresponding leap in the region's arms imports.[1] A natural reflection of Asia's growing economic clout and political confidence, together with a need to replace obsolescent second-hand equipment acquired decades before, this was more a 'festival of competitive modernisation' than a potentially destabilising naval arms race as generally understood. In any case, it was largely brought to a halt by the Asian financial crisis of 1997.

By the early years of the twenty-first century, most countries in the region had recovered from this crisis sufficiently to resume naval modernisation programmes funded by steadily increasing levels of defence expenditure. Even when the main four navies of the Asia-Pacific region are temporarily left out of the analysis (they will be the major focus of later chapters), this is an area now seeing remarkable growth in the composition and operational aspiration of its naval forces.[2] In 2011, according to IISS calculations, Asian spending on defence surpassed that of Europe.[3] The French naval armaments firm DCNS, considered the Asia-Pacific region 'a future centre for defence business ... The defence market in the Asia-Pacific should be, in about 2016, a major market – even above the US.'[4] The US-based naval consultancy firm AMI International anticipates a naval spend in the Asia-Pacific of some US$170 billion by 2030.[5]

In the Asian context, defence-expenditure trends have been defined by Chinese spending patterns. The Chinese defence budget has long enjoyed double-digit percentage annual growth rates.[6] This rapidity of defence-spending growth, (and hence the impressive pace of naval modernisation) and increasingly assertive use of its new naval and coast-guard forces is one of the primary reasons why China's neighbours and potential rivals have been so alarmed by China's rise.[7] Yet, defence spending has increased as a percentage of GDP only gradually, lending weight to the argument that China's expenditure is in line with its remarkable economic growth and should therefore be seen as the natural development of capabilities by an emerging power rather than the aggressive procurement of equipment aimed at enforcing hegemony or defeating specific adversaries. However, the picture is complicated somewhat by the opacity of China's defence budget, which has greatly clouded the issue of exactly how much the country spends.

In the US, defence expenditure increased rapidly in the 2000s, partly owing to the extraordinary spending related to the wars in Iraq and Afghanistan. However, the budgetary pressures facing the government and the Department of Defense are putting significant constraints on the expansion of military capabilities.[8] Admiral Jonathan Greenert has repeatedly warned that the US Navy is 'running hot' with an unsustainable level of operational activity that further budgetary cuts can only exacerbate.[9]

This arguably only highlights the international factors driving the rebalance to Asia: given tight budgets, Washington might prefer to cut its overseas deployments and forces, but a desire to reassure allies and deter China is encouraging a more robust posture in the Asia-Pacific. Within Japan, defence spending has remained a relatively low percentage of GDP – about one per cent – since the end of the Second World War, owing to the country's pacific constitution, the security umbrella supplied by the US and the domestic unpopularity of defence expenditure in general. Yet, even with these factors, Japanese defence spending has now begun to creep up as a percentage of GDP and the perceived threat from North Korea and China has encouraged a broader public debate on defence capabilities.[10]

With the much discussed US rebalance to Asia having been announced in January 2012, and expanded upon at the Shangri-La Dialogue in June 2012, the sense of a competitive military relationship between China and the US has grown.

The rebalance has at its heart the development of an operational concept known as Air-Sea Battle, which aims to deter, defeat and disrupt anti-access and/or area-denial capabilities. Although the US Navy emphasises that this is a concept, and not a strategy, and is not specifically aimed at China, it is nonetheless widely seen as an American reaction to the development of China's asymmetric naval capabilities, typified by submarines, anti-ship missiles and small attack craft that seem designed to undermine the US Navy's substantial military advantages.[11] The practical, immediate effect of Air-Sea Battle – which aims to develop networked, integrated aerial and naval forces to assure access against an adversary – will be to increasingly disperse US forward-deployed forces throughout the region, complicating China's ability to prevent their entry to a theatre (anti-access) and their freedom of movement once there (area denial).

These developments reflect the burgeoning bilateral military rivalry developing between China and the US, even while their trade relationship continues to develop and deepen. Yet, there is evidence that other major navies in the region are similarly engaged in a form of military competition: Japan's 2010 white White Paper, for example, focused on a shift in the weight of its forces to its southern islands, in a clear demonstration of its growing concern over China, while pledging to increase its submarine force from 16 to 22 boats. India, meanwhile, has been alarmed by the extension of China's military reach into the Indian Ocean, with its development of support facilities and a rolling, counter-piracy flotilla on patrol in the region since January 2009 – the first out-of-area active operation for China in nearly 600 years.

It is not just the rapid development of China's armed forces that has alarmed the country's potential rivals. A perceived change in its diplomacy towards its neighbours in various maritime disputes, particularly in the South China and East China seas, since 2009 has fuelled concern about China's intentions as well as its capabilities. These factors have stimulated, for the first time in more than a decade, serious academic debate over whether the Asia-Pacific region is currently undergoing a form of arms race.

Patterns of acquisition

As changes in the size of Asian navies over the period of 2000–2012 demonstrate, the region has in the early years of the twenty-first century witnessed a doubling in the size of China's fleet (by tonnage) and sizeable increased in the South Korean and Indian fleets on the same measure. The increase in submarine capabilities, which has the potential to be especially destabilising because of their stealthy offensive potential, is particularly marked. The size of the Chinese and Japanese submarine fleets by tonnage have increased by roughly a third in just over a decade, while South Korea's has increased by two-thirds.

Growth in fleet size, 2000–12

	2000									
	US (Pacific Fleet)		China		Japan		India		South Korea	
	Hulls	Tonnage	Hulls	Tonnage	Hulls	Tonnage	Hulls	Tonnage	Hulls	Tonnage
SSBN	8	152,000	1	6,600	0	0	0	0	0	0
SSGN/SSN	30	236,800	5	28,000	0	0	0	0	0	0
SS/SSK	0	0	59	120,650	16	48,050	16	43,600	8	10,400
CV/CVN	5	500,000	0	0	0	0	0	0	0	0
CVS/H	0	0	0	0	0	0	1	29,100	0	0
PAS	13	366,150	0	0	0	0	0	0	0	0
C/DD/FF	53	419,300	60	157,900	55	245,800	20	81,500	15	49,900
FS	0	0	0	0	0	0	19	15,650	28	34,400
Total Subs	38	388,800	65	155,250	16	48,050	16	43,600	8	10,400
Total Surface	71	1,285,450	60	157,900	55	245,800	40	126,250	43	84,300

	2012									
	US (Pacific Fleet)		China		Japan		India		South Korea	
	Hulls	Tonnage	Hulls	Tonnage	Hulls	Tonnage	Hulls	Tonnage	Hulls	Tonnage
SSBN	8	152,000	4	32,100	0	0	0	0	0	0
SSGN/SSN	33	261,200	5	29,000	0	0	1	9,250	0	0
SS/SSK	0	0	55	142,900	18	65,100	14	38,600	12	17,400
CV/CVN	6	600,000	1	59,500	0	0	0	0	0	0
CVS/H	0	0	0	0	2	36,300	1	29,100	0	0
PAS	10	318,300	2	37,000	0	0	1	17,500	1	19,300
CC/DD/FF	59	487,300	75	266,000	45	256,050	22	110,200	20	87,000
FS	0	0	0	0	0	0	24	20,000	34	36,050
Total Subs	41	413,200	64	204,000	18	65,100	15	47,850	12	17,400
Total Surface	75	1,405,600	78	362,500	47	292,350	48	176,800	55	142,350
% Change 2000–2012	8	6	-2	31	13	35	-6	10	50	67
	6	9	30	130	-15	19	20	40	28	69

Source: IISS

Navies are modernising to an unprecedented extent throughout the Asia-Pacific region, and it is not hard to find evidence of at least some of the seven action–reaction dynamics in the area. This is especially true of the naval programmes of the 'big four', namely the US, China, India and Japan.

China's primary security concern remains internal stability, but this is increasingly being assured by the People's Armed Police, an organisation that was developed in the early 1990s in the wake of Tiananmen Square specifically to counter domestic protests. The armed forces are therefore much more focused on external contingencies than previously, and the armaments they are procuring are far better designed for regional and increasingly extra-regional conflicts.

Much has been made in international media of the development of China's first aircraft carrier, and it is true that this platform is symbolic of Beijing's growing confidence and willingness to deploy overseas. In September 2012, the *Liaoning*, the refurbished and modernised *Varyag*, returned from its tenth sea trials and was commissioned into the PLAN.[12] However, other platforms and weapons being integrated into the People's Liberation Army are perhaps of more concern for regional actors, and are in turn inspiring greater reactions. Japan's submarine expansion plans can be seen to be an attempt to counter both China's growing submarine fleet and its improving surface fleet through a strategy of sea denial; the planned expansion also exploits the perceived weakness of China's submarine-warfare capabilities. The People's Liberation Army Navy's Type 022 *Houbei*-class fast-attack craft, meanwhile, which are designed to be used in littoral waters rapidly to attack larger vessels with their eight C-803 anti-ship missiles, look largely like an attempt to blunt the naval superiority of the US and Japan and to prevent the deployment of their forces close to China's shores.

China's submarine development, meanwhile, has focused on procuring quieter, longer-endurance boats capable of evading US and Japanese ASW capabilities, in particular through the 12 *Kilo*-class vessels purchased from Russia in the 2000s and the *Yuan*-class boats currently being built domestically.

India, meanwhile, has plans afoot to commission three aircraft carriers within the next decade, two of which will be developed indigenously, and commissioned its first nuclear-powered submarine for two decades in early 2012. These blue-water capabilities might be thought to be at odds with the primary threats to the nation's security, which are far more local than global, since Pakistan and its apparent support for non-state armed groups is a far more immediate concern than China's activities in the region and beyond. Nevertheless, declaratory statements from both India's military and government have suggested that China's military development and the continued problem of their disputed border territories in the north are significant factors in justifying and in some cases even driving India's naval arms procurement.

These procurements suggest a level of interactivity in the military relationships of the four large navies and between them and the other significant navies of the region that may indicate the beginnings of an arms race. There is, at the same time, a desire to avoid conflict in the short term, with placatory statements often accompanying otherwise assertive activities. China regularly declares, for instance, that its military exercises or defence procurements are not aimed at other countries, as it did during the first Sino-Russian naval exercises in April 2012. US officials, including Defense Secretary Leon Panetta, have also played down the possibility that Air-Sea Battle and the rebalance were entirely focused on containing China, even though some aspects of both certainly look like that, not least to Beijing.[14] The deployment of up to four Littoral Combat Ships to Singapore starting in 2013, in particular, is not only a way in which the US can rapidly deploy naval force to the disputed regions of the South China Sea, but could be seen as an implicit threat to China. Beijing has since the mid-2000s expressed concern over its so-called 'Malacca Dilemma', whereby a vast majority of its imported energy resources passes through the narrow straits of Southeast Asia, primarily the Malacca Strait. This has increased the country's vulnerability to disruption of traffic through the strait, and the LCS deployment, sitting atop the Strait of Malacca Strait as it does, might be considered an implicit message from the US that it would be able selectively to disrupt Chinese shipping if required.

In this way there appears to be an arguable specificity to the activities of the big four navies, with their procurements, deployments and expenditure increasingly resembling a form of action–reaction that could bind them into a self-fulfilling dynamic of deterrence and armament.

Drivers of naval acquisition: external or internal?

Naval policymakers are clearly reacting, in the main, to the international environment as they see it. However, in some cases the incentive to modernise may be more to secure political leverage than to respond to, far less than to defeat, an adversary's military advantage – such as seems to apply to Taiwan's desire to up-grade its military forces in the face of increasing mainland strength. Thus as Taiwan's Information Minister, Philip Yang told Washington in July 2011:

> The US must help Taiwan to level the playing field. Negotiation with a giant like mainland China is not without its risks. The right leverage must be in place, otherwise Taiwan cannot credibly maintain its equal footing at the negotiation table.[15]

While external drivers are certainly prominent, there are other factors at play, even in the case of the most dramatic example of modernisation in the area, that of the PLAN. China, like most countries in the region, has strong domestic economic and political incentives to build up its defence industries. In the 1980s, there was a major defence conversion programme and, under the philosophy of 'Rich Nation: Strong Military', the encouragement of integrated thinking and dual-use technologies. According to President Deng Xiaoping, the PLA had to be developed in order to achieve four objectives:

- Cultivation of an armed force that is capable of modern warfare;
- training political soldiers;
- obtaining skills in science and technology; and
- cultivating working forces that are versatile in dual-use technology.[16]

The 2006 national plan emphasised the development of high-tech capabilities over the next 15 years, including 'new and high-end technologies for the space industry, aviation, ship and marine engineering, nuclear energy and fuel, and information technology for both military and civil purposes'. It mentioned the construction of new nuclear power stations and large aircraft, among others.[17] It was clear from the beginning that the defence industry would be at the heart of the economic revolution: at a working conference of the Commission of Science, Technology and industry for National Defence (COSTIND) in January 2006, Vice-Premier Huang Ju described the defence industry as a 'significant force of the country's scientific and technological innovation system'.[18]

China's military innovation accordingly needs to be seen as part of the country's broader long-term industrial planning. The 2010 White Paper emphasised civil–military integration and industrial consolidation: 'China has established and is striving to optimise those research and production systems for weaponry and equipment which cater to both military and civilian needs and sustain military potential in civilian capabilities.'[19] Major projects are consciously directed, coherently linked and appropriately funded to this end. The aviation and ship-building sectors are leading the innovation surge.[20]

Since its inauguration in 1982, for example, the China Shipbuilding Trading Company (CSTC), with its 27 shipyards, 66 manufacturing plants and 37 R&D institutes, has become the sole means by which China supplies more than a dozen kinds of naval platforms and auxiliaries including conventional submarines and missile frigates and destroyers. This is but a small part of a much larger export portfolio of civil projects, including bulk and crude carriers, large LPG (liquified petroleum gas) carriers and VLCCs (very large crude carriers) as well as bridges and steel for civil construction. Quite apart from the military strategic benefits of a home-grown capacity to design and build ships, weapons and sensors, the CSTC's activities foster industrial expertise and socio-economic development across the country.[21] It has opened offices in eight countries and exported to 52; having turned so much of its energies to exports, the CSTC's continued economic success depends on the overall prosperity and stability of the international system. This would seem, at first glance, to mitigate any competitive build-up of arms within the region.

The same kind of urge for defence-led technological development and innovation is equally manifest in India, South Korea and parts of Southeast Asia. Countries such as Singapore and Malaysia are anxious to develop the industrial skills associated with ship-building, weapons and sensors and systems integration. In reality, however, naval modernisation is often hampered by graft, corruption and programmatic incompetence in many countries. Indian naval programmes, for example, are constantly bedevilled by acquisition and dockyard inefficiencies. Other elements of 'Innenpolitik' can be found elsewhere, especially where the ruling elite protects its position by showering the military with resources to keep it happy and politically supportive.

Nonetheless, there is also throughout the region a clear desire for independence of strategic decision and for reduced reliance on foreign defence suppliers, whose record is distinctly spotty in terms of quality, cost and reliability. China has frequently suffered from major discontinuities in supply. In 1960 Russia abruptly stopped supply of military equipment to China, contributing to the country's sense of siege. Even now China labours under an arms embargo from the EU and the US, introduced for political reasons in the aftermath of the Tiananmen Square incident. While the Russians have resumed arms supply, it is on a reduced basis and is often characterised by commercial dispute. Russian military exports to China totalled US$3.5bn in 2006 but only US$401 million in 2009.[22] The Russians have suspended supply of SU-27K kits to China, complaining of China's unauthorised development of Russian equipment; it has also refused to provide the SU-33 aircraft, which was apparently intended for PLAN carriers.[23]

Accordingly in China there is a substantial emphasis on indigenous innovation with Chinese characteristics. Military delegates to China's National Congress in 2007 argued: 'if a country failed to establish an independent and powerful system for military industrial development and the army did not completely operate under an independent military equipment and logistics service system, then that country's army cannot be regarded as a strong army, and the military power of the country cannot be further enhanced'.[24] The same aspiration for greater degrees of strategic independence is manifest elsewhere in the region as well.

Moreover, the strategic criticality of keeping up with technological trends irrespective of their domestic political and economic benefits is clearly recognised in China as elsewhere. The Chinese notion of 'people's war under modern conditions' requires more advanced, educated and technologically equipped forces since 'technology drives doctrine'.[25] In short, essentially domestic factors drive policy as well as international ones.

One race or many?

There are of course strong bilateral tendencies at play in the naval modernisation programmes of the Asia-Pacific region; the most obvious adversarial pairings are the two Koreas, China and the US, China and Taiwan, China and Japan, China and Vietnam and India and Pakistan. The naval rivalry between North and South Korea provides the currently most deadly example of the genre, with the sinking of the ROK corvette *Cheonan* and the bombardment of Yeonpyeong Island in 2010. Many of the ROK Navy's acquisitions are clear reactions to the actions and capabilities of the North and seem often in turn to stimulate asymmetric responses from Pyongyang. This seems a classic action–reaction dynamic.

China's rivalry with Vietnam over the South China Sea is similar and has also had lethal consequences, most notably with China's seizure of the Paracel Islands in 1974 and the battle of Fiery Cross Reef in 1988. Vietnam's response to this has been a reactive defence programme which includes the prospective acquisition of six *Kilo*-class submarines and the K-300P *Bastion* P mobile coastal-defence missile system. For its part, China has much increased the strength of its Southern Fleet, built up its naval position at Ya Long in Hainan province and its activity level in the South China Sea area. Other factors limit the arms-racing potential impact of these two most difficult of bilateral relationships, however.

China/US

The most substantial, if not so far the most lethal, naval rivalry in the area is between the US and China. This is part of the much wider suspicions that each has of the other's future role in the region and, indeed, globally.[26] In addition to its extreme sensitivity about US policy towards, and potential arming of, Taiwan, China's attitude towards what it regards as its near seas, in terms both of the ocean areas it claims, and what it regards as permissible activity by other navies within those areas, has been a cause of sporadic flare-ups of tension between the two navies, most obviously with the incidents surrounding the harassing of the USNS Impeccable in 2009.

China/India

'Hedging' tendencies (the inclination to take precautions against another state just in case the employment of force becomes necessary) are strongly characteristic of many navies in the region. We may take India as an example. The naval situation between China and India is complicated by the parallel difficulties that India has with Pakistan. Thus Indian Defence Minister A.K. Antony:

> The increasing nexus between China and Pakistan in the military sphere remains an area of serious concern. We have to carry out continuous appraisals of Chinese military capabilities and shape our responses accordingly ... (w)e need to be vigilant at all times'.[27]

These historic antipathies often manifest themselves in the maritime domain. One example, India's launch of its first SSN in July 2009, was criticised by the Pakistani Foreign Ministry as 'detrimental to regional peace'; the ministry promised 'appropriate steps' to maintain a strategic balance. A spokesman for the Pakistani Navy remarked that: 'It is a matter of serious concern not only for Pakistan but also for all littoral states in the Indian ocean and beyond ... All littoral states, including

Pakistan, have to take necessary safeguards in the wake of new induction in its navy by India.'[28] The following month saw Admiral Mehta complaining about alleged modifications to the Pakistani Navy's *Harpoon* missiles that brought them within range of land targets in India. These maritime frictions demonstrate that mutual trust between the two countries remains in short supply, further complicating the naval balance between India and China.[29]

Japan/China

The Japanese likewise seem increasingly focused on their neighbour across the East China Sea. Successive Japanese White Papers have referred to the need for close attention to the growing economic, political and military power of China:

> China has been modernizing its military forces, with the rapid and continuous increase in its total defense spending. However, with clarity on neither the present condition nor the future of its military power, there is concern how the military power of China will influence the regional state of affairs and the security of Japan.[30]

Japan's absolute economic and strategic reliance on the sea lines of communication that go through the East and South China seas, its sensitivity to the growth of Chinese naval power and to events in and around Taiwan, the Paracels and the Spratlys accounts for something of the southward shift in strategic posture noted earlier. Tokyo has repeatedly called for increased transparency from China and the promotion of dialogue.

The 2009 Defence White Paper also expressed unease at Chinese incursions into and ostentatious passages through

Japanese waters, not least an incident in September 2005 when five PLAN vessels circled Japanese installations at the Kashi gas field in the East China sea as a 'demonstration of their naval capabilities of acquiring, maintaining and protecting maritime rights and interests'.[31] The April 2010 encounter between two Japanese destroyers and eight Chinese warships plus two submarines transiting Japanese waters in the Ryukus and the apparent ramming of a Japanese coast-guard vessel by a Chinese fishing boat in September 2010 angered the Japanese public. Said the *Asahi Shinbun* in an editorial, with masterly understatement,

> If China keeps up with these provocations, it will risk harming relations with Japan by creating concerns about its intentions among the Japanese public.[32]

The Japanese have claimed that Chinese official defence spending in FY2009 was 15.3% up on FY2008 and was effectively doubling every five years. On this basis, the semi-official Japanese National Institute for Defense Studies East Asian Review for 2009 stated that 'Beijing's rebuttals of those who say that China now poses a security threat are not persuasive'.[33] The White Paper itself pointed out that in recent years China has begun to work on acquiring capabilities for missions other than the Taiwan issue. 'Furthermore, several senior military officials recently made positive remarks on the possession of an aircraft carrier, and maritime activities in the sea surrounding Japan have been intensifying. Such events happened that Japan should keep a careful watch over.'[34]

These conclusions were repeated in the 2010 and 2011 Defence White Papers and are likely to be further reinforced by the rising tensions over the Senkaku/Diaoyu Islands in summer 2012.[35]

The Rest/China

In general, there is a noticeable tendency for the navies of Japan, India and the United States to benchmark their policies against China and for China, most obviously, to do so against the United States – although all of these navies have other distractions as well, Pakistan in the case of India, Iran and North Korea in the case of the United States, North (and to a certain extent, South) Korea and Russia, for Japan, and Taiwan and the South China Sea for China. These pre-occupations especially manifest themselves in both their declaratory thinking and in their fleet-construction programmes, being especially observable in the attention paid to their nuclear and conventional deterrent postures, their understanding of the nature and requirements of sea control/denial (with a special focus on ASW and fleet air defence). Such approaches sometimes also surface in their actual, rather than their declaratory, willingness to compromise on operating procedures and jurisdictional propriety in the common pursuit of maritime security against low-level threats like pirates and drugs smugglers.

From Beijing's perspective, a particularly worrying aspect of all this (and hence a great incentive to develop its naval forces) is the extent to which this hedging process seems to end with China as the common denominator. In large measure this is simply a function of malign geography, since unless Taiwan is re-absorbed strategically, Japan and South Korea sit astride China's eastwards access to the Pacific Ocean and the other claimants to the South China Sea complicate its access to the south. The problem is that the 'defensive' security concerns of all its neighbours in these very same sea areas are also perfectly understandable, even legitimate. That these countries appear divided by the same sea areas provides them all with a security dilemma uncomfortably close to that of Britain and Germany over the North Sea in 1914. The problem is particularly difficult for Beijing, however.

Having to deal with this 'the rest versus China' prospect presents the country's leaders with a major strategic dilemma, given its oft-repeated renunciation of any hegemonic aspirations. Should it arm against such a contingency – or should it desist on the grounds that such a response would only encourage the 'China threat theory'? But in which case, how does it defend its legitimate interests against, on the one hand, the unwanted intrusion of outsiders and on the other its neighbours appropriating China's territory and stealing its marine resources? How, moreover, does it explain such forbearance to its own nationalisitic netizens?[36] Hence the lively debate in China about the future of the country's naval development and the uses to which it should be put.

These wider and sometimes cross-cutting relationships mean that the situation is not cleanly bilateral. For instance, neither China nor India see each other as their primary antagonist but do note that they are allied to the countries that are – the US and Pakistan respectively. India is mainly worried about the notional threat on the border and what it considers China's developing presence in the Indian Ocean and its moves to increase its influence and open up strategic outposts in the Indian Ocean.

In this way such cross-cutting secondary concerns as the delimitation of the North East Pacific between Japan, South Korea and China could increase rather than decrease the prospect of an essentially bilateral naval arms race between China and everyone else The more they turn Beijing's fear of 'the Rest versus China' into a reality, the more 1914 – Europe's past – may come to be Asia's future. The prospects of that however still seem remote, given the numerous disagreements amongst 'the rest', the importance of their economic relationships with China and their domestic reluctance to be manoeuvred into a pseudo-coalition led by the United States.[37] Nor is there much evidence that such is Washington's intention.

Measuring intensity

The intensity of the naval competition in the region can be measured in a number of ways, and the matter is further complicated by the fact that the competition can be symmetrical (such as the race in long-range precision strike between China and the US) or asymmetrical (such as Vietnam's procurement of *Kilo*-class submarines, presumably in response to the increased presence of Chinese ships in the South China Sea). Worse, symmetry and asymmetry may lie in the eye of the beholder. Thus, US Defense Secretary Robert Gates at Newport in 2009:

> No-one intends to bankrupt themselves by challenging the US to a ship-building competition akin to the Dreadnought race prior to World War I. Instead we have seen their investments in weapons geared to neutralize our advantages: to deny the freedom of movement and action while potentially threatening our primary means of projecting power: our bases, sea and air assets, and the networks that support them.[38]

Perhaps the clearest of measures, though, is the extent to which national budgets are devoted to naval development. Here the situation is generally much more encouraging, since defence expenditure levels as a proportion of GNP remain very low by the standards of the twentieth century, and in many cases are actually falling rather than rising. India and Japan spend US$35bn (2.8% of GDP) and US$51bn (1%) respectively.[39] Japan's figure excludes some quite significant personnel costs, investment in a substantial coast guard and the provision of host-nation support to the US. India's official defence expenditure has hovered around 2.5% for over a decade, a little lower than it has been in the past. US defence expenditure at around

4.7% is higher than this but faces substantial budgetary challenge in the near future.

These relatively modest levels of effort are offset to some degree, of course, by the historic increase in GNP for the four countries, and the continuing growth of the Indian and Chinese economies in particular. China for example claims its defence expenditure as a percentage of GDP is steady and as a share of State financial expenditure actually falling.[40] In this regard the Chinese example is nonetheless often used as a worrying trend, particularly as its results tend to set the standard by which other countries define their needs. According to the latest Japanese Defence White Paper, Chinese defence expenditure is doubling every five years and as a result has now become the world's second-biggest defence spender. China repeatedly explains this away by its undeniable need to modernise, to improve the position of its service personnel and to meet rising commodity process. (*See Appendix, Table 1 for a comparison of defense budgets as a percentage of GDP*).

Concern is increased substantially by the Chinese budget's perceived lack of transparency, also a critical characteristic of the Anglo-German position before the First World War. Dire references are made to Sun Tsu: 'the pinnacle of military employment approaches the formless ... if I determine the enemy's disposition while I have no perceptible form, I can concentrate my forces while the enemy is fragmented.'[41] Analysts have pointed out that the 2010 Chinese Defence White Paper, for example, made no mention of the DF-21D, the J20 or the prospective launch of the country's first aircraft carrier and so provided a distinctly inadequate guide even to China's short-term intentions.[42] It cannot, however, be said that China provides a unique example of the opacity of Asian defence decision-making, which generally appears in strong contrast to the almost embarrassing candour of the American, and to some extent the Indian, systems.

Levels of political tension

Here the position seems particularly mixed. On the one hand, it is frequently pointed out that trade dependency is very high across the region. The prosperity of all the region's countries rely absolutely on the continued and smooth operation of the globalised sea-based trading system in general and on a mutually beneficial trading relationship with China in particular. At the very least this economic inter-dependence seems likely to moderate levels of dispute between competitors in the region. For evidence, the improving relations between Taiwan and the mainland could be pointed to. This proclivity towards the peaceful resolution of its disputes is held to be characteristic of 'the Asian way' and an encouraging indication that the region will not follow the example of early twentieth-century Europe.

For naval evidence of this, advocates point to the extent of naval togetherness and functional cooperation in the region, in terms of fraternal exercises and common efforts against common threats such as that of piracy in the Malacca Strait, and the emphasis given multinational naval cooperation in all their declaratory statements and doctrinal formulations.

On the other hand, it is easy enough to point to exceptions to the general rule, if that is what this is taken to be, of naval togetherness, not least the lethal confrontations described earlier. The three Indo-Pakistan wars, the Vietnamese invasion of Cambodia, the Chinese invasions of India and Vietnam, the continued tensions between the two Koreas, and the face-off over the Taiwan Strait all suggest that the area is not quite as pacific in nature as its name would suggest. Moreover, the rise of nationalism throughout the region, manifested among other things by 'netizen' fury over such incidents as the collision of a Chinese trawler with a Japanese Coast Guard vessel in the East China Sea, must be a cause for concern, since the outcomes to such incidents are taken as public indicators of how well the government is doing. For this reason, governments cannot afford simply to ignore such manifestations and it is easy to imagine situations in which they might become trapped by aroused public opinion. This may have been an example of what China's Defence Minister General Liang Guanglie had in mind when he told the *People's Daily* in December 2010: 'looking at the current world situation, a full-scale war is unlikely, but we cannot exclude the possibility that, in some local areas, unexpected events may occur, or military friction may take place due to a misfire'.[43] The tensions between China, Taiwan, Japan, Vietnam and the Philippines over the East and South China Sea disputes through 2012 makes misfires seem a distinct possibility. On the departure of the Taiwanese trawler flotilla to make their point on the Diaoyu/Senkaku Islands in September, for example, Minister Wang Jinn-Wang of the Coast Guard Administration warned that his units would be guided by the precepts of 'no provocation , no conflict and evasion' but 'if the Japanese spray water at the Taiwanese fishing boasts, we will spray water back at them' and that he would not rule out the use of arms if 'the other side resorts to it first.'[44]

Nor can economic interdependency be regarded as an automatic guarantee of ultimate peace and tranquillity. As already observed, Germany and Britain were each other's biggest trading partners in 1914. Economic imbalances even in very close economic relations can be both a source of tension and of what may be called 'sticky power' for the stronger side as the furore over the Chinese supply (or not) of rare earth minerals demonstrated throughout 2012. Between 2000 and 2009, two-way trade between China and India rose from US$2.4bn to nearly US$41bn. But since 2005, India's trade deficit with China has grown substantially to upward of US$20bn per year, generating a new source of tension between the two countries. These trade patterns have suggested a need to question early scholarly arguments that China and India had particularly complementary economies that showed great prospects for expansion and could form the basis of a settled relationship between the two countries.[45]

Relationships between Japan and China have certainly deteriorated in recent years after a brief period of improvement during the Hatoyama administration. The 2008 agreement jointly to develop resources has proved difficult to implement.[46] In addition to this, a series of maritime incidents ranging from the passage of ten Chinese warships 130km (85 miles) from Okinawa and related close encounters between helicopters and surface ships to the bumping incident in September 2010 between a Chinese fishing boat and Japanese coast-guard vessels (which led to nationalist demonstrations in both countries) and the ongoing Diaoyu/Senkaku islands dispute have exacerbated bilateral relations.[47]

Successive Japanese administrations have sought to rein in the hawks, pointing out the ever-closer economic relationship between the two countries, while re-emphasising the importance of the relationship with the United States.[48] The need to counter-balance a more assertive China contributes to Japan's seeking closer relations with both Australia and India.[49] In 2008, India and Japan signed a declaration of shared strategic interests such as the free flow of energy, natural resources and unimpeded SLOCs in the Indian and Pacific Oceans. Measured progress in security cooperation has flowed.[50] Typically, after the fishing boat incident led to talk of China's ceasing the export of rare earth minerals to Japan, India agreed to help instead.[51]

Against this background, Japan also remains concerned about the Taiwan question, despite the current improvement in cross-strait relations. Japan takes a close interest in Taiwan for a variety of historical, political and strategic reasons. Another threatened island democracy, it is close to Japanese territory and geographically commands Japan's main shipping lanes. Whatever, the rights and wrongs of this issue, China's past military pressures on Taipei have led to Japan as well as the United States demonstrating considerable concern at the prospect of the employment of force over the issue. Leaving aside its historic, economic and political connections with Taiwan, the reunification of the island with the mainland would change Japan's strategic geography and especially the theoretical vulnerability of its SLOCs. All this, together with Japan's general wariness about China's strategic rise, mean that Japan's bases are likely to be at the disposal of the United States in the event of trouble in the area. For all these reasons it is easy to see why some should conclude 'that it is very unlikely that Japan would sit-out any conflict that erupts across the Taiwan Strait. Tokyo would probably become an active ally in the military conflict against a PRC attempt to forcefully reunify Taiwan and the mainland'.[52]

Relations between India and China are also notably wary. Tensions include a still unresolved border dispute, Chinese support for Pakistan (and the possibility of some combined action between the two),[53] India's hosting of the Dalai Lama, in an atmosphere of mutual suspicion fanned by shrill media coverage in both countries. The naval situation in the Indian Ocean region illustrates the resultant tension. Arun Saghal of India's USI predicts that 'the IOR is going to become a bigger area of possible conflict than anywhere else'[54] and Robert Kaplan agrees, arguing that one of the US Navy's chief preoccupations will be to 'manage' this tension.[55] The problem is China's increasing reliance on oil shipped through the region, increasingly and by deliberate policy in Chinese-flagged vessels. Already China owns 15% of the oil-tanker fleet, and soon that will be 40%. A major Chinese naval presence in the Indian Ocean and an Indian response seems increasingly likely.[56] The result is a degree of privately admitted tension between China and India over the former's 'intrusion' into the Indian Ocean area and the latter's forays into the South and East China seas in support of its 'Look East' policy.[57]

Both countries have accordingly sought to increase their influence and construct defence relationships with other countries in the Indian Ocean region. China has defence links with the Yemen, Oman, Pakistan, Sri Lanka and Myanmar. India for its part has established defence links and in some cases facilities with Oman, Qatar, the Seychelles, Madagascar, Mauritius and Mozambique and has hosted both the *Milan* and the *Malabar* exercise series with countries around the Indian Ocean rim, Japan, Australia, New Zealand and the United States. Furthermore India has built up of its naval, air and coastguard facilities in the Andaman and Nicobar islands.[58] Some Chinese observers such as the naval analyst Zhang Ming have worried that these islands might form a 'metal chain' across the western end of the Malacca Straits. He is quoted as saying:

> India is perhaps China's most realistic strategic adversary ... Once India commands the Indian Ocean, it will not be satisfied with its position and will continuously seek to extend its influence, and its eastwards strategy will have a particular impact on China.[59]

The unofficial Chinese 'naval commentariat' has in recent years devoted itself to the analysis of the implications of India's naval development for China, and seeing it as another potential challenge to the country's strategic interest in the area.[60] They will have noted sections of *India Maritime Doctrine* that could prove relevant to them, given the country's reliance on oil supplies from the Gulf:

However, trade warfare can also be used by a superior naval force, to impose commodity denial on the adversary. This can be done by sea control or sea denial measures, and requires a higher level of MDA on the identity and movement of enemy shipping.[61]

Opinion on the practical extent of this challenge, perhaps inevitably, reflects a range of perceptions within China about first the likelihood of such an Indian challenge and, secondly, its effectiveness. Official thinking on the subject remains opaque.

Not surprisingly, therefore, both China and India are courting opinion and seeking facilities in the island states of the Seychelles, Mauritius and the Maldives and most intensely in Myanmar. India established a base in Madagascar in 2006 and has helped the Iranians develop a new port at Chabahar on the Gulf of Oman. China has invested in the construction of a seaport in Gwadar, and is involved in the development of port facilities in Sri Lanka, Bangladesh and Myanmar and operates surveillance facilities in the Cocos Islands – all perhaps part of what India famously calls its 'String of Pearls strategy'. On the other hand, attempts to build a strategic highway in the Karakoram through Pakistan could be seen as a move by China to resolve its 'Malacca dilemma', by bypassing this potentially vulnerable sea route.

For its part, the Indian Navy has rounded the Malacca Straits into the South China Sea and the Pacific, secured good relations with Vietnam and is now part of the 'Quadrilateral Initiative' alongside Australia, Japan and the United States which is widely interpreted as a means of hedging against rising Chinese naval power. Indian diplomatic relations with the US and with Australia have enormously improved since the 1990s.[62] India's new Maritime Doctrine, says 'very clearly that India's second tier [of defence] relates to the South China Sea'.[63]

The degree of strategic rivalry between the US and China is a vast subject beyond the scope of this book but finds distinctively maritime expression, since seapower is at the heart of the American position in the Asia-Pacific region. The US Navy still thinks of itself as a navy under threat. It is not that American admirals believe themselves to be faced with the prospect of war with China; rather, it is a matter of a declining ability to shape events in the Western Pacific in the way that Washington would prefer, particularly in regard to the foreign-policy choices made by other Pacific nations.[64] This is not merely a matter of relative orders of battle, since here the US continues to enjoy the advantage; it is more a question of the United States being able to secure its access to what China calls the 'near seas' and to maintain that level of sustainable 'forward presence' which the navy believes to be a precondition for its capacity to project power and influence from the sea, to maintain its web of political relationships in the area, to reassure America's friends and partners and to deter possible adversaries. For its part China sees this 'forward presence' and the US interpretation of international maritime law on the 'freedom of navigation' as an illegitimate means of containing China's growth and power and ultimately threatening its security. Hence the USNS *Impeccable* incident, and the sometimes rancorous relationship between the two countries over problems in the East and South China seas.

Perceptions of racing

In 1912–14, there was a strong sense that Europe was engaged in an arms race at sea and this grim pessimism was why Churchill and others pushed so hard for naval holidays and construction stretches.[65] These came to nothing as the protagonists could not agree what their legitimate naval needs were, and the same was true of the naval arms control negotiations of the 1980s between the United States and the Soviet Union. Whether or not countries are exceeding their legitimate defence needs and engaging in arms-race behaviour remains notoriously subjective.

The pattern of naval spending in the Asia-Pacific region, with its increasing emphasis on sophisticated equipment designed for high-intensity operations, suggests that most defence decision-makers would seem generally to agree with the general line expressed by Australia's Minister for Defence , Joel Fitzgibbon in May 2009:

> It is the Government's view that it would be premature to judge that war among states, including the major powers, has been eliminated as a feature of the international system.[66]

In striking contrast to the situation at the beginning of the twentieth century, however, diplomats in the area do not in general appear to be ready to state in public that a naval arms race is underway, even if they do think some countries are exceeding their legitimate aspirations. The most that seems to be said are laden with caveat like that of Robert Gates, in June 2011, just before his retirement:

> I think the Chinese have learned a powerful lesson from the Soviet experience and they do not intend to compete with us across the full range of military capabilities. But I think they are intending to build capabilities to give them considerable freedom of action in Asia and an opportunity to extend their influence.[67]

Such careful and relatively limited formulations do not currently seem likely to approximate the rhetoric and indeed the level of concerns common in Europe in the period before the First World War. But it does perhaps suggest a need to make positive efforts through various programmes of naval together-ness to keep things that way. Hence much of the public rhetoric in the area is, instead, about the need further to develop areas of cooperation between the region's major and minor, navies in responding to common problems.

Measuring intent

The question of whether an arms race is occurring in the Asia-Pacific region is not an easy one to answer. Evidence can be sought not only in the rapidity, extent and interactivity of arms procurement and defence developments in the region, which provide a mixed picture of the Asian context, but also in exam-ining the intentions behind these factors, to the extent it is possible to do so. One of the best ways to gauge such intent is to view the missions for which the naval platforms are intended: are regional navies developing forces designed solely to control the sea and project power for aggressive purposes, or are the capabilities designed to work with other navies in protecting public goods such as maritime security?

The following chapters will seek to outline the balance these four navies strike between the two paradigms of naval devel-opment noted earlier, the competitive state-based conceptions of what navies are for and the more consensual system-based alternatives. This is best illustrated by the extent to which the region's navies elect to focus their acquisitions and activities on dealing with transnational and non-traditional threats to good order and international stability, such as terrorism, piracy and other forms of maritime crime; humanitarian assistance and disaster relief; the consequences of climate change and so on; rather than on naval roles associated with traditional inter-state competition and rivalry. To what extent, in short, do the characteristics of naval arms races identified earlier seem to apply to the naval behaviour of China, Japan, India and the United States?

Notes

1   Desmond Ball, in 'Naval Acquisitions in Northeast Asia: Modernization or Arms Racing?', unpublished notes for seminar on *Enhancing Asia Maritime Security and Confidence Building Measures,* Singapore, 26 January 2010.

2   Richard Bitzinger, 'A New Arms Race? Explaining Recent Southeast Asian Military Acquisitions', *Contemprorary Southeast Asia,* vol. 32, no. 1, 2010; Karishma Vaswani, '"Arms drive" in South East Asia', BBC, 15 March 2010, http://news.bbc.co.uk/1/hi/world/asia-pacific/8567750.stm.

3   *The Military Balance 2012* (London: IISS, 2011); see also Military Balance 2012 Press Statement: 'While per capita spending levels in Asia remain significantly lower than those in Europe, on the current trend Asian defence spending is likely to exceed that of Europe, in nominal terms, during 2012', at http://www.iiss.org/publications/military-balance/the-military-balance-2012/press-statement/.

4   'DCNS Plans to Expand Business in Asia Pacific', *Jane's Defence Weekly,* 11 November 2009.

5   Robert Karniol, 'Boom Time Ahead for Asia-Pacific Navies', *Straits Times,* 9 November 2009. I am extremely grateful to Bob Nugent, vice president of advisory services of AMI International for these figures and for his personal support of this project. For more information, see http://aminter.com.

6   Office of the Secretary of Defense, 'Military and Security Developments Involving the People's Republic of China 2012', Annual Report to Congress, May 2012, p. 42.

7   Lin Zhaowei, 'China Driving Japan Closer to US', *Straits Times,* 10 March 2011.

8   For discussion of this see Richard L. Kugler, *New Directions in US National Security Strategy, Defense Plans and Diplomacy – A Review of Official Strategic Documents* (Washington DC: NDU Press for Institute for National Strategic Studies, 2011), p. 32 and 'US Debt and defence: battle lines drawn', IISS Strategic Comments September 2012.

9   Statement of Admiral Jonathan Greenert, chief of naval operations before the House Armed Services Committee on the Future of the Military Services and Consequences of Defence Sequestration, 2 November 2011, http://armedservices.house.gov/index.cfm/files/serve?File_id=15d1f748-0850-4f6f-9b47-31273cf5f281.

10 Japan's naval force expenditure in 2011 was ¥1,100,801 bn; in 2012 it was ¥1,109,807 bn. (IISS Defence and Military Analysis Programme statistics).

11 See for example, Chief of Naval Operations Adm. Jonathan

Greenert's Opening Remarks at the Brookings Institution Air–Sea Battle Doctrine, 16 May 2012, at http://www.brookings.edu/events/2012/05/16-air-sea-doctrine#ref-id=20120516_schwartz. This, and other presentations like it, was plainly intended to correct the impressions caused by earlier civilian explorations of the subject.

12 Choi Chi-yuk, 'Lianoning to Undergo Extended 'Sea Trials', *South China Morning Post*, 27 September 2012.

14 'Panetta: New Asia Focus not Aimed to contain China', Associated Press, 19 September 2012, http://news.yahoo.com/panetta-asia-focus-not-aimed-contain-china-042922761.html?_esi=1; President Obama said the US welcomed a 'rising and peaceful China': Bonnie Glaser, 'US Pivot to Asia Leaves China off Balance', *Comparative Connections*, January 2012, http://csis.org/files/publication/1103qus_china.pdf.

15 Quoted in Washington DC, 'Taiwan says US Looking at Military Needs', Agence France-Presse, 15 July 2011.

16 Shi Yewen, *The Military Career of Deng Xiaoping* (The PLA Audio Press, 4th ed) DVD video, procured July 2006.

17 'China Plans for High-Tech Army', *China Daily*, 26 May 2006.

18 'Vice Premier calls for Innovation in Defence Industry', Xinhuanet, 4 January 2006.

19 Quoted in 'China Reaffirms Reform in White Paper', *Janes Defence Weekly*, 6 April 2011.

20 Tai Ming Cheung, 'The Chinese Defense Economy's Long March from Imitation to Innovation', *Journal of Strategic Studies*, vol. 34, no. 3, June 2011, p. 331.

21 Information from CSTC documentation and web address http://www.chinaships.com. Their e-mail address is webmaster@cstc.com.cn.

22 SIPRI Arms Transfer Database4, http://armstrade.sipri.org/armstrade/page/values.php.

23 'Chinese Time-out for Russian Weapons,' Vlasti-net, 6 June 2008. Tai Ming Cheung, The Chinese Defense Economy's Long March from Imitation to Innovation', 'China Relying Less on Russia for Weapons, Energy: Think Tank', Agence France-Presse, 2 October 2011.

24 Chang Hsin, 'China Cautiously Allowing Foreign Capital Access to Military Industry', *Wen Wei Po*, 14 August 2007, WNC 200708141477.1_1f4b02507c03c455.

25 Dennis J. Blasko, 'Technology Determines Tactics: the Relationship between Technology and Doctrine in Chinese Military Thinking, *Journal of Strategic Studies*, vol. 34, no. 3, June 2011, pp. 355–81, p. 358.

26 Michael S. Chase, 'Chinese Suspicion and US Intentions', *Survival*, vol. 53, no. 3, June–July 2011, pp. 133-50.

27 'Growing Sino-Pakistani Defence Ties Alarms India', *Jane's Defence Weekly*, 8 December 2009.

28 'Pakistan Hits Out at 'detrimental' Indian Nuclear Sub', Agence France-Presse, 28 July 2008.

29 'Indian Navy chief slams Pakistan missile "proliferation"', Agence France-Presse, 31 August 2009. For a recent review of the background, see Rahul Roy-Chaudhury, 'India

Versus Pakistan: From Partition to the Present', *RUSI Journal*, August 2009, pp. 60–65.

30 Japan Ministry of Defense White Paper 2009, Overview, p. 4. Accessible at http://www.mod.go.jp/publ/w_paper/pdf/2009.html.

31 *Ibid.*, p. 55.

32 'China's Aggressive Navy', Asahi.com, 26 April 2010, http://www.asahi.com/english/TKY201004250145.html.

33 *East Asian Review*, 2009 (Tokyo: The Japan Times for the National Institute for Defense Studies, 2009), p. 136.

34 Japan Ministry of Defense White Paper 2009, Overview, p. 3.

35 Justin McCurry, 'Trouble in the Pacific: Japanese Firms Shut Down in China as Islands Row Turns Violent', *Guardian*, 18 September 2012.

36 This seems a classic illustration of the Daoist principle of managing uncomfortable situations rather than trying to solve them, for fear of stirring up counter-developments. The trouble is that the less sophisticated can interpret this as mere passivity. The point that Vietnam occupies 29 of the features in the South China Sea that China claims, the Philippines eight and Malaysia five can easily be seen as just an example of this.

37 For Australia, as an ally torn between thinking of China as a strategic concern but a critical economic partner, see Malcolm Turnbull, 'A Friend to Two Giants', *Guardian*, 6 October 2011. 'Japan's Balancing Act Over Ties with China, US', *Straits Times*, 23 November 2011; 'India "Unaware" of Security

Pact with US, Australia', *The Straits Times*, 2 December 2010; Evelyn Goh, 'America Faces Familiar Dilemmas in Region', *Straits Times*, 3 December 2011.

38 Robert Gates address at Newport, 17 April 2009, quoted in Jonathan Holslag, 'The Persistent Military Security Dilemma between China and India', *Journal of Strategic Studies*, vol. 32, no. 6, December 2009, p. 67.

39 SIPRI Yearbook for 2010, p. 8, and associated Military Expenditure Database. The domestic and political costs of these levels of defence spending, on the other hand, are more difficult to calculate and may prove significantly less easy to bear.

40 *China's National Defense in 2010*, Information Office of the State Council, March 2011 at http://www.gov.cn/english/official/2011-03/31/content_1835499.htm, p. 10.

42 For a concise summary of the Chinese 2012 Budget see Richard A Bitzinger, 'China's New Defence Budget: What does it Tell Us ?' *RSIS Commentary* 060/2012, April 2012 at http://rsispublication@ntu.edu.sg

43 Interview, *People's Daily*, 29 December 2010.

44 Quoted in 'Taiwanese Flotilla Sails to Diaoyutais,' *Taipeh Times*, 25 September 2012.

45 United Nations, *2004 International Trade Statistics Yearbook* and *2009 International Trade Statistics*, available at http://comtrade.un.org; Huang Yasheng, 'The Myth of Economic Complementarity in Sino-Indian Relations', *Journal of International Affairs*, vol. 64, no. 2 (Spring/Summer 2011), pp. 111124.

46 Compare 'Japan and China in Talks to Form 'EU of the East', *Daily Telegraph*, 5 October 2009 and 'Beijing Lays Markers for East China Sea', *Straits Times*, 9 February 2010. The latter offers a strong contrast to the interim compromise agreement on managing the dispute reached on 18 June 2007, and to the exchange of port visits by the Japanese destroyer *Sazanami* and the Chinese *Shenzhen* in November 2007. 'Japan Seeks Answers over Chinese Warships', *Financial Times*, 13 April 2010.

47 'Japan says Chinese Submarines, Ships Seen near Okinawa', *Taipeh Times*, 14 April 2010; 'Diet to See Boat Collision Footage' *Straits Times*, 28 October 2010; 'Japan Defence Paper points at China's Growing Reach', Agence France-Presse, 10 September 2010.

48 'Japan Hawk's Remarks "shock" China', *Straits Times*, 20 October 2010; 'Japan FM Downplays 'Bad Neighbour' Label on China', AFP Staff Writers, Tokyo 3 October 2010,' Japan Revises its Role in the China Market', *Financial Times*, 5 July 2010.

49 'Japan, Australia Sign "Historic" Military Deal', Channelnewsasia, 20 May 2010.

50 C. Raja Mohan, 'Japan and India: Towards Nuclear and Security Cooperation', *RSIS Commentaries* 70/2010, 29 June 2010.

51 China 'Plans to Cut Rare Earth Exports', *Straits Times*, 20 October 2010; 'Rare Earths Agreement', *Straits Times*, 31 October 2011. And so, for that matter, did Vietnam.

52 Michael McDevitt, 'Mounting Tensions in Northeast Asia: What are the Potential Consequences?', in Stephen Leong (ed.), *Asia Pacific Security: Imperatives for Co-operation* (Kuala Lumpur: ISIS, 2006), pp. 175–8.

53 Ashok Sawhney, *Indian Naval Effectiveness for National Growth* (Singapore: RSIS, Working paper No. 1970), p. 20.

54 Cited in Trefor Moss, 'Power Struggle', *Jane's Defence Weekly*, 23 December 2009.

55 Robert D. Kaplan, 'Centre Stage for the Twenty-first Century: Power Plays in the Indian Ocean', *Foreign Affairs*, March/April 2009, http://www.foreignaffairs.com/articles/64832/robert-d-kaplan/center-stage-for-the-21st-century.

56 'Eyeing China Push into Indian Ocean, India Boosts Navy' Reuters, 2 December 2009. 'India frets as China Builds Ports in S. Asia', *Straits Times*, 17 February 2010.

57 Varying Chinese academic perspectives on this are well described in James R. Holmes and Toshi Yoshihara, 'China's Naval Ambitions in the Indian Ocean', *Journal of Strategic Studies*, vol. 31, no. 3, June 2008, pp. 367–94.

58 Fully discussed in Jonathan Holslag, 'The Persistent Military Security Dilemma between China and India'.

59 Cited in Kaplan, 'Centre Stage for the Twenty-first Century: Power Plays in the Indian Ocean'.

60 James R. Holmes, et al., *Indian Naval Strategy in the Twenty-first Century* (London: Routledge, 2009), pp. 133–8.

61 *Indian Maritime Doctrine* (2009), p. 84.

62 'India, Australia Agree to Boost Security Cooperation', *Jane's Defence Weekly*, 25 November 2009.

63 Cited in Trefor Moss, 'Power Struggle', *Jane's Defence Weekly*, 23 December 2009.

64 Ronald O'Rourke, *China Naval Modernization: Implications for US Navy Capabilities – Background and Issues for Congress* (Washington: Congressional Research Service, June 2010), p. 25.

65 Maurer, John H., 'Churchill's Naval Holiday: Arms Control and the Anglo-German Naval Race, 1912–14, *Journal of Strategic Studies*, vol. 15, no. 1, March 1992, pp. 102–27.

66 The Hon. Joel Fitzgibbon MP, *A New Strategic Environment*, media release of 2 May 2009 available at http://www.defence.gov.au/media.

67 'Gates Denies US wants to "Hold China Down"', Agence France-Presse, 2 June 2011.

CHAPTER TWO

Sea control

Sea control is generally understood to denote a navy's capacity to use an area of sea for its own purposes for as long as necessary to achieve those purposes and to deny that ability to others. Maritime strategists such as Alfred Thayer Mahan and Sir Julian Corbett have argued that sea control can only be achieved either through battle with hostile forces or through acceptance by both sides of the likely consequences of such a battle were it to be fought.[1] Sea control is a relative concept, not an absolute one. It is a matter of degree. Sea control is usually the essential precondition for all other activities at and from the sea; the greater the degree of sea control, the greater the freedom to use the sea. For this reason, navies conventionally attach high importance to the achievement and exploitation of sea control. Since traditionally it has involved a focus by one navy on the capacities of others, it is an essentially *competitive* aspect of maritime strategy. It is certainly regarded in that light by all four of the navies considered here. But at the same time, all of them are also developing newer, more collaborative, conceptions of what sea control should mean, and how their naval forces should carry such re-interpreted functions out. The balance they strike between these traditional and non-traditional conceptions of sea control, then, is a strong indicator of the extent to which naval developments in the Asia-Pacific region seem likely to lead to a destabilising arms race, or not.

Conceptual approaches to sea control
China

As remarked earlier, semantic differences make straight comparisons difficult, but there is little doubt that Chinese thinking is increasingly focused on conventional conceptions of contesting sea control against serious adversaries. Western commentators believe there to be a growing stress on Mahanian thinking in Chinese naval discourse. At a symposium conducted in Beijing in 2004, Chinese analysts pointed out the need for China to 'build up a strong sea power guarding against the threats to our "outward leaning economy" by some strong nations'. Globalisation did *not* mean the end of such traditional conceptions as the command of the sea, bearing in mind that Mahan believed that control of the sea was achieved through decisive naval battles on the sea; 'that the outcome of decisive battles is determined by the strength of fire power on each side of the engagement ... One can only guarantee smooth sea traffic and eventually gain sea domination by annihilating the enemy' in large scale fleet engagements. This is quite different to the language of protracted local defensive resistance that was all that China was once thought to have aspired to.[2]

There are clearly three aspects to Chinese thinking on sea control/denial. The first is to do with the concept's role in the direct defence of China itself. Here the role of the navy is seen to be of an expanded Gorshkovian system of concentric defence of the type aspired to by the Soviet Navy of the Cold War era. Hence Admiral Liu's successor, Admiral Zhang Lianzhong, in 1988:

The exterior perimeter is conceived as encompassing the seas out to the first chain of islands. This region will be defended by conventional and nuclear submarines [some of which will be armed with anti-ship missiles], by naval medium-range aircraft and by surface warships. The submarines will play a dynamic role to ensure defence in depth, including the laying of mines in the enemy's sea lines of communication. The middle distance perimeter extends 150 miles from the coast and comes within, but in most cases does not reach the first chain of islands. Anti-ship aircraft, destroyers and escort vessels will carry the main burden in this area. The interior defence perimeter extends to 60 miles from the coast. This will be the theatre of operations for the main naval air force, fast-attack boats and land-based anti-ship missile units.[3]

This focus on making use of China's maritime geography is characteristic of continental powers embarking on a maritime career. China's Defence White Paper of 2004 emphasised this significant transition:

While continuing to attach importance to the building of the army, the PLA gives priority to the building of the Navy, Air Force and Second Artillery force to seek the balanced development of the combat force structure, *in order to strengthen the capabilities for winning both command of the sea and command of the air, and conducting strategic counter strikes.*[4]

Currently this aspiration extends to some 320–400km from the coast, the operational radius of its land-based aircraft, but the PLA Navy (PLAN)'s intention is clearly to stretch out beyond the 'near seas' of the first island chain. The immediate focus of the Chinese navy for the moment remains on the direct defence of what they take to be their interests in the Taiwan Straits and the East and South China seas.[5] Here the aim would be to deter more powerful adversaries and overwhelm weaker ones by making maximum use of forward islands and positions, and highly diversified all-arms and electronic warfare attacks, in 'counter-intervention operations' or what the Americans call an Anti-Access/Area Denial (A2/AD) strategy in which an adversary's capacity to enter and then operate freely in a sea area is contested.[6]

This illustrates a significant re-think about how China should defend itself against conventional amphibious operations and other forms of sea-based attack on the homeland. No longer would it be a matter of meeting adversaries on the beaches or as they seek to break out from the bridgehead; now it was a question of blocking and interception operations since 'sinking one enemy landing ship at the landing phases is equivalent to wiping out one enemy company or battalion later'.[7]

During the first decade of this century, Chinese thinking about the direct maritime defence of China has explored a variety of integrated A2/AD aspirations, based on advanced anti-ship cruise missiles carried in submarines, surface ships and aircraft, an array of anti-air radars and missiles, defensive mining and electromagnetic dominance of the battlespace – and land-based anti-ship ballistic missiles (ASBM). Western observers have especially remarked on the appearance in China of authoritative articles that discuss the potential for ASBMs as means of denying the Western Pacific, out from China to the Philippines to major US Navy surface forces.[8] The result could be the ideal *Shashaojian* or 'assassin's mace' – a deadly weapon concealed from the adversary until the moment of its use, rather in the manner of the initial Chinese attacks on UN forces in Korea in autumn 1950; this might well limit the ability of the US to intervene, for example, in a future Taiwan crisis; some Chinese analysts emphasise the deterrent value of such a possibility, while others worry about the risks of escalation implicit in an ASBM strike on US carriers, especially if these strikes were made at US forces *before* they came within their own striking ranges of the Chinese coast and if the missiles carried nuclear warheads.[9]

Targeting ships at sea is technically extremely demanding, especially when it involves the use of multiple independently targetable re-entry vehicles (MIRVs) that are intended to complicate defensive efforts whilst allowing greater accuracy through adjustments to their flight path. The Chinese are thought to be exploring electro-optical terminal guidance for their ballistic missiles. The technical feasibility of such a project again has been the subject of much debate, but 'the majority of Chinese studies indicate that the technical obstacles are well within China's ability to resolve'.[10] Overall, most of the evidence suggests the Chinese are developing such a system, that the so-called DF-21D 'carrier-killer' missile has been tested but that the system, which will critically depend on satellite support, is still in the early stages of development.[11] Should it indeed materialise, the likely US response could spark off a particularly destabilising naval arms race.

The ominous possibilities of this were put into high relief by the harsh tone of China's response to the projected but cancelled presence of the US carrier *George Washington* in an exercise with the ROK Navy in the Yellow Sea in 2010 and by subsequent editorials in the *Global Times*, the English-language version of the official *People's Daily*, one of which said:

> China undoubtedly needs to build a highly credible anti-carrier capacity ... Not only does China need an

anti-ship ballistic missile, but also other carrier-killing measures ... Since US aircraft carrier battle groups in the Pacific constitute deterrence against China's strategic interests, China has to possess the capacity to counterbalance.[12]

This reflected China's acute sensitivity to the presence of foreign naval forces in areas regarded in Beijing as the near seas which could threaten the shore. The 1,000km range of the *George Washington* group deployed into the Yellow Sea would have brought the capital itself within reach.

Secondly, Chinese strategists also worry about the way in which China's access to the high seas might be constrained by those who occupy, or who could exploit, the chain of islands that stretches from the Sea of Okhotsk to the Malacca Strait. For example, *The Science of Military Strategy* text produced by the PLA Academy of Military Science in 2000 stated:

> If Taiwan should be alienated from the mainland ... our natural maritime defence system [would] lose its depth, opening a sea gateway to outside forces ... [O]ur line of foreign trade and transportation which is vital to China's opening up and economic development will be exposed to the surveillance and threats of separatists and enemy forces, and China will forever be locked to the west of the first chain of islands in the West Pacific.[13]

In a similar vein, but from the opposite point of view, some foreign observers express concern that China's seizure of those islands would open the Pacific and Indian Ocean to limitless Chinese advance, thereby transforming the wider strategic situation and threatening US links with its forward allies and partners.[14] Here the worry is that later in the century, China will develop and possibly exploit sea-control capabilities well beyond the first island chain, and that these will be devoted less to the immediate defence of the homeland and its islands and more to challenging the United States' dominance of the wider ocean. This may be an important driver in China's military modernisation. Thus the 2007 report by a task force sponsored by the American Council on Foreign Relations:

> China's military modernisation has two main drivers, one with a clear *operational* objective [Taiwan] and the other with a clear *strategic* objective [to be a modern power].[15]

Thirdly, Chinese thinking about sea control has also focused on the Far Seas, as opposed to Near Seas operations for the defence of SLOCs and China's wider interests. In 2004, President Hu Jintao set out some 'new historic missions' for the PLA that reflected China's growing stake in the global maritime transportation system for its energy security, increasingly for essential grain and other foodstuffs and raw materials, as well as for the export of its manufactured goods. As China increases its exposure to the world economy, its distant interests will grow and so will its need to protect them. This expanding concern is reflected in developments as varied as the presence of a PLAN warship standing by the evacuation of Chinese citizens from Libya in 2011 and the emergence of China's capabilities in the Arctic.[16] These expanding concerns have become increasingly obvious in Chinese discourse and policy statements.[17]

Hu has, for example, alluded to the country's 'Malacca Dilemma', by which the country's prosperity and strategic independence rests on secure sea lines of communication over which China can currently exert little or no control. The attention paid to the importance of this task is likely to increase in consequence of China's determined campaign to build up a state-owned oil and gas tanker fleet to bring in its energy supplies, thereby reducing one source of its strategic and commercial vulnerability.[18] China's capacity to provide the effective escorts, maritime patrol aircraft, ASW capability and logistics supply chain needed for a sustained and comprehensive campaign of SLOC defence in the Indian Ocean, however, seems remote.[19]

Chinese thinking on the necessity for the defence of SLOCs is quite diverse, moreover. One school of thought maintains that all countries would find this difficult, that no serious assault on the safety of China's SLOCs in Asia-Pacific seems in prospect and that in the meantime American naval predominance should provide sufficient guarantees of security against the more likely irregular threats of piracy, local disorder and so forth.[20] Interestingly SLOC security was hardly mentioned in China's 2006 Defence White Paper. One speaker at a conference held in Beijing in 2004 described this sceptical position by saying:

> China should not act by following traditional sea power theory in pursuing a strong navy, because today's world situation is different from the time of Mahan ... that the globalisation of the world's economy has made various countries' interests interconnected, mutually dependent on each other to a great degree, and that if a country wants to preserve its life line at sea, the only way to do so is to go through 'cooperation' rather than the traditional 'solo fight'.[21]

There is certainly evidence that China is increasingly recognising the need for *cooperative* naval efforts to defend its essentially systemic economic and trading interests.[22]

Traditionalists in China, however, argue that the potential insecurity of its SLOCs remains a major strategic vulnerability which needs to be corrected in the long run, not least because the continued goodwill of the United States (or for that matter other countries such as Japan or India) should not be assumed. As *China's National Defence in 2004* made clear, 'struggles for strategic points, strategic resources and strategic dominance [will] crop up from time to time'. Because of this, the PLA should build forces capable of 'winning both command of the sea and command of the air', evidently the first such explicit mention of the notion in official documentation.[23] Major-General Jiang Shiliang made the same point: 'In modern times, efforts aimed at securing the absolute control of communications are turning with each passing day into an indispensable essential factor in ensuring the realisation of national interests', not least since economic development depended on 'the command of communications on the sea'.[24] In 2009, PLAN Commander-in-Chief Wu Shengli, writing in the Communist Party journal *Qishi*, identified the need to maintain 'the safety of oceanic transportation and the strategic passageway for energy'.[25] Semi-official and growing American interest in developing an alternate 'Offshore Control' anti-SLOC strategy[26] (which may seem much less escalatory and technologically demanding than an attempt to take on China's A2/AD strategy through the Air–Sea Battle construct) will have been noticed in Beijing.

Chinese naval discourse has acknowledged the obvious problems they would encounter in any bid to protect their SLOCs against serious opposition, namely problems in forward-logistics support, weak anti-submarine capacities and an absence of organic airpower and ocean-going battlegroups.[27] China is clearly now in no position to defend its foreign energy-supply and general trade routes but may feel the need to build such a capacity up for the longer term. This kind of thinking has led to China's alleged 'String of Pearls' concept for an extension of their areas of concern around Southeast Asia and across the Indian Ocean to the Gulf and East Africa. 'China has to turn to the international resource supply system, and will seek military force to safeguard its share when necessary', said Zhang Wenmy of the China Institute of Contemporary International Relations in 2005. He added: 'There has never been a case in history where such a pursuit was realised in peace.'[28]

The consequent aspiration to defend these interests *individually* and possibly against the United States, India and even Japan illustrates a strong and markedly traditional aspect of Chinese maritime thinking, although with its Confucian notions of the 'Harmonious Ocean' there is also a growing emphasis in Chinese discourse on cooperative concepts of sea control.[29] China's doctrinal approach to sea control is noticeably specific in terms of both area and putative adversaries. China's sea-control thinking also reinforces the notion that for all its current focus on the defence of its interests in the near seas, the country nonetheless harbours eventual blue-water aspirations as well.

India

In strong contrast to the situation in both China and Japan we have clear, official and unequivocal doctrinal statements of what sea control means from both India and the United States. Turning to India first: *Indian Maritime Doctrine 2009* asserts that the ancient origins of Indian sea power are reflected in the word 'navigation', which the document claims is derived from the Sanskrit word *navagati*, meaning to travel by sea. It goes on to warn of the dangers of losing sea control:[30]

The only measure of combat effectiveness at sea is the successful use of ocean areas or the denial of the same to an adversary, all aimed at furthering national interests, in war and peace. In other words, the capability of a navy to effect sea control or sea denial in the ocean areas of its interest would be a major determinant in the outcome of war.[31] ...

Essential to establishing battle-space dominance is the ability to synergise all elements of combat power to relentlessly target and degrade or destroy the enemy to achieve the desired degree of dominance[32] ... our primary maritime military interest is to ensure national security, provide insulation from external interference, so that the vital tasks of fostering economic growth and undertaking developmental activities, can take place in a secure environment.

Consequently, India's maritime military strategy is underpinned on 'the freedom to use the seas for our national purposes, under all circumstances'.[33]

Accordingly sea control is valued for the independence of action it confers. *Indian Maritime Doctrine 2009* speaks of the importance of controlling 'the choke points ... as a bargaining chip in the international power game, where the currency of military power remains a stark reality'.[34] Because this independence of action is so crucial, it goes on: 'sea control is the central concept around which the Indian Navy is structured.'[35] *Indian Maritime Doctrine 2009* is quite explicit about what this might mean:

One school of thought avers that the fleet battles of the past are part of military history and that such exigencies will not occur again. It is only a rash security planner who will be so complacent.[36]

As a result, the Indian Navy is structured to subdue a range of potential adversaries in a conflict. This emphasis no doubt derives from India's experience of three wars with Pakistan and explains both the devotion in *Freedom to Use the Seas: India's Maritime Military Strategy*[37] of a whole chapter to how the Navy would be employed in a conventional state-on-state conflict and India's wary reaction to an ambitious, modernising Chinese navy's 'attempts to gain [a] strategic toe-hold in the IOR(Indian Ocean Region)'.[38]

India's concerns about the sea lines of control are very much driven by its dependence upon energy imports. The need to secure energy supply lines from the Gulf, for example, is regarded as 'a primary national maritime interest'.[39] As the sixth-highest energy consumer in the world, India is particularly worried about shortages of oil and gas supplies in the future, which it believes could even lead to conflict. This explains why it has explicitly stated that 'maritime security for supply lines and installations will remain a primary responsibility of the Indian navy'.[40]

Indian doctrine is distinctive in being explicit about the offensive possibilities of sea control, particularly in contesting an adversary's reliance on shipping:

> The interdiction of enemy SLOCs is carried out in consonance with sea control or sea denial. Submarines with their ability to operate with stealth and relative invisibility close to an enemy coast are particularly well suited for these missions. These are also quite effective at choke points, convergence of SLOCs and at harbour mouths, particularly if the enemy's capability for ASW is limited in the area. Surface and air

elements can also be used effectively for SLOC interdiction in a variety of situations and areas.[41]

But there is room for the global perspective, too, in Indian
thinking about access. Indian expositions emphasise the extent
to which the Indian Ocean is an international waterway crucial
to the wellbeing of the world economy, particularly given
its absolute dependence on energy imports. Accordingly,
'the Indian navy sees itself as a major stabilising force in this
great movement of energy across the Indian Ocean, not just
for India, but for the world at large'.[42] Here India would act
as a responsible post-modern stakeholder in the world trading
system against all those who would seek to disrupt it, ensuring
'a measure of stability and tranquillity in the waters around
our shores [for] ... [s]maller nations in our neighbourhood as
well as nations that depend on the waters of the Indian ocean
for their trade and energy supplies'.[43]

Japan

Japanese naval thinking about sea control, like the Chinese, has
a similar focus on the defence of the country's SLOCs, a lesson
hammered home by its experiences in the Second World War.
Like other Asia-Pacific countries it has long been concerned
about the general vulnerability of its SLOCs and has participated
in regular conferences to discuss the matter collectively since
1979. The requirement is increasingly seen by the Japanese to be
for the kind of forward defence posture adopted by traditional
maritime powers, and indeed to justify or even mask a significant build-up in its naval forces. The major notional threat in
this regard for those with deep suspicions of both North Korean
and Chinese intentions is those countries' submarine forces,
which in turn seems to make ASW a particularly high priority
for the Japanese Maritime Defense Force (JMSDF).

There are elements in Japanese thinking about SLOC protection that echo the non-traditionalist US approach, seeing the issue more as a cooperative than a competitive task. Thus Admiral Kazumine Akimoto: 'the defence of sea lanes is not so much a national interest of individual states as it is ... a global interest', that calls for maritime countries like Japan to contribute to the system's defence.[44]

The United States

American thinking on sea control is interestingly varied, encompassing traditional competitive thinking, in terms of adversaries or potential adversaries, as well as this concern for universal freedom. In both *Naval Operations Concept 2010: Implementing the Maritime Strategy* [45] and *A Cooperative Strategy for 21st Century Sea Power*, sea control is seen as the crucial enabler for all forms of naval power and America underlines its determination to maintain it:

> We will not permit conditions under which our maritime forces would be impeded from freedom of maneuver and freedom of access, nor will we permit an adversary to disrupt the global supply chain by attempting to block vital sea-lines of communication and commerce. We will be able to impose local sea control wherever necessary, ideally in concert with friends and allies, but by ourselves if we must.[46]

Sea control is thus seen as the capacity to manoeuvre freely in areas of concern, and to be able fully to exploit the ocean as the world's greatest manoeuvring space. This is clearly the thinking behind, and the justification for, the US Navy's investment in the Air–Sea Battle construct. Although this is always claimed *not* be aimed at China, but instead at A2/AD capacities around the world, it is hard to imagine Beijing being easily persuaded by this attempted reassurance. *A Cooperative Strategy for 21st Century Sea Power* was initially unveiled in October 2007 and its principal architects have mostly moved on. Since then, there has been five years of refining and further developing some of its concepts, with some further expositions in 2013. To judge by the US Navy's growing preoccupation with Air-Sea battle and Admiral Greenert's articulation of the three new 'tenets' of US Navy business, namely 'Warfighting First', 'Operate Forward' and 'Be Ready', there seems likely to be an increasingly muscular tone to the American sea-control narrative in the immediate future.[47]

However, the US Navy has also probably been the leading exponent of a new and decidedly non-traditional conception of sea control, which clearly militates against arms-racing behaviour. During his tenure as Chief of Naval Operations, Admiral Mike Mullen explained the distinction between this new concept and what had gone before:

> Where the old maritime strategy focused on sea control, the new one must recognise that the economic tide of all nations rises not when the seas are controlled by one but rather when they are made safe and free for all.[48]

This is sea *controle*, French style, something more akin to supervision than dominance. This spirit of the common defence of all legitimate forms of the use of the sea permeates *A Cooperative Strategy for 21st Century Seapower*. Another strategic treatise, the *Naval Operations Concept 2010*, also raises the importance of sharing the maritime domain, which it says 'motivates allies and partners alike to collaborate on maintaining maritime security and to conduct sea control operations'.[49]

This cooperative concept of sea control underpins the non-traditional, collaborative activities to be discussed in Chapter Four.

This is not just altruism on the part of the US, however, for as well as emphasising the importance of free access to the sea and the defence of international shipping in general, the US Navy exhibits concern that, rather than challenge US combatants on the open ocean, adversaries might focus specifically on opposing the transit through choke points like the entrance to the Gulf of military sealift, expeditionary forces and merchant shipping supporting distant conflicts, requiring the US Navy to escort them and further dissipate its capacity to concentrate force.[50] Such concerns about adversaries resorting to such sea-denial strategies long ante-date current US preoccupations with Anti-Access and Area Denial concepts.

Anti-Access/Area Denial (A2/AD)

Japanese thinking about the A2/AD dimension of sea control/denial differs from the Chinese only in its orientation towards its local neighbours rather than the Americans, and its lower level of aspiration. Admiral Keiji Akahoshi has emphasised the need for enhanced ASW in the waters around Japan: 'In each country they are trying to develop their submarine fleets, and submarines are posing perhaps the biggest threat to maritime security around Japan. We have to develop our anti-submarine warfare capabilities to react [to] and counter this threat.'[51] In the same way, a continued emphasis on defensive mine-laying is seen as a demonstration of capability: 'If they recognise Japan has the capability it will frighten enemy forces so they will have to delay before any invasion or landing takes place on Japanese territory.'[52]

There is, interestingly, little in the way of discussion of A2/AD issues as such in Indian maritime doctrine, although concerns about potentially hostile forces in the Indian Ocean generally, or off their immediate coasts, are frequently expressed.

Unsurprisingly, given its enormous stress on the importance of being able to manoeuvre freely in areas of concern, the US Navy exhibits great interest, by contrast, in developing notions of A2/AD, though from the angle of trying to defeat rather than implement them. *Naval Operations Concept 2010* notes the challenges posed by the A2/AD capabilities deployed by 'increasingly capable blue-water adversaries'.[53] These include anti-ship ballistic missiles, sea mines, cyber attack against command-and-control systems, swarming attacks by small attack craft, strikes from shore-based aircraft and, most particularly, from submarines. In 2008 the former Chief of Naval Operations Admiral Gary Roughead said: 'Submarines remain an immediate threat and their roles and lethality [are] increasing. More countries are buying submarines; some are building anti-access strategies around them. Maintaining the ability to detect, locate, track and destroy submarines is essential.'[54] The 2010 Quadrennial Defense Review took the defence of access as an important part of the strategy to deal with a resurgent China; suggestions that earlier drafts of these sections of the Quadrennial Defense Review were toned down show how very sensitive and important this issue is thought to be.[55]

Air–Sea Battle

In response to the challenge from submarines, the US Navy, together with the US Air Force is refining the still-classified bundle of responses which make up 'Air–Sea Battle' concept which is often seen as a contemporary equivalent to the Air–Land battle concepts developed in response to the apparent challenge posed by Soviet forces in Europe in the 1970s and 1980s.[56] The idea first appeared publicly in 2010 as a product of the civilian Center for Strategic and Budgetary Assessment, but

since then a series of official US Navy and Air Force presentations have sought to explain what they think it means, and what
their priorities are in developing it.[57] Its emergence marked a
recognition that the US Navy's freedom to manoeuvre in and
from the global commons may in the decades to come seem
much more constrained than at any other time since the end
of the Cold War. The sea, especially the Western Pacific, may
be less of a sanctuary for the US Navy than before, especially
but by no means exclusively in dealing with a peer competitor
such as China. Responding to this possibly developing challenge is seen as 'a signal of US commitment to security in the
Western Pacific and to reassure regional partners in the near-
term'.[58] This reinforces the point that there is more to ASB than
the development and deployment of military weaponry.[59]

Implementing ASB requires what is often referred to as the
three Ds: the disruption of the adversary's intelligence and
command and control systems, the destruction of neutrali-
sation of his A2/AD weaponry at source and its defeat once
deployed. Amongst the responses in this developing line of
thought are potential developments in missile defence for US
ships and bases, cyber offensives and counter-space operations against Chinese ocean surveillance systems, directed
energy weapons, air and missile attacks on Chinese air bases
and surveillance systems, offensive mining, enhanced mine
countermeasures and anti-submarine capabilities. Some,
generally outside the Navy, have also argued for a switch from
platform-centric to the network-centric operations of a 'distributed fleet', in which there would be more emphasis on the use
of larger numbers of smaller units rather than fewer, larger
ones. Another complementary response will be the development of 'enhanced long-range strike capabilities' as a means of
staying outside the strike range of Chinese A2/AD forces and
preserving the American capacity to project power ashore.[60]

Critics of the strategy point to the technological challenge it poses the US, the very considerable financial cost and its potentially destabilising effect on already difficult relations with China, since it is bound to stimulate unsettling responses from the Chinese armed forces.[61]

The developing concept of Air–Sea battle illustrates the continuing American sensitivity to strategies at risk of the kind of devastating ambush of forward-deploying forces suffered at the hands of the Japanese at Pearl Harbor and of the Chinese themselves at Unsan and elsewhere in Korea during the winter of 1950. Concerns relate especially to larger surface ships; no other country's ASW capabilities are currently thought to pose much of a threat to US submarines. Both surface ships and submarines would, however, be parts of a 'system-on-system' approach to the A2/AD challenge, in which complete dominance is not expected.

It is important to repeat the point that Air–Sea battle is an operational concept designed to develop generic military capabilities rather than a national strategy.[62] It is not confined to a set of technological and operational responses; political engagement with China and other countries in the region is seen as part of the strategy as well.[63] This is a response to the concern that China would seek to advance its 'area denial' objectives through political means as well, as it arguably did through its strident objections to the possibility of an American aircraft carrier participating in an exercise in the Yellow Sea aimed at North Korea in the aftermath of the *Cheonan* incident.[64] Political responses are therefore seen to be clearly necessary as well, not least because the US's regional partners will also need to be involved in any Air–Sea Battle campaign. Despite frequent protestations to the contrary, Air–Sea battle ideas are inevitably associated with rather traditional political assumptions which explicitly identify China amongst others as a putative adversary that needs to be 'offset' in order to preserve a 'stable military balance' in the Western Pacific and more generally.[65]

But there is a third angle to US thinking and policy on sea control, namely a concern to bridge the gap between blue-water operations and the land, to which we will return in Chapter Three.

Whatever sea control is taken to mean, the US Navy does seem to be rediscovering the need to develop the operational disciplines needed to fight for it. Since the end of the Cold War, sea control was taken for granted. Now, the great 'commons' of the sea is seen as a place contested by everything from pirates to rising powers. Over the past decade a new ballistic-missile-capable nation has emerged every three years; 75,000 anti-ship cruise missiles are now deployed in more than 70 states and another 280 new submarines are expected to be launched over the next 20 years.[66] The proliferation of such threats as wake-homing torpedoes and over-the-horizon anti-ship missiles with precision guidance has led the US Navy to pay increasing attention to stealth[67] and deception, to proactive defence, to movement and to the technologies capable of welding dispersed forces into a coherent whole.

Sea-control forces

Almost all naval capabilities may contribute to the achievement and exploitation of sea control in some way or another, and in this study there is neither room nor need for a detailed platform-by-platform comparison of the four fleets under special consideration. However, a few observations about the significance of fleet composition for the achievement of sea control nonetheless need to be made.

The PLAN's acquisition programme since the 1990s benefited from three things. The first and most obvious was an increase in the relative proportion of defence spending allocated to the navy. As early as 1991 this was some 32% (compared to 25% and 16% allocated to the Japanese and Indian navies respectively).[68] Second was China's access to the Russian as well as European defence industries. China has made large-scale purchases of Russian weaponry, including fighters, missiles and naval combatants. But the growth in the size and sophistication of the Chinese economy and the extent to which the military industry can tap into civilian industry, has also led to major advances, not least in the maritime sphere through the huge advances made in Chinese shipbuilding. Merchant ship construction rates have doubled since the 1990s. Technical standards have improved too.[69]

The considered, not to say leisurely, way in which the Chinese appear to be approaching the upgrading of its strategic nuclear submarine and aircraft carrier capabilities, together with a new emphasis on research and development, the stream-lining of training, the development of better command and control, an emphasis on the combined-arms approach and a drastic pruning of personnel and overall combatant numbers all suggest that China had been tooling up for a considered, evolutionary and long-term expansion of its naval forces, rather than anything dramatic and over-hasty. Particularly in the 1990s, it was debateable whether China was doing much more than keeping up with the naval modernisation programmes then being conducted by Japan, South Korea, Taiwan and other countries of the region. More recently, however, the PLAN in some areas has begun to pull away from many of the capabilities of most of its immediate neighbours. This trajectory is entirely in line with the three-stage aspiration described in China's 2006 Defence White Paper: establishing a 'solid foundation' by 2010, achieving 'major progress' by 2020 and ultimately 'being capable of winning local 'informationalised wars' by around 2050.[70] It is interestingly argued that the

Chinese character once translated as 'local' should now really be interpreted as 'regional'.[71]

This in turn is consistent with the Chinese practice through the 1990s and into the first decade of the twenty-first century of introducing classes of ships and submarines in small numbers as 'technology demonstrators'; many analysts now expect China increasingly to adopt more volume production of high quality products such as the *Song*-class submarines and the *Luyang* II destroyer with its indigenous *Aegis*-type radar and air-defence system. This represents a significant advance on the standards of what was a relatively unimpressive military-industrial complex up to the mid-1990s.[72]

According to the *Military Balance 2012*, the PLAN comprises 876 vessels including 78 principal surface combatants and 71 submarines.[73] A Japanese assessment of Chinese naval power, published by the National Institute for Defense Studies in 2009, concluded that 'in recent years, China has begun to work on acquiring capabilities for missions other than the Taiwan issue'.[74] The implication of this is that Chinese naval modernisation would continue even if the Taiwan issue were resolved. A US Office of Naval Intelligence review of China inadvertently released in February 2010 concurred with that projection. Over the next ten to 15 years, it concluded the Chinese navy would be much better equipped for maritime security and humanitarian operations well outside its normal operating areas in the East and South China seas, although these would remain China's main focus for the time. The report pointed out significant advances in all the main warfare areas, correcting historic weaknesses in anti-air warfare (AAW) and developing significant cruise and ballistic missile anti-ship capabilities.[75]

Back in 1986, China launched the so-called '863 programme' to fund high-technology military research. The resultant construction of one of the world's most advanced fibre-optic

grids and advances in computer chip and hardware technologies have facilitated real progress in the development
of the country's C4ISR capabilities, not least in communication, navigation and surveillance satellites. This will provide
more precise monitoring of naval movements in the Western
Pacific of the sort that allowed the Chinese to move ships into
the disputed Senkaku/Diaoyu Islands area, taking Japanese
Coast Guard ships by surprise, in December 2008.[76] Moreover,
according to Dennis C. Blair, then director of US national intelligence, 'counter-command, control and sensor systems, to
include communications satellite jammers, are among Beijing's
highest military priorities'.[77]

In terms of the defence of what they regard as the 'near
seas', the Chinese are clearly developing the capabilities they
feel they need in order to turn their A2/AD thinking into
reality. Most Chinese seaborne forces and some aspects of its
land-based missile and aircraft forces, together with supporting surveillance capabilities, would be useful for A2/AD,
most obviously against the US Navy. The Chinese have been
developing a number of cruise missiles like the DH-10,[78] but
the development of the DF21D/CSS-5 medium range ballistic
missile has attracted most comment for its potential to 'provide
the PLA the capability to attack ships at sea, including aircraft
carriers, in the western Pacific Ocean' up to ranges in excess
of 1,500km.[79] The Chinese have moved on from talking about
them to testing an ASBM version of the DF21/CSS5, according
to Admiral Robert Willard's testimony to the House Armed
Services Committee in March 2010; meanwhile, up to a dozen
have been deployed in Qingyuan, Guangdong Province.[80]

These efforts are supported by aircraft and satellite development. Complex satellite manoeuvres in September 2010
suggested the development of a 'satellite-killing' capacity. In
similar fashion there have been reports of China working on

electromagnetic pulse and high-powered microwave weapons designed to disable carrier and other naval operations.[81] The *Chengdu* J10, the early appearance of the J20 'fifth generation stealth fighter' in January 2011 and the fact that the proportion of fourth-generation aircraft in the PLA Air Force (PLAAF) has risen to one third illustrate a general push to develop an air force with regional capability.[82] By 2020 China's airpower will project beyond the first island chain, allowing it to defeat Taiwan's capacity to ward off air/missile attack and making the whole area much more hazardous for US forces. It is also develop-ing unmanned aerial vehicles (UAVs), particularly the turbo-jet powered CASIC WJ-600, for long-range reconnaissance and strike missions, as well as *Shadow dragon*, a hypersonic 'space plane'.[83] The PLA Naval Air Force (PLANAF), however, still suffers from dominance by the PLA and has integration prob-lems even within itself, with no single national air command system.

The Chinese submarine force now stands at five nuclear-powered attack submarines (SSNs) and 52 diesel-powered vessels (SSKs). The newer classes in both categories, such as the 6,000-tonne *Shang* class SSN and the *Song* and *Yuan* classes of SSKs, in particular represent a significant upgrade of Chinese submarine capabilities and have raised a number of operational and strategic concerns for the US as well as other powers in the region. Although equipped with sophisticated wake-homing torpedoes (particularly effective against vessels with large wakes – such as aircraft carriers), Chinese submarines (such as the *Kilo* with its *Sizzlers*) appear to be optimised for shoot-ing anti-ship cruise missiles and the development of the new H-6K/M cruise missile suggests a developing capacity to reach as far as Guam, a possibility that might require the hardening of military facilities there.[84] The Chinese Navy's focus on the procurement of submarines is entirely consistent with a strategy of sea denial intended to defend the maritime approaches to China against intruding naval forces bent on attacking the mainland. It is also seen as evidence of a desire to deter external intervention in any future conflict with, or over, Taiwan.

The comparatively modest Chinese SSN programme, and the development of an ambitious new nuclear submarine base at Ya Long near Sanya,[85] suggest an interest in operational speed and a capacity to range well beyond China's immediate area. Even so, the bulk of China's submarine force is especially suited for operations within the first island chain.

China's surface fleet now numbers 78 ships, with greater emphasis being placed on indigenous production. The PLAN's four *Sovremenny* class destroyers (bought from Russia and originally designed during the Cold War to assist in amphibious operations) are still impressive ships, equipped as they are with *Sunburn* anti-ship missiles and air defences, though comparatively lacking in ASW capabilities. The PLAN has emphasised the construction of fewer, but bigger and more powerful, vessels since 'it takes a single anti-ship missile to cripple a 100 meter-long ship, but it needs three to cripple a 150 metre-long ship'.[86] Newer types of warship, like 9,000-tonne *Luyang* I Type 052B and the Type 051C *Luzhou* guided-missile destroyer demonstrate all-round improvement, which is especially marked in area-air-defence where new surface-to-air missile systems are linked with more advanced air-surveillance radars and an increasing variety of longer-range high-speed anti-ship missiles, launched from submarines and warships.[87] This would put some key American assets at significant risk, at least within the first island chain, and so help deter the Americans from aggressive action, perhaps in support of some Taiwanese demarche.[88] Modern Chinese frigates like the *Jaingwei* II and the *Jiangakei* classes now compare well with regional equivalents.[89] Continuing deficiencies in anti-submarine warfare and anti-air warfare, organic airpower and combat logistics, however, would seriously constrain the Chinese in major sea-control activity beyond this area and especially in the Indian Ocean.[90]

The most discussed aspect of the development of China's surface fleet, however, has been the emergence at long last of its first carrier, the *Liaoning,* which was finally commissioned in September 2012. Probably best seen as another 'technology demonstrator' and trials ship, this vessel, with its modest size, ski-jump ramp plus the PLAN's total lack of carrier experience means the ship will clearly not be an operational equivalent of US Navy carriers. Nonetheless, it suggests the intended development in the longer term of a capacity for organic naval aviation able to support PLAN operations outside the near seas and it serves as a persuasive indication of China's growing political clout within them.[91] Alongside this, there is evidence of a steady programme to develop modern carrier-based fighters such as the J-11B/J-15 (given the reluctance of the Russians to supply further Su-33s), together with surface escorts such as the Type-065A air-defence frigate, to go with its future carriers.[92] Some speculate that China may have as many as five carriers by the mid 2020s, but given China's need to absorb the lessons of the *Liaoning's* trials, this seems very challenging[93] For all that, it is far from clear that such carriers are designed for sea-control operations against first-class opposition in local waters. It is more likely that they are expected to help defend the country's interests further afield.

In addition to its destroyers and frigates, the PLAN has enhanced its substantial coastal-defence and near-seas A2/AD force with a large and sophisticated inventory of mines and at least 64 new highly capable[94] *Houbei* (Type 022) class of fast-attack craft, each with eight short-range YJ-83 ASCMs, together with long range YJ-62C land-based anti-ship missiles, led the US Office of Naval Intelligence in 2009 to conclude that this programme 'allows the PLA(N)'s larger combatants to focus on offshore defense and out-of-area missions without leaving a security gap along China's coastline'.[95]

The JMSDF is showing the same tendency towards rather fewer but larger and more capable sea-control forces. The Japanese defence budget has been static for several years and in October 2009, the MoD completed a study showing that the projected decline in budgetary allocations to defence from 1.27% of GDP in 2001 to 1.06% in 2011 had already resulted in a significant reduction in the country's defence-industrial base as well as the number of its forces, since affected industries are constitutionally prevented from compensating for a drop in domestic demand by seeking markets abroad. In July 2010, a government panel recommended the easing of these restrictions in order to allow Japan to participate more easily in international military research and development programmes, but the Hatoyama administration was committed to maintaining this ban. In consequence, a Japanese official from the Ministry of Defence was reported to have said, 'we are expecting the DPJ to decrease the defence budget, or perhaps make it a little flatter'.[96]

The JMSDF is a now substantial force, which includes 29 destroyers and 15 frigates (six of which are equipped with *Aegis* area air defence systems) 18 submarines, and a personnel strength of 45,550. The JMSDF budget has been static for the past several years, sitting at ¥1,069.9 bn (US$13.7 bn) in 2009, then rising to ¥1,100,801bn in 2011 and ¥1,109,807 bn in 2012.[97] All the same, that sum allowed the JMSDF to build one destroyer and one submarine every year, but over the next five years from 2012 it will begin decommissioning two or three destroyers or frigates annually, leading eventually to a smaller fleet. Its latest ships such as the *Akizuki* class of large destroyers, which are primarily intended to defend the *Kongo Aegis* ships, are considered very capable, however. But even in the current economic downturn and with the need to reconstruct after the Fukushima disaster, Japan's acquisition aspirations seem affordable. Anxieties about China have, moreover, led to an acceleration in Japan's investment in ASW and its submarine-replacement rate, which will eventually lead to a force of some 22–24 submarines.[98] There has even been talk of Japan acquiring an SSN on lease from the US.

An increasing emphasis is placed on building naval forces stronger in the disciplines of sea control, particularly in the areas of anti-submarine and anti- missile defence, which also take Chinese capabilities as a benchmark of what is required. Hence the JMSDF now has 30 undersea SOSUS-type arrays connected to 14 shore stations, ideally deployed to monitor Chinese submarines transiting from the East China Sea to the wider Pacific Ocean.[99]

The commissioning in 2009 of the 18,000-tonne *Hyuga* 'helicopter-carrying destroyer' attracted a good deal of attention. It is claimed by the Japanese to be substantially intended for antisubmarine operations, and indeed has the bow sonar, torpedo tube, and 'Shin-Asroc' missiles characteristic of an ASW platform. The second ship, the *Ise*, was launched in August 2009 and two more may be forthcoming.[100] The first two ships are intended to act as the core of four helicopter/destroyers groups operating in defence of Japanese islands in the East China Sea. Together, they are expected to 'transform the reach and power projection of the country's surface fleet' and certainly represent a significant advance over the two 6,900-tonne *Haruna*-class vessels they replace.[101] The rest of Japan's surface fleet, traditionally oriented towards SLOC protection, is substantial in both size and quality.[102] It now comprises 44 destroyers and nine frigates. The JMSDF has twice as many destroyers as the US 7th Fleet and four times its inventory of P-3C maritime patrol aircraft. Given the Americans' initial hesitation in making the P3C available to their Japanese allies, this ratio is particularly striking.[103]

The JMSDF operates 18 indigenously built SSKs. With one submarine being routinely replaced every year, this is a very modern force capable of long-range deep-water operations.[104] In March 2009, the commissioning of the 4,200-tonne *Soryu* – Japan's first submarine with air-independent propulsion (AIP) – marked the beginning of a significant upgrade in the country's underwater capability, since it effectively trebles a submarine's endurance – the amount of time a submarine can stay under-water. Japan's developing concerns about the Chinese navy have contributed to the expansion of the Japanese submarine force and its ASW capabilities.[105]

In October 2008, the then Indian navy chief, Admiral Sureesh Mehta, announced force-structure plans amounting to a 160-strong fleet including three aircraft carriers, 60 major combatants and 400 aircraft by 2022.[106] India has accordingly engaged in an extraordinarily ambitious fleet modernisation programme with some 40 new ships/submarines plus ten fast-attack craft currently under construction. This has been facilitated by a 12% increase in its defence budgeting that matches or exceeds those rises commonly attributed to China, half of which is devoted to capital acquisition. According to the Stockholm International Peace Research Institute (SIPRI), India has now become the world's main arms importer.[107] The fleet modernisation programme is filling its three major ship-yards. It includes two carriers, three destroyers, six frigates, eight corvettes and offshore patrol vessels, six SSKs, one large amphibious-warfare vessel and six survey ships. Others are planned and approved, still others in the pipeline. Given the fact that India's yards and graving docks are full but still seem able to deliver only one unit per year, many wonder whether

India will in fact be able to meet all its aspirations in the time frame envisaged, even with Russian, Israeli and French help.[108] These ambitions are, moreover matched by an equally energetic assault on the country's past deficiencies in surveillance by developing its satellite, UAV and helicopter capabilities.

Unlike the Japanese or Chinese navies, the Indian Navy has acquired significant experience in carrier operations, and the central role of organic naval aviation in Indian sea-control aspirations is plain:

> The Carrier Task Force (CTF) is a self contained and composite balanced force, capable of undertaking the entire range of operational tasks, including presence, surveillance, maritime strike, ASW, ASuW, AAW, IW [Anti-Submarine warfare, Anti-Surface Warfare, Anti-Air warfare, Information warfare] *et al*, and is critical to the success of amphibious/sea-borne expeditionary operations.[109]

India's carrier and naval aviation programme, however, has been a major victim of systemic deficiencies in defence acquisition. Delivery of the INS *Vikramaditya* (the ex-Soviet *Kiev*-class carrier *Gorshkov*) is not now expected until late 2013. India's first locally built carrier, the INS *Vikrant,* was expected to be delivered from Kochi shipyard in 2015, with a second follow-up order to be placed soon, but is now two years behind schedule.[110] As a result, the Indian Navy may have two carriers by 2016, and possibly a third by 2020. The *Vikramaditya* is expected to operate 24 Mig-29K aircraft and the same aircraft could very well be operated by the next (indigenous) carrier in line. This carrier force should be able to deliver 'the entire gamut of attributes and characteristics of maritime power', and so will be available for a variety of other tasks, including fleet air defence and strike operations against fleets at sea and targets ashore.[111]

The Indian surface fleet (*see Appendix, Figure 2, Naval fleets*) comprises ten destroyers, ten frigates and 26 corvettes. With the decommissioning of older vessels and the arrival of new ships such as the last three *Talwar* (ex *Krivak*) 6,200-tonne frigates being built in Russia and new vessels from the modified *Delhi* and *Kolkata* classes, the Indian Navy is expected to benefit from a modest increase to about 29 destroyers and frigates by 2020. In parallel with the ambitious building programme already noted, India is developing missile and space programmes to improve its all-round sea-control capacities. Much attention is paid to the introduction by India of the *Brahmos* PJ-10 super-sonic anti-ship cruise missile (ASCM) – a joint venture with Russia that some interpret as an answer to the SS-N-22 *Sunburn* 3M80 missiles supplied by Russia to China.

India also currently maintains 14 SSKs but has an ambitious submarine programme of modernising existing forces, while developing new ones in order to serve standard sea-denial/control purposes. In 2007, the upgraded Mazagon dock in Mumbai began the construction of the first of six advanced French-designed *Scorpene* SSKs and the navy has launched another project for six locally produced submarines. Admiral Mehta was particularly keen for India to develop more of an all-round indigenous submarine capability, but for the time being it will need to rely heavily on foreign expertise.[112] According to India's comptroller and auditor general's report, project delays are likely to mean that, given the need to decommission its older submarines, the navy would have to operate with less than half its current active submarine fleet. To compensate for this serious shortfall, India is in the market for an additional six SSKs with air-independent propulsion under Project-75 India, but that project has also run into trouble.[113]

American sea-control capacities, by contrast, are very substantial, when compared to any of the other three navies of the area, or indeed with all of them put together. Its particular advantage lies in its 11-strong aircraft-carrier force. Despite doubts in some quarters about the survivability of large aircraft carriers operating close to the shores of a near-peer competitor engaging in concerted A2/AD strategies, the US Navy stresses the all-round utility of these platforms, not least for middle-range contingencies, such as Iran or North Korea, and argue that they can be defended against more serious threats such as long-range precision strikes. Judgements about the numbers of carriers needed by the US Navy have instead been largely determined by assumptions about the concurrency and strategic seriousness of the events for which they might be needed and the assessed acceptability of deployment delays before carriers or their reliefs/reinforcements arrive on station. Generally the answer has been found to be between ten and 15 first class fleet carriers; it is now accepted, though, that although 11 carrier strike groups are required, this number will dip to ten because of the delayed entry into service of the new *Ford*-class CVN-21.[114] Six are currently to be deployable within 30 days and a further two within 90 days. The new *Ford*-class carrier is apparently progressing well, but has been delayed by two years for budgetary reasons. In the meantime, and to ease the pressure, the US Navy has also formed a number of Expeditionary Strike Groups to take on some of the less demanding commitments. The US Pacific Fleet now comprises approximately 13 cruisers, 36 destroyers and 12 frigates but with the re-prioritisation of US surface ships and submarines announced in 2012, the Pacific may well become the main effort. In turn this could easily prompt a Chinese response, encouraging fears of a naval arms race in the region.

All the same, the US Navy's concern about, and response to, Chinese A2/AD capabilities is evident. Some analysts worry that 'East Asian waters are slowly becoming another potential no-go zone for US ships, particularly for aircraft carriers, which carry short-range strike aircraft that require them to operate well within the reach of [China's] A2/AD systems'.[115] Suggested solutions to the problem vary greatly. Some remain confident that the larger platforms can survive and do their jobs even in such hostile waters, if properly protected by sufficient intelligence, surveillance, target acquisition and reconnaissance (ISTAR), submarines, air-defence ships and electronic countermeasures. Others argue for more radical solutions based on the diffusion of naval power amongst much larger numbers of smaller units networked together.[116] Unless the Littoral Combat Ship, to be discussed in the next chapter, is taken as evidence of this second school of thought, there is as yet little sign of such a transformational response in the US Navy's design of its sea-control forces.

However, the recent decision to extend the acquisition of the impressive DDG-51 *Arleigh Burke* destroyers, with improved Flight IIA and III variants which as an expression of conventional, high quality, high intensity seapower are focused on the maintenance of American sea control against all comers, would seem to suggest otherwise.[117] Current planning calls for 48 SSN, and the US Navy attaches a great deal of importance to the successful *Virginia* programme, which is running ahead of schedule and below budget,[118] and which currently confers a considerable ASW advantage over China. Eight have been completed and brought into service to date. The US Navy is exploring options for a later follow-on class of much smaller nuclear submarines nonetheless capable of carrying a number of the smaller manned and unmanned platforms now considered essential for littoral operations. In 2012, its total complement of submarines was 71.

The US Navy also derives considerable benefit from its sea-control facilitators in a way that more than compensates for falling numbers. 'Forcenet' was the term used in the US 'Sea Power 21'[119] strategy formulation of 2002 for electronic networks used to integrate the sensors and weaponry on the varied and dispersed, constituent platforms of the fleet. The US Navy has heavily invested in this as a significant force multiplier and remains well ahead of all other navies in the efficiency and the ambition of its network-enabled operations, which will help compensate for falling combatant numbers.[120]

Sea-control operations

The US Navy changed from a force primarily configured in its missions and assets to take on the Soviet Navy in a Cold War context to one able to cope with the more fluid and ambiguous circumstances of the post-Cold War world. The slow rise of American concerns about security in the Pacific and the impact of the Chinese navy, with a consequent need to re-focus on conventional sea-control capabilities, however, have begun to reverse this trend. In June 2012, US Defense Secretary Leon Panetta said the US Navy has been reinforcing its position in the Asia-Pacific, and will be deploying 60% of its submarines to the Pacific, not 50% as it used to,[121] and has also moved another carrier battle group in as well. These enhancements are aimed at boosting the forward-deployed naval force in Japan. The emphasis was on areas such as anti-submarine warfare and ballistic-missile defence, with the latter represented by the deployment to Yokusuka (south of Tokyo) of the first upgraded *Ticonderoga*-class cruiser. The nature of some of these deployments reflects a desire to hedge against a possible North Korean and/or Chinese threat. Roughead acknowledged that the build up of the Chinese navy was not 'inconsistent with their economic growth and the interests they too have in security and stability on the world's oceans ... [but] when you talk about threat, you have to look at capability and intent. What the intent is and what their operational patterns will be are all still very unclear.'[122] Accordingly, the US Navy keeps a particularly close eye on Chinese naval operations.

The US Navy works to a 24/7 operational tempo unparalleled in the Asia-Pacific region. On any one day, about half the fleet is at sea, the vast majority of this well away from American waters.[123] This usage rate strains personnel and wears out ships and systems, to an extent that worries Admiral Greenert and his colleagues[124] but also provides an unrivalled bank of operational experience, an inestimable advantage in comparison with the other navies of the area.

Although neither the Japanese nor the Indian navies aspire to this level and extent of operational activity, both have for many years acquired significant experience in their own operating areas. Much Japanese activity is seen as a direct response to North Korean and Chinese activity. In 2004, the passage of a *Han*-class SSN around Guam while exercises involving the US Pacific Fleet were taking place and then in November of that year its return passage through Japanese waters was taken by both Japan and the United States as evidence of a need to build up ASW capabilities. The fact that the submarine had left the area of concern before the Japanese were able to intercept it, despite prior notification from the US Navy, brought home to the Japanese their need for greater command flexibility and more sophisticated equipment if they really wished to control their own seas against such intrusions, especially as the Chinese navy seemed engaged in a major programme of hydrographic surveying and testing throughout the area.[125] The subsequent pursuit of the submarine until it reached Chinese waters and the extraction of a private apology from Beijing shows how seriously the Japanese took this incident.

Extensive anti-submarine warfare exercises with the US Navy, such as the SHAREM (Ship Antisubmarine Readiness and Evaluation Measurement) series, were a major focus of US–Japanese cooperation through the Cold War, although the Americans, concerned about Japanese security measures, were quite often constrained in the data and equipment they were prepared to pass on to the JMSDF, to its clear annoyance.[126] The development of Chinese submarine capability and incidents such as the voyage of the *Han* around Guam and through Japanese waters are likely to increase incentives for closer cooperation against this possible new adversary.

In 2005, a new force of 55,000 troops plus supporting warships, aircraft and a command system to go with it was established, through the re-allocation of existing forces. The 2008 White Paper, moreover, refocused submarine deployment areas from the north of the country to the south, saying: 'The new formation of submarines to be deployed in important maritime traffic points in the East China Sea and the Sea of Japan for information-gathering purposes is intended to detect new threats and diverse contingencies as soon as possible.'[127] Since then there has been a significant move to make the Japanese Ground Self Defence Forces more mobile and flexible, to increase the garrisoning of its southern islands and to strengthening of its radar facilities in the Nansei islands chain far to the south.[128]

There is a wider issue for the Japanese too. The more the JMSDF integrates its efforts into a general American effort, perhaps developing contributory niche capabilities such as ASW or mine warfare, the less capable it may be of independent action where the United States is not involved, such as may develop over islands disputed with China, South Korea or Russia.

Japanese sensitivity about sea control in their immediate area was reinforced by similar, though less publicised, incidents involving Chinese units on previous occasions in the Osumi and Miuyako straits and even more by the dramatic intrusions into Japanese waters by North Korean surface vessels. After an earlier incident in 1999 which alerted the Japanese to a rising problem, a North Korean spy-ship was intercepted by the coast guard in Japanese waters in December 2001 and was then chased out into Chinese waters where, after an exchange of fire, it sank with the loss of all 15 crew members. Again the Japanese felt so strongly about this challenge to their capacity to control their own seas that they sought an accommodation with the Chinese by which they could salvage the vessel, proving conclusively that it was North Korean, and then put the wreck on public display as evidence of the need for continued vigilance, better coordination between the navy and the coast guard and more heavily armed coast guard patrol boats.[129] In short, Japan has devoted increasing resources to develop a sea-control capability in its own waters.

These operations, of course, illustrated concerns about local sea control and the extent to which the Japanese navy would be able and willing to back up its 1981 pledge to seek to defend its SLOCs up to 1,000 miles from Tokyo Bay. (This pledge, to be sure, has always been ambiguous for the terminology used was vague.)[130] The Japanese have however, clearly moved from the earlier assumption that their readiness to engage in such a campaign was contingent upon on its being part of a general attack on Japan itself. More recently Japan has evinced a desire to contribute to the defence of the SLOCs, over a much wider area than it used to, and in cooperation with Indian and other forces in Southeast Asia. At the same time the JMSDF's efforts have been backed up by the 'soft power' resources of organisations like the coast guard and the Nippon Foundation in contributing, for example, to SLOC security and navigational safety in the Malacca Strait.[131] The JMSDF has, moreover, been actively engaged in the international counter-piracy effort in the Gulf of Aden.

The Indian Navy engaged in sea-control operations in its immediate vicinity during the last two wars with Pakistan, but its ambitions to develop this capacity further afield have been quite limited. There was, for example, no attempt to defend Indian tankers caught up in the Iran–Iraq tanker war of the 1980s. From April to September 2001, during *Operation Enduring Freedom*, the Indian Navy did, however, engage in joint SLOC-protection patrols off the Malacca Strait, escorting over 20 American and allied high value ships through the area.

China's involvement in the construction of a new deepwater ports in Pakistan and Sri Lanka has reinforced concerns, especially in India, about the country's alleged efforts to extend its strategic influence to ports, airfields and other strategic outposts throughout the South China Sea from the Malacca Strait, across the Indian Ocean to the Persian Gulf (the so-called 'String of Pearls'). But serious naval competition in the Indian Ocean, even if the Chinese were considering it, remains only a long-term prospect, if an uncomfortable one for India. The revelation that China had opened a large new submarine and general naval base at Ya Long on Hainan island caused some concern in India, since it seemed to bring China's South Fleet rather closer to India and, further, the tunnelling effort for the base implied both high priority and an impressive level of constructional ability. Admiral Sureesh Mehta refocused the debate by pointing out that the size of China's fleet of long range of nuclear submarines gave more cause for concern than their basing.[132]

Incidents between the Chinese and Indian navies have been reported. In January 2009, for example, an Indian *Kilo*-class submarine apparently engaged in a clandestine sonar battle with Chinese warships passing by on their way to the Gulf of Aden. The Indian Navy strongly denied reports that the submarine in question was forced to the surface. In November

2011, an Indian warship, the INS *Airavat*, was apparently challenged by the Chinese in the South China Sea.[133] (The 'challenge' was electronic and the Indian forces could not identify its source). Such incidents illustrate an uneasy relationship between the two navies.[134] That India has established its Far Eastern Command in the Andaman and Nicobar islands is seen by some Chinese observers as evidence of a potential Indian desire to be able to contest the passage of Chinese vessels into the Indian Ocean. In July 2012, India opened a new Naval Air Station on Great Nicobar island, nearest the Malacca Strait, in order to extend its maritime surveillance.

In its exercises with countries such as the US, the UK, France and Singapore, moreover, the Indian Navy has shown proficiency in the rehearsal of the hard sea-control disciplines of ASW and AAW. The SIMBE exercise with Singapore of March 2007, for instance, involved defence against Singaporean F-16s, coincidentally the same aircraft used by Pakistan. It all illustrates the navy's often-expressed view that war-fighting remains its core business.

While the operational focus in sea control of the US, Indian and Japanese navies appears to be related to the PLAN, their preoccupations vary. India is more focused on its distant sea-control operations in the Indian Ocean; Japan and the United States with China's more localised sea control capabilities; and it is indeed largely in comparatively local waters that the Chinese navy has been most prepared, active and assertive.

As referred to above, a *Han*-class submarine was detected in Japan's territorial waters in 2004, and five warships operated in close proximity to Chinxiao gas field in the East China Sea, in an area disputed with Japan, in September 2005.[135] In November 2006, in an incident which some construed as a part of China's preparations for a campaign of sea denial, a diesel-powered *Song* submarine surfaced within five miles of the *USS Kitty Hawk* battlegroup operating near Okinawa. Denying this was a deliberate part of their developing anti-access strategy against the United States, the Chinese claimed it to be nothing more than an accidental encounter, and that the submarine in question did not have the speed to trail the battlegroup. Perhaps in part because of their embarrassment at having been thus surprised (to the extent that they were), and partly in a bid to prevent this incident turning into a crisis, the response of US Fleet Commander Admiral Fallon was quite muted. He pointed out that the battlegroup had not been exercising its ASW capabilities at the time but if it had been 'and if this Chinese submarine came in the middle of this, then it could have escalated into something that could have been very unforeseen'.[136]

China's more controversial anti-satellite test of January 2007 was also widely and likewise interpreted as an exercise in the PLAN's developing anti-access capability. Commentators point out that the US Navy, with its emphasis on networking and cooperative engagement, is heavily reliant on satellite communications and that an attack on its satellites would therefore greatly degrade its performance, unless sufficient counters were found.[137] From this perspective, China's considerable interest in space technology and cyber-war technology[138] are often considered part of a new and evolving arms race, and are closely related to the broader, and highly contentious issue of national and theatre ballistic-missile defence systems in the region.

Against this, analysts have frequently remarked on the very low patrol rate of Chinese submarines, which at an average of 2.4 operational patrols a year over the past 25 years, and 3.4 since 2000, hardly provides high levels of training, especially when the great majority of the submarines so employed are of relatively low quality, and the ASW capacities of the PLAN are currently reckoned to be indifferent, though improving.[139] To these capacities, they might have added a rudimentary underwater Sound Surveillance System (SOSUS) to detect submarines in the Western Pacific.[140] However, submarine patrols beyond immediate coastal waters have increased significantly both in number and in length of patrol in recent years.[141]

The scale and extent of PLAN sea-control exercises have been growing steadily, but never more so than in 2010 which saw several ambitious operations. In April, 16 warships from the three different fleets sailed past Okinawa towards the South China Sea and conducted ASW, AAW and live firing exercises. In July that year, Type 022 *Houbei* fast-attack craft tried out their swarming tactics with anti-ship missiles in apparent response to the putative arrival of the US carrier *George Washington* in the Yellow Sea after the loss of the *Cheonan*. A large-scale exercise in the South China Sea came later that month involving its most modern frigates and destroyers, *Kilo*-class submarines and JH-7/7A fighter bombers. These exercises focused on sea-control. Those in the Yellow Sea and the Sea of Japan were exercises in contesting sea-control notionally against the US and Japan respectively; in the South China Sea it was a question of asserting it against other claimants in the area.

In addition to their training function, all of these sea-control exercises transmitted messages of Chinese resolve and capacity to the United States and to China's neighbours – and indeed to the country's domestic audience. Whether or not these exercises were targeted against particular countries, they were certainly interpreted in that way by the US, Japan, Vietnam and the Philippines in particular.[142]

A more conciliatory note was struck with the continuation of the PLAN's counter-piracy efforts in the Gulf of Aden, which revealed a closer relationship with Western and other partners in the enterprise, and a willingness to protect foreign flagged ships as well as their own. On one hand, having to maintain a task group far from home has been a major learning experience, logistically and in other ways, for the Chinese. On the other hand, the presence of an LPD, the *Kunlan Shan*, complete with its force of marines, and the detachment of a section of the fifth squadron on site for a prolonged visit to the Mediterranean squadron testified to the growing operational reach of the Chinese fleet and its increasingly sophisticated development and use of port facilities in Djibouti, Salalah and Aden.[143] The detachment of an air-defence frigate, the *Xuzhou*, to standby while some of 35,000 citizens were evacuated from Libya,[144] illustrated the extent to which China's increasing exposure to the world economy will require the development of more global naval capacities and will have increased worries, especially in India, about the longer-term future. In Japan and the United States too, there is speculation about the future activity of the PLAN once its more local concerns in the Taiwan Strait and the East and South China seas have been resolved. The Americans have concluded that the PLAN could support a 12-ship task force with several battalions of ground troops out-of-area within the next five years.[145]

Conclusion

Sea-control is critical to future relationships in the Western Pacific because of the centrality of the importance, as ever, of secure supplies of energy resources and raw materials, and unimpeded access to distant markets, to the economic development and social stability of all four countries, and for regime survival as far as China is concerned.[146]

Unsurprisingly, contemporary interpretations of traditional conceptions of sea-control and sea-denial and the manner in which they are put into effect are inherently conflictual since they tend to be aimed at other navies and so encourage competitive responses from them. There is certainly evidence of this in the Asia-Pacific region, most obviously in the tensions between US concepts of Air–Sea Battle and Chinese ideas about 'counter intervention operations' (or A2/AD as the Americans call it), but also in similar if smaller- scale interactions between the Chinese, the Japanese and Vietnamese, where the PLAN finds itself as the force whose 'intervention' evidently needs to be countered. Japan's switch to the defence of its southwest is one clear example of this. Increased discussion in Taiwan about the vulnerability of its SLOCs to Chinese pressure and evidence of a Chinese buildup in the capacity to do so would be another.

These interactions clearly have decided potential as sparks for arms-racing behaviour. The prospect of this is increased by the simple fact that the contested South and East China Seas – or what China calls its near seas – are the areas in which these tensions are most obvious and ones which link the US with its local allies and partners. Admiral Greenert's three tenets of 'Warfighting First', 'Operate Forwards' and 'Be Ready' suggests that the US Navy in particular intends to tackle what it sees as the challenge to its freedom of manoueuvre quite robustly. There is, however, some evidence that the US Navy is beginning to think of pressure on Chinese SLOCs as a more affordable and perhaps less escalatory alternative to overt confrontation in China's near seas should this ever seem neces-sary.[147]

Nevertheless, the development of sea-control capabilities has been steady rather than fast in all four countries, and the inherent dangers that it presents have been partially offset by a shared acceptance of the malign consequences of not recognis-ing them and by their readiness to cooperate against common threats to their capacity to use the sea peacefully, most obvi-ously in the counter-piracy mission in the Gulf of Aden. This example and the support that all these navies provide for the operation reinforces the point that sea control is a wide-ranging concept which includes the protection of shipping against pirates and in which the navies concerned seem themselves as partners rather than potential adversaries in a prospective naval arms race.

Notes

1 See Geoffrey Till, *Seapower; A Guide for the 21st Century* (London: Routledge, 2009, 2nd ed.), pp. 145–57; *Australian Maritime Doctrine: RAN Doctrine 1 2010* (Canberra: Seapower Centre, 2010), pp. 71–4.

2 James R. Holmes and Toshi Yoshihara review a variety of Chinese-language sources from which these quotations derive, in their *Chinese Naval Strategy in the 21st Century: the Turn to Mahan* (London: Routledge, 2008) especially pp. 39–43; see also their 'The Influence of Mahan Upon China's maritime Strategy'. *Comparative Strategy*, January–March 2005, pp. 8, 53–71; and You Ji, *The Evolution of China's Maritime Combat Doctrines and Models*, Working Paper no. 22 (Singapore: IDSS, May 2002).

3 Admiral Zhang Lianzhong, cited in J. Downing, 'China's Evolving Maritime Strategy: Part II', *Jane's Intelligence Review*, April 1996, p. 187.

4 Defence White Paper (Beijing: Information Office of the State council of the People's Republic of China, December 2004), http://english.people.com.cn/whitepaper/defense2004.

5 You Ji, 'China's Naval Strategy and Transformation', in W. Lawrence Prabhakar, Joshua H. Ho and W.S.G. Bateman (eds), *The Evolving Maritime Balance of Power in the Asia-Pacific: Maritime Doctrines and Nuclear Weapons at Sea* (Singapore: World Scientific Publishing Co., 2006), p. 72.

6 Office of the Secretary of Defense, 'Military and Security Developments involving the People's Republic of China 2012', Annual Report to Congress May 2012, p. iv.

7 Liu Jixian, *Research of the Maritime Strategic Environment and the Policy Response* (Beijing: Liberation Army Press, 1997), cited in Nan Li, 'The Evolution of China's Naval Strategy and Capabilities: from "Near Seas" to "Far Seas"', *Asian Security*, vol. 5, no. 2, Spring 2009, p. 8.

8 Office of the Secretary of Defense, *Military Power of the People's Republic of China 2009* (Washington DC: Department of Defense, 2009), pp. 20–4.

9 For a dissenting view of the readiness of the Chinese to engage in early use of ASBMs against US carriers see Dennis J. Blasko, 'Technology Determines Tactics: the Relationship between Technology and Doctrine in Chinese Military Thinking', *Journal of Strategic Studies*, vol. 34, no. 3, June 2011, pp. 377–8; Duncan Lennox, 'China's

ASBM Project: Keep Calm and Carry On', *Jane's Defence Weekly*, 16 February 2011.

[10] Eric Hagt and Mathew Durnin, 'China's Anti-ship Ballistic Missiles', *US Naval War College Review*, Autumn 2009, pp. 87–115.

[11] 'China Confirms "Carrier Killer"', *Jane's Defence Weekly*, 20 July 2011; 'China's New Satellites Capable of Sinking US Nuclear Carriers', *Daily Telegraph*, 13 July 2011.

[12] 'China Needs "Carrier-Killer" Missile: Press', Agence France-Presse, 6 September 2010.

[13] United States Department of Defense, Office of the Secretary of Defence, 'Military Power of the People's Republic of China 2008', available at http://www.mcsstw.org/www/download/China_Military_Power_Report_2008.pdf, p. 29.

[14] For example, Ross Munro, 'Taiwan: What China Really Wants', *National Review*, 11 October 1999, p. 47 and Robyn Lim, 'Taiwan and Asia-Pacific Security', in Martin L. Lasater and Peter Yu (eds), *Taiwan's Security in the Post-Deng Xiaoping Era* (London: Frank Cass, 2000), p. 97, cited in Holmes and Yoshihara, *Chinese Naval Strategy*.

[15] Cited in Ronald O' Rourke, 'China Naval Modernisation: Implications for U.S. Navy Capabilities – Background and Issues for Congress', Congressional Research Service, 18 October 2007, p. 41.

[16] Aldo Chircop, 'The Emergence of China as a Polar-Capable State', *Canadian Naval Review*, Spring 2011.

[17] Information Office of the State Council, 'China's National Defense in 2010', March 2011, http://www.gov.cn/english/official/2011-03/31/content_1835499.htm, p 6.

[18] Michael Richardson, 'China's Reliance on Mid-East Oil a Strategic Vulnerability', *Straits Times*, 14 February 2011.

[19] Andrew Erickson and Gabe Collins, 'Beijing's Energy Security Strategy: The Significance of a Chinese State-Owned Tanker Fleet', *Orbis*, Fall 2007, pp. 665–84.

[20] Evan Feigenbaum, 'China's Military Posture and the New Economic Geopolitics', *Survival*, vol. 41, no. 2, Summer 1999, p. 73.

[21] Professor Ni Lexiong, 'Seapower and China's Development', *Liberation Daily*, 17 April 2005, cited in Holmes and Yoshihara, *Chinese Naval Strategy in the 21st Century: The Turn to Mahan*, p. 42.

[22] See the following chapter. For more on this topic, see also Eric A. McVaden, 'US–PRC Maritime Cooperation: An Idea Whose Time Has Come?', *China Brief*, vol. 7, no. 12, 13 June 2007. Admiral McVaden is a former defence attaché to China.

[23] People's Republic of China, *Chinese National Defence in 2004*, cited in Holmes and Yoshihara, *Chinese Naval Strategy*, p. 72.

[24] Jiang Shiliang, 'The Command of Communications', *China Military Science*, 2 October 2002, pp. 106–14, cited in Holmes and Yoshihara, *Chinese Naval Strategy*, pp. 74–5.

[25] Cited in Richard D. Fisher Jr, 'Depth Perception: China Links Power to Economic Security', *Defense Technology International*, May 2009.

[26] J. Noel Williams, 'Air–Sea Battle: An Operational Concept Looking For A Strategy,' *Armed Forces Journal*,

September 2011; T.X. Hammes, 'Offshore Control: a Proposed Strategy for an Unlikely Conflict' *National Defense University, INSS Strategic Forum*, June 2012.

27 You Ji, *The Evolution of China's Maritime Combat Doctrines and Models*, Working paper no. 22 (Singapore: IDSS, May 2002), pp. 27 et seq.

28 Quoted in Declan Walsh, 'US Uneasy as Beijing Develops a Strategic String of Pearls', *Guardian*, 10 November 2005.

29 Ian Storey, 'China as a Global Maritime Power: Opportunities and Vulnerabilities', in Andrew Forbes (ed.), *Australia and its Maritime Interests* (Canberra: Sea Power Centre, 2008).

30 *Indian Maritime Doctrine 2009*, available at Press Information Bureau, Government of India, http://pib.nic.in/newsite/erelease. aspx?relid=52223, p. 1. See also Vijay Sakhuja, *Asian Maritime Power in the 21st Century* (Singapore: Institute of Southeast Asian Studies, 2011), pp. 92–5.

31 *Indian Maritime Doctrine 2009*, pp. 60 & 78.

32 *Ibid*, pp. 60 & 78.

33 *Ibid.*, p. 78.

34 *Ibid.*, p. 64.

35 *Ibid.*, p. 75.

36 *Ibid.*, p. 50.

37 Indian Navy, *Freedom To Use The Seas: India's Maritime Military Strategy* (New Delhi: Integrated Headquarters, Ministry of Defence, 2007).

38 Foreword to *Freedom To Use The Seas: India's Maritime Military Strategy*, 2007, p. iv, p. 41,

39 *Indian Maritime Doctrine 2004*, p. 63.

40 Indian Navy, *India's Maritime Military Strategy*, pp. 46–9.

41 *Indian Maritime Doctrine 2009*, p. 95.

42 Admiral Sureesh Mehta, address to IISS Shangri-La Dialogue, Singapore, 30 May 2009.

43 Admiral Sureesh Mehta, foreword to *India's Maritime Military Strategy*, p. iv.

44 Cited in Graham, *Japan's Sea Lane Security*, pp. 182–96.

45 US Navy, *Naval Operations Concept 2010: Implementing the Maritime Strategy* (Washington DC: Department of the Navy, 2010), at http://www.navy.mil/maritime/noc/NOC2010.pdf.

46 *A Cooperative Strategy for 21st Century Sea Power* (Washington DC: Department of the Navy, 2007), p. 11.

47 See 'US Navy Needs to Lean Forward, evolve, Admiral Greenert Says' at http://www.diplonews.com/feeds/free/28_June_2012_49.; and the Admiral's blog http://cno.navylive.dodlive.mil, posted 9 October 2012.

48 Quoted in 'USN Seeks Wider Seapower Definition', *Jane's Navy International*, July–August 2006, p. 11. This much-quoted comment was praised by Admiral Mehta at the IISS.

49 'Naval Operations Concept 2010', p. 52.

50 *Ibid.*, p. 54.

51 Tim Fish, 'Japan Rises to the Challenge of Cuts and New Threats', *Jane's Navy International*, May 2009.

52 Commander Shinichi Nakazawa, quoted in *Ibid*.

53 'Naval Operations Concept 2010', p. 52.

54 Statement by Admiral Gary Roughead before the Senate Armed Services Committee, 28 February 2008, p. 7.

55 Ronald O'Rourke, *China Naval Modernisation: Implications for US Navy Capabilities – Background and Issues for Congress* (Washington DC: Congressional Research Service, June 2010), pp. 26–32.

56 See Jan Van Tol, Mark Gunzinger, Andrew Krepinevich and Jim Thomas, *AirSea Battle: A Point-of-Departure Operational Concept* (Washington DC: Center for Strategic and Budgetary Assessments, 2010).

57 Thus Captain Philip Dupree USN and Col Jordan Thomas, USAF, 'Air Sea Battle Clearing the Fog', *Armed Forces Journal*, May 2012; US Navy Air Sea Battle Office, 'The Air Sea Battle Concept Summary' at www.navy.mil/submit/display.asp?story_id=63730.

58 Van Tol et al., *AirSea Battle: A Point-of-Departure Operational Concept*, p. xv.

59 Chief of Naval Operations Adm. Jonathan Greenert's Opening Remarks at the Brookings Institution Air–Sea Battle Doctrine, 16 May 2012, at http://www.brookings.edu/events/2012/05/16-air-sea-doctrine#ref-id=20120516_schwartz.

60 O'Rourke, *China Naval Modernisation 2010*, p. 27.

61 Bill Gertz, 'Inside The Ring: Air Sea Battle Fight', *Washington Times*, 12 October 2011; Sam Bateman, *US AirSea Battle: Countering China's Anti-access Strategies'*, RSIS Commentaries, no. 82, 19 May 2011; Richard Fisher, 'Too Little Too Late?', *Defense Technology International*, April 2011.

62 General Norton A. Schwartz, USAF & Admiral Jonathan W. Greenert, USN, 'Air–Sea Battle: Promoting Stability in an Era of Uncertainty', *American Interest*, 20 February 2012.

63 Interview with Captain Stuart Munsch, Washington DC, August 2010.

64 'Strained US-Sino Ties Loom at Asia Security Forum', Agence France-Presse, 22 July 2010.

65 Van Tol et al., *AirSea Battle: A Point-of-Departure Operational Concept*, p. 9; for an excellent summary of the issues see Michael Raska, 'Air–Sea Battle: Operational Consequences and Allied Concerns', *Defense News*, 29 October 2012.

66 Remarks by Admiral Gary Roughead to the Exponaval Conference, Santiago, 2 December 2008.

67 Interestingly, Admiral Greenert himself sometimes comes over as something of a sceptic on 'stealth': See his 'Payloads over Platforms: Charting a New Course', *Proceedings of the US Naval Institute*, July 2012 at http://www.usni.org/magazines/proceedings/2012-07/payloads-over-platforms-charting-new-course.

68 Alexander Chieh-cheng Huang, 'The Chinese Navy's Offshore Active Defense Strategy', *Naval War College Review*, 1994, pp. 7–31; Nan Li, *Reconceptualising the PLA Navy in Post-Mao China: Functions, Warfare, Arms and Organisation*, Working Paper no. 30 (Singapore: IDSS, August 2002), p. 5.

69 James C. Bussert and Bruce A. Elleman, *Peoples Liberation Army:*

Combat Systems Technology, 1949–2010 (Annapolis, MD: Naval Institute Press, 2011), pp. 8–14.

70 See Ian Storey, 'China as a Maritime Power'; see also O'Rourke, *China Naval Modernisation: Implications for US Navy Capabilities – Background and Issues for Congress*. The Chinese use 'Informationised Warfare' as a label for military operations that are heavily reliant of information technology. The US phrase 'network-centric operations' is an approximate equivalent.

71 Office of the Secretary of Defense, 'Military and Security Developments involving the People's Republic of China 2012', Annual Report to Congress, May 2012, p. 3.

72 *Ibid.*; O'Rourke, *China Naval Modernisation: Implications for US Navy Capabilities – Background and Issues for Congress*, p. 13; Richard A. Bitzinger, 'China's Military Industrial Complex: is it [Finally] Turning a Corner?', RSIS Commentary no. 121, November 2008.

73 There are various criteria for determining which class a vessel corresponds to. For our purposes, judgements will be made on the basis of tonnage, as used by the *Military Balance* in its comparison of global capabilities. See IISS, *Military Balance 2012* (London: Routledge for the IISS, 2012).

74 *East Asia Strategic Review* (Tokyo: The Japan Times for NIDS, 2009) p. 49. *The East Asia Strategic Review* is an annual product of the National Institute for Defence Studies (NIDS), Japan. See also *Annual Report to Congress: Military and Security Developments Involving the People's Republic of China 2011*, US Department of Defense, March 2011, http://www.defense.gov/pubs/pdfs/2011_CMPR_FInal.pdf, p. 3.

75 *A Modern Navy with Chinese Characteristics* (Washington DC: Office of Naval Intelligence, 2010), as discussed in Richard Scott, 'China to Take Naval Forces to Another Level over next Decade', *Jane's International Defence Review*, February 2010, http://www.janes.com/products/janes/defence-security-report.aspx?id=1065926378.

76 Richard D. Fisher, Jr, 'Regional Power: China Aims to Hold Sway in the Western Pacific', *Defense Technology International*, March 2009.

77 Dennis C. Blair, *Annual Threat Assessment of the Intelligence Community for the Senate Select Committee on Intelligence* (Washington DC: US Senate, 12 February 2009), p. 23.

78 Bradley Perrett, 'China Expands its Military Reach', *Aviation Week*, 18 October 2011.

79 US Department of Defense, *Annual Report to Congress [on] Military Power of the People's Republic of China* (Washington DC: Department of Defense, 2009), p. 48.

80 Thomas G. Mahnken, 'China's Anti-Access Strategy in Historical and Theoretical Perspective', *Journal of Strategic Studies*, vol. 34, no. 3, June 2011, p. 319; 'China Ramps Up Missile Threat with DF-16', *Defence News*, 21 March 2011.

81 David Crane, 'Chinese Electromagnaetic Pulse and High-Powered

Weapons vs US Navy Aircraft Carrier Battle Groups', *Defence Review*, 22 July 2011.

82 'DoD: China to Have a Regional AF by 2020', *Defense News*, 21 February 2011; Bill Sweetman, 'After Chengdu', *Defense Technology International*, February 2011; 'China Sets the Tone', *Jane's Defence Weekly*, 16 February 2011.

83 Jonathan Watts and Julian Berger, 'Chinese Jet Fighter 'Sighting' Raises Fears over Region's Military Power Balance', *Guardian*, 5 January 2011; *Defense News* reports of 6 September, 8 November, 29 November and 6 December 2010. Much of this was revealed in 'Airshow China 2010', in which the PLAAF played a major and notable assertive role; *Jane's Defense Weekly*, 22 December 2010; Bradley Perrett, 'China Expands its Military Reach', *Aviation Week*, 18 October 2011.

84 'China Ramps Up Missile Threat with DF-16', *Defence News*, 21 March 2011.

85 Nan Li, 'The Evolution of China's Naval Strategy and Capabilities: from "Near Seas" to "Far Seas"', *Asian Security*, vol. 5, no. 2, Spring 2009.

86 Yu Chuannxi et al. *Science and Technology and Future Arms and Equipment* (Beijing: National Defence University, 1997), p. 41, quotation cited in Nan Li, 'Reconceptualizing the PLA Navy in Post-Mao China: Functions, Warfare, Arms and Organisation', Working Paper No 30 of August 2002, Institute of Defence and Strategic Studies, available at RSISPublication@ntu.edu.sg, p. 19.

87 Office of the Secretary of Defense, 'Military and Security Developments involving the People's Republic of China 2012', Annual Report to Congress May 2012, p. 23.

88 US Office of Naval Intelligence, *Report on PLA[N]* (Washington DC: US Office of Naval Intelligence, August 2009), p. 19. The four SAM systems now available are the SA-N-7 (Russian) 30-45km dependent on variant of missile, SA-N-20 Gargoyle (Russian) 150-200km dependent on variant of missile, HHQ-9 (Chinese) 90km and over, and the new vertically launched HHQ-16 (Chinese) 40km and over. See also *Jane's Fighting Ships* (London: IHS Jane's, 2009–10).

89 James C. Bussert and Bruce A. Elleman, *Peoples Liberation Army: Combat Systems Technology, 1949–2010*, p. 57. Rather less than half of the PLAN's destroyers and frigate force would, however, be regarded as modern.

90 James R. Holmes and Toshi Yoshihara, 'China's Naval Ambitions in the Indian Ocean', *Journal of Strategic Studies*, vol. 31, no. 3, June 2008, pp. 389–439.

91 Abraham M. Denmark, Andrew S. Erickson and Gabriel Collins, 'Should We Be Afraid of China's New Aircraft Carrier? Not Yet', *Foreign Policy*, 27 June 2011.

92 'China Tests Carrier-Based J-11B Prototype', *Jane's Defence Weekly*, 2 June 2010.

93 Richard D. Fisher, 'Making Waves: China's Aircraft Carrier Program is in Full Swing', *Defense Technology International*, January 2011; Wendell Minnick, 'Images Provide Clues to

China's Naval Might', *Defense News*, 1 October 2012.

94 Trefor Moss, 'Plan of Action: China's Naval Modernisation', *Jane's Defence Weekly*, 9 February 2011.

95 Office of Naval Intelligence, *The People's Liberation Army Navy, A Modern Navy with Chinese Characteristics* (Suitland, MD: Office of Naval Intelligence, August 2009), cited in O'Rourke, *China Naval Modernisation: Implications for US Navy Capabilities – Background and Issues for Congress*, p. 29.

96 'Budget Cuts Take Heavy Toll on Japan's Defence Industrial Base', *Jane's Defence Weekly*, 7 October 2009.

97 IISS Defence and Military Analysis Programme statistics.

98 Paul Kallender-Umezu, 'Japan's Budget Request Targets Capabilities to Defend Sea Lanes', *DefenseNews*, 17 September 2012.

99 Desmond Ball, 'Naval Acquisitions in Northeast Asia: Modernisation or Arms Racing?', unpublished notes for Seminar on 'Enhancing Asia Maritime Security and Confidence Building Measures', Singapore, 26 January 2010.

100 The naming of the vessel is interesting. The last *Ise* was a 25,000-tonne battleship converted during the war into a hybrid aircraft carrier.

101 Sunho Beck, 'Sea Change: Japan's New Destroyer could be an Aircraft Carrier', *Defense Technology International*, September 2008; 'Japanese Helicopter Carrier Enters Service', *Jane's Defence Weekly*, 25 March 2009.

102 Euan Graham, *Japan's Sea Lane Security 1940–2004* (London: Routledge, 2006) p. 45.

103 The Japanese had first to threaten to buy the British *Nimrod* instead. See Elizabeth Guran, *The Dynamics of the US Japan Naval Relationship*, unpublished PhD, King's College, London, p. 108 and for these statistics, Guran, p. 178, n. 274.

104 Alessio Patalano, 'Shielding the 'Hot gates''; Submarine Warfare and Japanese Naval Strategy in the Cold War and Beyond (1976–2006)', *Journal of Strategic Studies*, vol. 31, no. 6, December 2008.

105 Graham, *Japan's Sea Lane Security*, p. 179; 'Japan to Beef Up Submarines to Counter Chinese Power', *Chosun Ilbo*, 26 July 2010; 'Japan to Add Six Submarines To Fleet: Reports', AFP, 21 October 2010.

106 James R. Holmes, Andrew C. Winner and Toshi Yoshihara, *Indian Naval Strategy in the Twenty-first Century* (London: Routledge, 2009), p. 83.

107 Interview with Admiral Nirmal Verma, *Defense Technology International*, June 2010; 'India Announces 12% Defence Budget Increase', *Jane's Defence Weekly*, 9 March 2011; 'India Tops Arms Importers: SIPRI', *Defense News* , 21 March 2011.

108 Rahul Bedi, 'Lack of Strategic Will is Sapping India's Potential', *Jane's Defence Weekly*, 9 August 2006; 'Navy Chief Questions India's Ship-building Pace', *Defense News*, 2 December 2009; 'Indian Auditors Warn of Navy Capability Shortfall', *Jane's Defence Weekly*, 30 March 2011.

109 *Indian Maritime Doctrine* 2009, p. 125.

110 Vivek Raghuvananshi, 'Should India be Building Another Carrier?', *Defense News*, 30 July 2012; Vivek

Raghuvanesh, 'India Seeks Home for ex-Russian Carrier', *Defense News*, 24 September 2012.

[111] Vice Admiral Madanjit Singh, 'Carrier Operations in the Indian Navy', *Seagull*, February 2006.

[112] 'India to Acquire Six More Submarines: Naval Chief', *Hindustan Times*, 9 May 2008.

[113] 'India Approves Additional Payment for Delayed Subs', *Jane's Defence Weekly*, 17 March 2010; 'Biggest Military Deal: Six Subs for Rs 50,000 Crore', *Times of India*, 11 July 2001; 'Induction of Scorpene Submarines Delayed by Three Years', *Hindustan Times*, 23 February 2011; 'India Close to Receiving Akula Class Submarine', *Jane's Defence Weekly*, 31 August 2011.

[114] Congressional Budget Office, 'An Analysis of the Navy's Fiscal Year 2013 Shipbuilding Plan', July 2012 pp. 4, 15.

[115] Adm. James A. Lyons (retd), 'Countering Beijing's New Weapon: Stealthy Zumwalt Destroyer is the Answer', *Washington Times*, 6 December 2009; Andrew F. Krepinevich Jr, 'The Pentagon's Wasting Assets: the Eroding Foundations of American Power', *Foreign Affairs*, July–August 2009.

[116] See O'Rourke, *China Naval Modernisation: Implications for US Navy Capabilities – Background and Issues for Congress*, p. 35.

[117] 'Flight of Fancy', *Defense Technology International*, July–August 2011; Congressional Budget Office, 'An Analysis of the Navy's Fiscal Year 2013 Shipbuilding Plan', July 2012, p. 20–23.

[118] The *Seawolf* programme is reckoned to have cost about US$7.3bn in R&D and US$14.2bn in construction and outfitting (2010 dollars). See 'USS Missouri Leading Way for New Wave of Submarines', *Military News*, 4 August 2010; 'New US Attack Subs Getting their "Sea Legs"', *Defense News*, 13 September 2010.

[119] Adm. Vern Clark, USN, 'Sea Power 21, Part I: Projecting Decisive Joint Capabilities', *Proceedings*, October 2002.

[120] 'US Navy to Spend $6bn on Unmanned Platforms', *Jane's Defence Weekly*, 19 August 2009.

[121] 'Leon Panetta: US to Deploy 60% of Navy Fleet to Pacific', BBC, 2 June 2012.

[122] Quoted in Robert Karniol, 'Pacific Partners', *Jane's Defence Weekly*, 25 April 2007.

[123] Remarks delivered by Chief of Naval Operations Admiral Gary Roughead to 2008 Exponaval Conference, Santiago, 2 December 2008.

[124] Sam Fellman, 'Greenert: Fleet Operations Pace Unsustainable', *Marine Corps Times*, 16 April 2012 at http://www.marinecorpstimes.com/news/2012/04/navy-jon-greenert-fleet-operations-pace-unsustainable-041612/.

[125] 'Submarine that Intruded into Japanese Waters Likely to be Chinese Vessel', *Mainichi Shimbun*, 11 November 2004; 'Eagle Eyes: Self Defense Forces Keep Tabs On Nations Mapping East Asia's Seabed', *Asahi Shimbun*, 16 February 2004.

[126] M. Elizabeth Guran, *The Dynamics and Institutionalisation of the Japan–US Naval Relationship 1976–2001*, London University Doctoral Thesis, 2008.

127 *2004 National Defence Program Outline* cited in Naoko Sajima, 'Contemporary Japanese Sea Power: Weighing Anchor' in Naoko Sajima and Kyoichi Tachikawa (eds), *Japanese Sea Power: A Maritime nation's Struggle for Identity* (Canberra: Sea Power Centre, 2009), p. 85.

128 Jonathan Holslag, *Trapped Giant: China's Military Rise* (Abingdon: Routledge for the IISS, 2010), p. 80.

129 Jonathan Watts, 'Japanese Navy Fires on Spy Ships', *Guardian*, 25 March 1999; Marcus Warren, 'Japan Sinks 'North Korean Spying Ship' *Daily Telegraph*, 24 December 2001.

130 Peter J. Woolley, *Japan's Navy: Politics and Paradox* (Boulder, CO: Lynne Rienner, 1999), pp. 50–2.

131 Graham, *Japan's Sea Lane Security*, pp. 119, 123–4, 141.

132 'China's Submarine Progress Alarms India', *Asia Times*, 9 May 2008; 'Satellite Imagery Confirms Nuclear Sub Base in China', *Jane's Defence Weekly*, 16 April 2008; 'Nuclear Submarine Base Making Waves', *New Zealand Herald*, 3 May 2008. My thanks to Dr Mohan Malik and several officers of the Indian Navy for their illuminating thoughts on this point.

133 'China Confronted Indian Warship off Vietnam', *Financial Times*, 1 September 2011.

134 Manu Pubby, 'Indian Submarine, Chinese Warship Test Each Other in Pirate Waters', *Indian Express*, 5 February 2009. Such encounters are discussed in Harsh Pant, 'India in the Indian Ocean', *Pacific Affairs*, vol. 82, no. 2, Summer 2009.

135 Ronald O'Rourke, *The Impact of Chinese Naval Modernisation on the Future of the United States Navy* (New York: Novitka Books, 2006), p. 25.

136 'Chinese Sub Got within Striking Range of US Ship', *Gulf Times*, 14 November 2006; accounts of this incident vary widely. See David Axe, 'China's Overhyped Sub Threat' *The Diplomat*, 20 October 2011 and O'Rourke, *China Naval Modernisation 2008*, p. 44.

137 'Chinese ASTA Test Rekindles Weapons Debate', *Jane's Defence Weekly*, 24 January 2007; G. Friedman, 'To be Prepared is to Survive', *Straits Times*, 25 January 2007.

138 Office of the Secretary of Defense 'Military and Security Developments involving the People's Republic of China 2012', Annual Report to Congress May 2012, pp. 8–10.

139 The figures come from Federation of American Scientists, 'China's Submarine Fleet Continues Low Patrol Rate', http://fas.org/blog/ssp/2007/02/; but see also O'Rourke, *China Naval Modernisation 2007*, pp. 12–13, 30–31; O' Rourke, *China Naval Modernisation 2008*, pp. 12–16; see also 'China Increases Submarine Patrols', *Jane's Defence Weekly*, 21 October 2009. The number of patrols increased to 12 in 2008, exactly double the previous peak in 2000.

140 O'Rourke, *China Naval Modernisation 2008*, pp. 27–8.

141 Bussert and Elleman, *Peoples Liberation Army: Combat Systems Technology, 1949–2010*, p. 75.

142 'China's Three-point Naval Strategy', *IISS Strategic Comments*, 15 October 2010.

143 *Ibid.*

[144] Zhang Lili, 'An Analysis of China's All-Out Efforts To Evacuate Chinese Nationals From Libya', *Contemporary World*, 5 April 2011.

[145] Department of Defense, *Annual Report to Congress: Military and Security Developments Involving the People's Republic of China 2011* (Washington DC: Department of Defense, March 2011), p. 27, http:// www.defense.gov/pubs/pdfs/2011_CMPR_Final.pdf.

[146] Timothy R. Heath, 'What Does China Want? Discerning the PRC's National Strategy', *Asian Security*, vol. 8, no. 1, 2012, p. 64.

[147] Michael Kraska, 'Air–Sea Battle Debate: Operational Consequences and Allied Concerns, *Defense News*, 29 October 2012.

CHAPTER THREE

Traditional missions

The current and future trajectories of the US, Chinese, Indian and Japanese navies may also be assessed according to their interpretation of three traditional naval roles: deterrence; the maritime projection of power ashore; and gunboat diplomacy, the more competitive variant of general naval diplomacy. The more priority they accord these intrinsically competitive roles, the more competitive their general stance is likely to be, and the greater the risk of sparking a destabilising naval arms race.

Deterrence

Although as a concept deterrence extends into the sphere of conventional conflict and weaponry, which may indeed be aimed against non-state actors, this chapter will focus on the nuclear deterrent mission – a mission to which the Chinese, Indian and American navies currently direct considerable thought and effort. This is perhaps the quintessentially most competitive, state-centred of all the possible functions of seapower, since it is about the potential survival or destruction of nations, generally requires national levels of effort and is usually aimed at rival nations.

China has consistently stated that it adheres to a no-first-use doctrine, which increases the incentive for it to maintain the reliable means of second strike provided by an SSBN force. The 2006 Defence White Paper spoke of the need for a 'gradual extension of strategic depth for offshore defensive operations and enhancing its capabilities in integrated maritime operations and nuclear counter-attack'. China has so far adopted a minimalist stance on nuclear deterrence, signed a non-targeting agreement with Russia in 1994 and the United States in 1998 but has not so far done the same with India.[1] Its scholars have taken a particular interest in the French model of nuclear deterrence as an example of the effective use of a relatively modest deterrent force.[2] Given the unlikelihood of a victory against the conventional forces of the United States in any major conflagration between the two countries, an effective nuclear deterrent is seen as an essential part of the Chinese armoury, but the Chinese insist that they will never enter a nuclear arms race.[3]

Some Chinese and Western analysts have argued that China might reconsider its 'no-first-use' policy stance, in the face of a prospective disarming strike, either nuclear or conventional, but at the moment this remains highly speculative.[4]

The Japanese Maritime Self-Defense Force (JMSDF) is quite unlike the other three navies in having no nuclear deterrent missions. This is a reflection of Japan's deeply held self-denying ordinance against nuclear weapons. Nonetheless, for all its pacifist proclivities and 'nuclear allergy', Japan is, technologically, a 'threshold' state. Were the US guarantee to come into doubt, voices would certainly be raised that Japan should explore the idea of developing its own sea-based deterrent system.[5] Former Prime Minister Yasuhiro Nakasone has argued that Japan's adoption of a defensive, minimalist nuclear posture would be compatible with the constitution and that: 'In order to raise Japan's defensive capability in case of emergency our Constitution should allow Japan to possess small-size nuclear weapons.'[6] Should North Korea develop substantial and overt nuclear capabilities, it is, accordingly, likely that Japan would review its self-denying ordinance against the acquisition of nuclear weapons, especially if there were doubts about the reality or the permanence of the US nuclear guarantee.[7] Were this to happen, then deploying them could ultimately become another task for the JMSDF. Indeed there are some indications of an emerging debate on the subject.

India's maritime doctrine is much more transparent.[8] It dwells on the need for deterrence, both conventional and nuclear:

> The ways and means of deterrence by the [Indian Navy] would include developing a sea-based nuclear second-strike capability, in keeping with the Indian Nuclear Doctrine that lays down a 'No First Use' (NFU) policy. It also entails conventional deterrence by both denial and punishment, by maintaining a robust military capability and posture to convince potential aggressors of high costs and limited gains from any aggression or intervention against India's national interests.[9]

That doctrine, moreover, is explicit about the attractions of a sea-based nuclear deterrent, as a necessary part of the spectrum of deterrence:

> India stands out alone as being devoid of a credible nuclear triad. It is one of the tenets of the post Cold War era that the ability of a nation to adopt a truly independent foreign policy/posture is inexorably

linked with such a strategic capability either directly
or indirectly.[10]

The aim is to establish 'credible minimum nuclear deterrence.' Furthermore, India remains acutely aware of its nuclear
inferiority to China and concerned that an effective Chinese
SSBN force would open up a further avenue of theoretical attack. India currently adheres to the notion that a secure
second-strike capability offers the best defence against both
Pakistan and China and offers credibility for its declaratory
policy of 'no-first-use'.

Since nuclear weapons can radically change the cost-benefit
equation in warfare and produce destruction on a scale that
can easily shatter the enemy's will and ability to fight, nuclear
deterrence is an extremely powerful tool for attaining a safe
security environment.[11]

An eventual upgrading of India's sea-based deterrent forces
is seen as an essential part of its policy of no first use, given the
comparative vulnerability of its land-based second-strike capability. As Admiral Nirmal Verma has said: 'It is a fact that an
undersea deterrent is the most survivable leg of the triad, and
hence should form the core of a credible second-strike capability.'[12]

Given the stress laid by the US on the prevention of war
in *A Cooperative Strategy for 21st Century Seapower* and *Naval
Operations Concept 2010*, there is an unsurprising emphasis on the importance of naval deterrence, both nuclear and
conventional in which, according to the latter, 'regionally
concentrated, combat-credible' naval forces have a central
role.[13] President Obama's Nuclear Posture Review of April 2010
marked a further transition in the US's nuclear thinking away
from a Cold War focus on peer competitors such as Russia
or China. Instead the emphasis is on the dangers of nuclear

proliferation to countries such as North Korea and Iran, and to terrorist organisations, as well as the need for a more austere deterrent to deal with such threats.[14] *A Cooperative Strategy*, like its Indian equivalent, makes the point that deterrence includes the conventional ability to prevent war by dissuading potential aggressors. The document does little to illuminate US thinking on nuclear deterrence itself, but in the spectrum of deterrent tasks dealt within the OPPLAN 8044 family of plans against a variety of threats, nuclear weapons are said to 'provide credible capabilities to deter a wide range of threats, including weapons of mass destruction and large-scale conventional military force'.[15]

There is less consensus now about the role of nuclear weapons in national defence, and therefore in the contribution that the navy should make to it, than there was in the days of the Cold War. This is particularly true of the debate about their relevance to situations of non-nuclear threat and the extent to which traditional thinking about nuclear strategy should be amended to cope with the prospects of new, non-national asymmetric types of nuclear threat.

Nonetheless, there remain high levels of agreement and therefore very little discussion about the necessity for a secure nuclear deterrent force at sea and for the US Navy to be able to prevail against anti-access strategies based on the use of ballistic missiles and/or weapons of mass destruction.[16]

Nuclear deterrent forces

In the case of both China and India, the development of sea-based nuclear deterrent forces began in the late 1960s and 1970s; its slow pace has been a reflection as much of its technical challenge and expense as of any lack of priority. In China, the programme was considerably hindered in the past by the political turmoil of the Mao years,[17] and was intermittent at best thereafter. Three *Jin*-class SSBNs have now finally appeared, and another one is expected.[18] Analysts were surprised to note that they contained launch tubes for only 12, not 16, of the JL-12 sea-launched ballistic missiles.[19] These missiles are expected to have a range of nearly 6,400km (4,000 miles) and to have multiple independently targeted re-entry vehicle warheads. Alongside this, the Chinese appear to be improving the training levels of their nuclear submariners and, aware of networking developments in other advanced navies, are seeking to 'informationise' their command and control arrangements. Surprisingly, though, China's SSBN force does not currently appear to come under the control of their strategic rocket forces, the 2nd Artillery, and the robustness of linkages between military and civilian authorities in this area remains obscure.[20] Nonetheless, the Chinese are showing that they are well aware of the strategic advantages of a secure second-strike capability.[21] The prospect of the deployment of Chinese SSBNs to the submarine base at Ya Long in Hainan province is likely further to raise the strategic sensitivity of the South China Sea. In the longer term, however, the contribution this development might make to a more secure sea-based second-strike capability could be seen as essentially stabilising.

India began its programme to develop an indigenous nuclear ballistic-missile submarine project, the Advanced Technology Vessel (ATV), in the 1970s, but it was not until December 2007 that Admiral Mehta finally confirmed the navy's intent to take the nuclear deterrent to sea.[22] India was helped in this programme by leasing 4,000-tonne Russian *Charlie 1* Type 670A SSN in 1988–91, an arrangement which facilitated the design and build of its first SSN, INS *Arihant*, which was launched at a cost of $2.9bn in July 2009, a major step in the country's naval and defence-industrial development; this submarine is expected to be the first of a class of five SSNs under this programme.[23] India has also leased a much larger, 12,000-tonne, *Akula II* SSN from Russia, despite delays in repairs after the accident in the Sea of Japan in November 2008, which killed 20 crew members.[24] The INS *Arihant*, which is scheduled for commission by late 2012,[25] will be equipped with four K-4 3,500km nuclear-tipped missiles or 12 K-15 *Sagarika* 750km missiles. More such submarines are expected to follow.[26] The relatively short range of the missiles first considered for India's sea-based deterrent – such as the 300km *Dhanush* and the *Sagarika* – suggests that Pakistan rather than China was considered the more immediate prospective adversary. These missiles have been indigenously produced, but with substantial Russian help. India is also pursuing a programme of longer-range sea-launched cruise missiles to join existing *Klub* and *Brahmos* weapons, all of which could carry nuclear warheads. Such nuclear potentialities have led to concerns of a nuclear arms race in the region.

The United States' seaborne nuclear deterrent is currently deployed in its 14-strong *Ohio*-class of SSBNs, and funding for the 12-strong SSBN(X) replacement programme began in Fiscal Year 2011. The American 313 ship plan originally included 14 SSBN submarines, although there is considerable doubt that this number can be sustained through the expected life of the programme. Indeed, the number is now expected to drop to 10–11 boats between 2029–41 because the replacement programme has been delayed by two years to save costs.[27] Despite the concern in some quarters about a lack of a clear and public plans for modernisation and replacement, design work has started and like, and indeed with, the UK, is intended to be dovetailed with the completion of the latest SSN programme (the *Virginia* and *Astute* classes) so as to assure continued industrial capacity.[28] Even with a prospective drop to 12 or even for a period in the 2030s to ten SSBN-X boats, this will remain by far the world's leading sea-based strategic nuclear deterrence force for the foreseeable future, hence the confidence that the United States may be able to meet its deterrent needs 'with a smaller nuclear force'.[29]

Deterrent operations

In 1999, China's Central Military Committee apparently decided that regular SSBN patrols should begin within a few years, but programme delays and technical difficulties have largely prevented that. There has been speculation amongst US and Japanese analysts that China might adopt a 'bastion' pattern for its future SSBN patrols, possibly based at Ya Long in Hainan province, rather in the manner of the Soviet Union during the Cold War, but as yet with little operational evidence.[30] This prospect appears to have unsettled India and other countries within the region, because it makes the South China Sea even more strategically sensitive.[31]

Neither Japan nor India is as yet actively deploying a continuous at sea deterrent (CASD), but the United States regards deterrent patrols of this sort as routine; as such the task hardly attracts attention. Former Defense Secretary James Schlesinger made the essential point in July 2009: 'Nuclear weapons are used every day ... to deter our potential foes and provide re-assurance to the allies to whom we offer protection'.[32] The 1,000th successful *Trident* strategic deterrent patrol was completed in 2009.[33] Most patrols now take place in the Pacific Ocean, and the rate of patrols is approximately as it was during the Cold War, with 31 in 2008. This rate is achieved by each SSBN having two alternating crews and much-reduced gaps between deployments.[34]

Although in some ways the operation of a nuclear deterrent at sea remains one of the most competitive of all naval missions, in that it is measured and designed for use almost exclusively against peer competitors, and extremely expensive to boot, it is not necessarily destabilising. Some may argue, to the contrary, that its deterrent effect and relative invulnerability when compared to land-based systems has the reverse effect. This of course is part of a much wider debate about the effect of nuclear weapons as a whole.

Ballistic-missile defence

Ballistic-missile defence (BMD) is another technologically demanding and expensive naval mission essentially aimed against major competitors, which all four navies are exploring and to which the United States and Japan are devoting considerable effort. It involves the erection of defences against ballistic-missile attack on forces at sea, ashore and, by extension, national centres.

Some analysts in China are sceptical about the defensive nature of US and Japanese BMD preparations, seeing them as little more than a cover for future offensive action.[35] This scepticism in turn could be seen as providing a strategic rationale for the development of anti-ship capabilities aimed specifically at US, Japanese and even ROK *Aegis* ships, raising doubts in Western minds at least about the 'defensiveness' of the Chinese approach. This could encourage a particularly dangerous form of naval arms racing.

While BMD is not yet much discussed in Indian naval doctrine, the need for a fleet to be able to operate in conditions of ballistic-missile attack is candidly addressed, for example, by *Freedom to Use the Seas: India's Maritime Military Strategy*:

> A direct nuclear attack on our own naval forces is as yet a distant possibility. Transition and passage through nuclear fallout areas will, however, have to be undertaken.[36]

Some have urged that given India's slow development of a BMD system, it should seriously consider taking up NATO's offer of cooperation in its BMD programme, but this is likely to be seen as compromising the country's much-valued strategic independence.[37]

With Pakistan's acquisition of advanced missile technology from China, and the probable forwards deployment of SSBNs from China's new Ya Long bay base near Sanya, Indian interest in the development of limited ballistic-missile defence systems for some of its major cities is growing, even though some think this could encourage an arms race in 'Star Wars technology' in the region.[38]

Since the North Korean missile launch of 1998, the Japanese have, however, given increasing attention to the importance of assuring their sea forces and their territory against all forms of missile attack. Japanese commentators also make the point that in 1996 some of the Chinese missiles fired in connection with the Taiwan Strait crisis of that year landed within 100km (60 miles) of Japanese territory. Under the administration of Prime Minister Taro Aso in June 2009, the Council on Economic and Fiscal Policy issued the 'Honebuto' guidelines, which for the first time identified North Korean missile launches and nuclear tests as a threat and suggested Tokyo should develop a ballistic-missile defence system. The LDP defence policymaking panel emphasised the importance of sea-launched cruise missiles as an appropriate response to this threat.[39]

Sea-based BMD accordingly has a high priority for the JMSDF and is an operational aspiration which the US is doing much to encourage, lest North Korean missile and nuclear tests impel Japan and South Korea into their own nuclear deterrent programmes. For that reason, the Obama administration is keen, in the words of one unnamed US official on 17 October

2009, to 'make sure our allies are left in absolutely no doubt about our full-throated commitment to their security, in all aspects to include extended deterrence'.[40] On occasion, individual Japanese policymakers have made oblique references to the need for strategic pre-emption against the source of such threats in some circumstances.[41]

Considerable public emphasis is also attached to BMD in the United States.[42] Admiral Roughead told Congress in February 2008: 'Maritime ballistic missile defense directly contributes to the navy's core capability of deterrence, and enables our core capabilities of power projection and sea control'.[43] The admiral asserts that BMD is regarded as 'a core mission' in the United States Navy, not least because sea-based detection and interception systems did not infringe on sovereignty of any other country, while 'providing an umbrella of protection to forward-deployed US forces and partners ... [and] contributing to the larger architecture planned for defense of the United States'.[44] As Roughead explained in a later speech, the mobility of sea-borne BMD is one of its greatest attractions:

> If you want me to go from covering the western Pacific to defending the Mediterranean, no problem. Give me the transit time and I can give you a first class *Aegis* ballistic missile defence ship on station without the need to infringe upon the sovereignty of any nation to do so.[45]

In contrast, a land-bound equivalent would require base negotiations and 35 lifts of equipment by C-17 aircraft from one location to another.

While there is near unanimity in the US about the importance of BMD, estimates of its technological feasibility vary widely. There are also doubts about the strategic wisdom and the technological feasibility of the search for *national* rather than fleet defences against ballistic-missile attack.

BMD capabilities

The initial alarm in Japan that greeted North Korea's firing of a missile in August 1998 was echoed by further concerns in 2002–03, which led to an agreement that year for closer cooperation in BMD research with the United States, and a focus in the Japanese Defence White Paper of 2005 on sea- and land-based missile-defence systems. To engage in defence against North Korean missiles in their initial launch phases, *Kongou*-class *Aegis* destroyers equipped with SM-3 missiles would need to deploy on the western side of the Sea of Japan in exposed positions that seem likely to pull other Japanese and American forces forwards in support. Despite such difficulties, the task has the highest priority for both navies.

The JMSDF decided in 2003 to equip its four *Kongou*-class destroyers with the US Navy's *Aegis* system, a process that was completed in 2010. This acquisition will also yield huge benefits for the JMSDF in terms of networking connectivity with the US Navy. Japanese stations seem to be deployed to monitor either North Korean or Chinese missile launches. The JMSDF's first successful BMD intercept test took place off Hawaii in the JDS *Kongou* on 18 December 2008. This was the first time a non-American ship had done so with the Version 3.6 *Aegis* BMD system, AN/SPY-1 radar and an SM-3 missile.[46] Since then the Japanese have regularly participated in the test programme, now estimated to have achieved 21 hits from 25 shots.[47] The Japanese may be planning to have a space-based early-warning system in 2015, and to increase number of firing units to cover the wider area that results from the switch in emphasis to the south west (and China) mentioned in Chapter Two.

Investment in a sea-based terminal BMD capability for both the defence of the United States and allied territory and for forces at sea remains a very high priority for the US Navy, despite the cancellation of the Navy Area Defense programme in 2002. This reflects American concern with North Korean and especially Chinese theatre ballistic missiles.[48] In 2010, the US Navy had 23 ships with BMD capabilities in cruisers and guided missile destroyers, with another 15 planned to 2015 as the US Navy turns its attention to the proliferation of advanced ballistic missiles, which it considers 'the greatest single threat'.[49] The CG[X] nuclear cruiser, however, was a particularly ambitious project. Intended to be a vessel with a displacement of possibly up to 25,000 tonnes, it was expected to replace the 22-strong *Ticonderoga Aegis* air defence/BMD cruisers between 2021 and 2029. From the start, however, it was a particularly expensive and controversial project,[50] and its cancellation caused little surprise. Some of the BMD technologies of both the CG[X] and the *Zumwalt*-class programmes will be incorporated into the third 'flight' of eight *Arleigh Burke* destroyers. BMD remains a technologically demanding and therefore expensive project, dogged by operational difficulties. But the willingness to accept the considerable opportunity costs involved in this programme attests to the priority attached in both Japan and the United States to modern missile defence.[51]

For all that, the US BMD system still faces a variety of challenges. Public discussion in China of the value of exploiting the electromagnetic pulse effects of nuclear weapons attack or attack by high-power microwave weapons has reinforced the need to harden the system against this kind of threat.[52] Some critics argue that the system needs to be supplemented with space-based interceptors. The Flight III DDG-51s have turned out to be more expensive than the US Navy first thought.[53] Finally there is concern that hard-kill systems intended to physically destroy incoming missiles may not be able to keep up with the increase in number and proliferation of those missiles.[54] Here again there is something of a race between the offensive and defensive capabilities of the navies involved.

In contrast to Japanese and American acquisitions, neither China nor India have yet deployed a fully-fledged sea-based capability for BMD for area defence at sea, still less for home-land defence, despite demonstrated interest in the topic. With the launch of the *Luyang* II-class DDGs which has an *Aegis*-like capability. The Chinese have begun to correct this deficiency.[55]

BMD operations

In January 2010, the Chinese conducted an apparently successful ground-based exo-atmospheric anti-missile test which suggested a developing capability in BMD. Some Western observers said the test demonstrated how far the country has still to go before it could create a reliable regional BMD system.[56] This placed the Chinese navy behind its competitors, insofar as the US and to a lesser extent the Japanese already had capacity to counter ballistic missiles. As mentioned before, the JMSDF conducted its first successful interception in 2008, and during the North Korean missile test of April 2009, the first two of the Kongou-class *Aegis* destroyers deployed to the Sea of Japan were ordered to attempt to shoot down the North Korea missile should it be seen to pose a danger to Japanese territory.[57] By contrast, the US Navy conducts regular operations and exercises in BMD and has established the Air and Missile Defense Command in Dahlgren, Virginia to integrate and progress both air and missile defence. It cooperates with nine other countries, including the UK, Canada and Germany, in the Maritime Theatre Defense Forum, and its *Aegis* ships configured for BMD are part of the Western Pacific Ballistic Missile Defense cooperation in concert with Japan.[58]

Maritime power-projection
Maritime power-projection thinking

As Australian maritime doctrine makes clear, maritime power projection is about the delivery of force from the sea: 'It can take a variety of forms including the landing of amphibious or special forces, the delivery of seaborne land and air forces, or bombardment by guided or unguided weapons from warships and aircraft'.[59] Its versatility means maritime power projection can be applied against a range of state and non-state adversaries and with differing levels of intensity. This review, however, will focus on those aspects of the capability that relate to operations against the serious opposition characteristic of states.

Official Chinese and Japanese public discussion about maritime power- projection is notable largely for its absence. In Japan's case, this is largely attributable to the limits on offensive deployment of military force imposed by the constitution. Tokyo's main focus appears to be on the development of amphibious capacities in defence of the main home islands and, increasingly, its more distant island chains to the southwest. Chinese commentators, however, make a virtue of China's apparent lack of aspiration in this area, claiming that it illustrates the strictly defensive purposes of the PLA and drawing strong contrasts between this and the 'offensive' characteristics of the US Navy. China's experience of amphibious operations has been an unhappy one; it was a notable victim of Western and Japanese operations in the nineteenth and twentieth centuries, and some costly and unsuccessful operations in the closing stages of the Chinese Civil War. Accordingly, their acquisition of equipment and conduct of exercises reinforces the impression that Beijing's approach is cautious and likely to be focused on Taiwan, and the defence of the country's local interests in the East and South China seas, rather than further afield.

The Indian debate on expeditionary operations and power projection, on the other hand, is a more open blend of traditional and non-traditional conceptions. In its extended and business-like discussion of the employment of the navy in a conventional state-on-state conflict, most obviously but by no means exclusively in renewed conflict with Pakistan, *India's Maritime Military Strategy 2007* makes the point that the function of the navy would be to have as early and as significant an impact on the land battle as possible. The phasing of information dominance, sea control/denial, support operations, and the all-arms battle leading to the final joint operations phases is given prominence. 'This is a major shift from the earlier strategy which believed that victory in the war at sea would produce its own beneficial effects on the land battle, albeit is a delayed and roundabout way.' Now, by contrast, 'the sea war is a phase that now has to be gone through in a shorter time frame, so that the navy participates in the final phase aimed at the enemy's Centre of Gravity, which invariably will be on land'.[60] Accordingly, the ability to influence events on land is seen as one of the primary roles of the Indian Navy. Alongside this, though, there has been a marked shift in Indian interest from conventional sea-control operations on the open ocean to force- projection operations in narrower littoral waters, as a precursor to operations against the shore.

For the US Navy, the capacity to project power ashore is what seapower is all about. The ability to secure access, then project and sustain power ashore 'is the basis of [US] combat credibility'.[61] As such, it depends heavily on a 'robust strategic sea-lift capability'.[62] Recent and current summaries of US thinking on the conduct of amphibious operations such as *A Cooperative Strategy for 21st-Century Seapower*[63] and *Naval Operations Concept 2010*,[64] and the Report of the Amphibious Capabilities Working Group (ACWG) of April 2012[65] all emphasise the advantages conferred by the 'expeditionary character and versatility of maritime forces',[66] which, says *A Cooperative Strategy*, 'will be characterized by regionally concentrated, forward-deployed task forces with the combat power to limit regional conflict, deter major power war, and should deterrence fail, win our nation's wars as part of a joint or combined campaign'. The 'global reach, persistent presence, and operational flexibility inherent in U.S. seapower' will allow it to 'limit regional conflict with forward deployed, decisive maritime power ... [with powerful forces] ... capable of selectively controlling the seas, projecting power ashore, and protecting friendly forces and civilian populations from attack.'[67]

All three documents cover the entire spectrum of maritime power-projection operations and indeed devote most attention to the lower-order stability tasks, such as counter-terrorism, disaster relief and tactical recovery as part of the expeditionary concept to be discussed in Chapter Four. 'Most amphibious operations do not involve large scale amphibious assault,' says the ACWG report of 2012.[68] Even so, the possibility that in projecting power ashore the US Navy and Marine corps could face substantial opposition from 'regional challengers', especially given the US 'pivot' towards Asia is expressly alluded to and justifies significant re-investment in the aftermath of the land-centric Iraq and Afghanistan preoccupations of the past decade.[69]

The special need to assure access 'against a modern adversary which uses its own multi-domain capability to impede access in unconventional ways ... that challenge US dominance and potentially limit our freedom of action'[70] is seen as one of the most demanding aspects of this higher-intensity state-based form of maritime power projection. A concern for shallow-water sea control of the sort discussed in Chapter Two is also evident. As Admiral Mullen pointed out: 'A naval force floating off the continental shelf with no impact on shore is not decisive. We must go forward to the very reaches of the sea, operating effectively in every part of the littoral and beyond.' Pointing to the fact that nearly one third of the waters of the north Arabian Gulf are inaccessible for ships with drafts more than 20 feet, he urged the need to 'think of the vast areas of the world covered by shallow water: those connected to the oceans by rivers, and harbours, and rugged shorelines. These are the decisive strips of sea that make all the difference. And we need to be there.' To operate in places where the ground was, in President Abraham Lincoln's words 'a little damp' requires the US Navy to win the inshore battle as well as the offshore one.[71] Hence the notable increase of US interest in riverine warfare.

Surprisingly, there is no specific mention of sea-basing, amphibious assault or strike warfare in *A Cooperative Strategy*, but these concepts have become familiar since the launch of the US naval document *From the Sea* in 1992 and they do appear in *Naval Operations Concept 2010* and, especially, in ACGW.[72] Thinking here, not unnaturally, was led by the US Marine Corps, whose aim was to make the maximum use of the sea as the world's greatest manoeuvre space, together with the traditional mobility, firepower and flexibility of maritime forces to seize and exploit the operational initiative ashore. The result was the concept of 'Operational Manoeuvre From the Sea', with its particular emphasis on 'Ship to Objective Manoeuvre', the capacity to go straight to the operational objective without the automatic need for tiresome median steps such as securing an amphibious lodgement area.[73]

The supporting concept of sea-basing was fleshed out in *Seapower 21* and was well described by Vice Admiral David L. Brewer in 2003:

> Sea basing will enable this force to use the sea as manoeuvre space to increase the asymmetric advan-

tage of surprise. By keeping the sea base over the horizon far from shore, it will also be less vulnerable to enemy attack. At the same time, many of the military logisticians would be performing their functions from the relative safety of the mobile sea base, resulting in fewer personnel remaining ashore in higher risk environments for long periods of time.[74]

There is, however, a degree of debate about how sophisticated these capabilities need to be. If major amphibious operations against a peer or near competitor are envisaged, these capabilities would need to substantial. But many are sceptical of such a requirement. Thus, as Secretary Gates has remarked:

> We have to take a hard look at where it would be necessary or sensible to launch another major amphibious landing again – especially as advanced in anti-ship systems keep pushing the potential launch point further from shore.[75]

In consequence the emphasis in maritime power projection is more likely to be limited to medium-to-low levels of intensity. In a similar way, visions of sea-basing are likely to become more austere.[76] All the same, successive United States Marine Corps commandants have urged a return to the development of the kind of true amphibious skills that have suffered in consequence of the force's employment as light infantry in Iraq and Afghanistan.[77]

Maritime power-projection capabilities

In various ways all four navies demonstrate the conviction that aircraft carriers are at the heart of seapower, because of the role the vessels play in supporting both sea control and power-projection missions.[78] For all the absence of public discussion about the maritime power projection mission in China and Japan, both countries seem slowly to be acquiring capabilities that one day would be useful for its performance. Accordingly, observers have been intrigued for years by the prospects of the PLAN's acquisition of an aircraft carrier capability. In 2004, Admiral Liu was clear about the importance of adding carriers to the fleet. He said: 'Sea control cannot be realised without air control.'[79] Since Taiwan is within range of land-based fighters operating from the mainland, it is generally believed by analysts that the Chinese carrier programme is motivated by other, less local considerations, such as a desire to prepare power-projection operations, humanitarian-relief operations and the like.[80]

After years of uncertainty, the US Office of Naval intelligence and the Defence Department finally concluded in 2010 that China was undertaking a programme to both refurbish the ex-Soviet *Varyag* and build an indigenous carrier to join the fleet between 2015 and 2020.[81] The *Liaoning* (the old *Varyag*) was duly commissioned with great fanfare in September 2012 – an event of some significance for the domestic population and for the wider Asia-Pacific region.[82] At the same time, China is expected to start a programme for the construction of up to six indigenous aircraft carriers, each likely to be of some 60,000 tonnes, perhaps to be built in the new No. 3 military dock at Shanghai's Changxing Island Shipyard, once the lessons of the *Liaoning* have been absorbed. The careful strategic communications campaign now under way seems to be designed to accustom observers to an emerging reality.[83] Developing a true operational carrier capability nonetheless remains, according to Admiral Timothy Keating, 'a profoundly difficult undertaking'.[84] Accordingly, it must be many years before the Chinese can operate it with the proficiency of the Americans, the Indians, the British, French, Spanish and Italians.

For the development of true capacity for maritime power projection, the Chinese must, moreover, also develop a range of other capabilities, including the sustainability required for distant operations beyond the first island chain, amphibious warfare shipping and greater land-attack capabilities. None of these seems currently to be regarded as high-priority aspirations. The South and East Chinese fleets have slowly developed rapid combat groups which include limited marine and sea-based support forces of the sort that would be appropriate in any campaign to recapture lost territories. China's *Amphibious Joint Island Landing Campaign* concept envisages operations ranging from a full-scale amphibious assault on Taiwan to much more limited operations against the offshore islands of Mazu and Jinmen and Itu Aba/Taiping Island in the South China Sea. But even a landing operation against Mazu or Jinmen would pose significant challenges for the PLAN.[85]

Despite its new Type 071 20,000-tonne assault ship (of which a total of four to six might be built) and the larger projected Type 081 amphibious warfare ships, China's development of its power-projection capabilities has been steady rather than spectacular. According to the US Department of Defense, 'air and amphibious lift capacity have not improved appreciably since 2000',[86] but the PLAN now has about 55 medium and heavy amphibious-lift vessels and has reportedly ordered heavy hovercraft from Russia. Along with China's two marine brigades, two amphibious infantry divisions of the PLA have significant amphibious experience. China's expeditionary capability remains limited, however. Its total amphibious-lift capacity is reported to be one infantry division of about 10,000 troops and their equipment at one time, and expeditionary logistics are modest. These capabilities could prove useful in a variety of contingencies in the South and East China sea, and do not exclude the prospect of more distant operations in the future.[87]

To some extent, deficiencies previously noted in China's capacity to project power further from local waters are being addressed. New intelligence- gathering vessels (AGIs) and support ships capable of sustaining naval forces on the open ocean have been commissioned. The appearance of the 11,000-tonne *Dayan* underway-replenishment ship was particularly interesting, since this, together with other ships, increases the PLAN's capacity to operate on a regional if not a global basis. At the same time the command and control limitations of the PLAN, which derived from a time when its warships rarely went far from home and when its C3 (command, control and communications) systems were accordingly largely land based and army dominated, are being improved. New compromises are being struck between centralised direction from shore, which has the benefit of facilitating greater inter-service coop-eration and their transfer to freer-ranging operations at sea. The PLAN's lack of organic airpower, however, remains a major constraint on China's capacity to engage in amphibious or expeditionary operations far from home.

As remarked in the last chapter, with the development of the *Hyuga* class, the Japanese could be beginning to develop the capacity for longer-range operations, but the focus of their amphibious capabilities would seem to be on the protection of their own sometimes disputed islands. The Japanese acquisition of three large 8,900-tonne *Osumi*-class LSTs, and the mainte-nance of two much smaller older ones, 18 landing craft and a small but capable force of marines, for example, is probably mainly a response to the need to defend the country's disputed islands. Japan's strategy to protect the Senkaku/Diaoyu Islands is based less on fortification and their direct defence than on the clear ability to retake them after low-level occupation by Chinese or Taiwanese forces. Such an approach encourages the development of Japan's power-projection capabilities – and with that, further expeditionary and/or humanitarian capacities.[88]

The modernisation of the Indian Navy's carrier programme is crucial to its focus on developing forward power-projection capabilities.[89] The absorption of the USS *Trenton*, current talks for the acquisition of the USS *Nashville* and the launch of the INS *Airavat*, the navy's third-largest landing ship, are all significant moves in the campaign to beef up the country's amphibious/expeditionary capabilities. A plan to build or procure four more LPDs and a number of other amphibious warships was announced at the end of 2010.[90] The clear aim is to develop 'amphibious landing and exercise tactics aimed at influencing battles on land from force deployment at sea'.[91] India wants to increase the size of the force, to be trebled from a battalion to a brigade, appropriate for the defence of the country's island territories. India's planned acquisition of two 30,000-tonne multipurpose tanker replenishment vessels and expansion of its maritime patrol aircraft also point to an aspiration for the capacity to engage in expeditionary operations at greater reach than before.[92]

Turning now to the US Navy, the cancellation of all but three of the 14,400-tonne *Zumwalt*-class DDG-1000 land-attack destroyers in favour of eight more older, cheaper but perhaps more versatile *Arleigh Burkes* was seen as a recognition of the need for more protection against ballistic missiles and SSKs. But this swing back towards sea control was based on high confidence in the US Navy's existing expeditionary capabilities. Its shore-strike capabilities, in particular, largely reside in the smart munitions now used by its aircraft and by sea-launched cruise missiles. In this regard, four former *Ohio*-class Trident boats have been converted to SSGNs, each capable of carrying 154 *Tomahawk* cruise missiles. These boats are regarded as 'conventional land-attack and special operations forces platforms'. In December 2008, Rear Admiral Mark Kenny, director of the irregular warfare office, called them 'the Navy's premier counterterrorism tool'.[93]

In the Quadrennial Defense Review 2006, the US emphasised the strengthening of America's capacity for amphibious operations, paying particular attention to its sustainability through an enhanced sea-basing and maritime pre-positioning force. The US is in the process of transforming its Asia-Pacific forces into a joint, modular and expeditionary framework able to cooperate with distant allies, especially Japan. The 313 Fleet Plan now envisages 33 amphibious warfare ships centred on 11 LPD17 *San Antonio* class amphibious transport dock ships, 'to project strike [fire and maneuver] forces from the sea deep into littoral land objectives'.[94] US Marine Corps preference was for 38 amphibious-warfare ships, based on the proposition that landing each of two Marine Expeditionary Brigades required 17 ships, of which at least five need to be LHA/LHD amphibious assault ships.[95] In addition the versatile but relatively cheap Joint High Speed Vessel (JHSV) for intra-theatre transport will be fast, and capable of operating in shallow waters. Twenty-three of these are now envisaged, a significant increase from the three originally envisaged in the 2006 version of the 313 Plan.[96]

The US Marine Corps also intends to buy 573 Expeditionary Fighting Vehicles (EFVs) capable of taking troops ashore from 40km (25 miles) out at 25 knots. The EFV programme has, however, been plagued with increasing costs and is vulnerable to future cuts.[97] The Landing Platform (Dock) (LPD) 17 *San Antonio* programme has likewise had a variety of quality problems, though these now seem to have been resolved.[98]

A prospective US sea-based force would also include a further 62 command, support and logistic ships. Much of the detail of the US Navy's sea-basing plans, especially the Maritime Preposition Force-Future (MPF-F) remains unclear, however.[99] The more ambitious they turn out to be, the more expensive they will prove.[100]

The US Marine Corps plans for the capacity to deliver two reinforced brigades, plus the equipment for a third, argues strongly for a 38-ship amphibious-warfare fleet, although the US Navy's 30-year shipbuilding plan ('2012 plan') objective is 33 ships,[101] which might include 11 large-deck amphibious-assault ships (Landing Helicopter Docks (LHDs)/Landing Helicopter Assault ships (LHAs), 11 LPDs and 11 Landing Ship Docks (LSDs).[102] For its part, the Navy is concerned at the cost of this project and what it would mean for the rest of the fleet, while others, including Secretary Gates, are sceptical about the need for, or the tactical/technical feasibility of, large-scale contested landings. These debates about the size and quality of the US Navy's amphibious force illustrate something of the dilemma between the requirements of conventional amphibious operations, which in an increasingly challenging era of precision-guided weapons are getting very expensive, against the more modest requirements of lower-level expeditionary and humanitarian operations. Hence the cuts announced in early 2012 which mean a delay in the first LHA-7 amphibious-assault ship and cutting two of the older LSD-41s, which some regard as odd given that, according to some reports, the USMC have been in 120 amphibious operations since 1990, and is accordingly one of the most used elements of the US armed services.[103]

Maritime power-projection operations

In line with the predominantly local focus of its maritime power-projection capabilities, the South and East China Sea

Fleets of the PLAN have seen the largest accumulations of still quite modest Chinese amphibious power. The principal focus historically has been Taiwan, an operation that would clearly require state-on-state capabilities, but with improving relations across the Taiwan Strait and a slowly deteriorating situation in the South China Sea, there has been something of a shift southwards.

The South China Sea fleet conducted a successful amphibious operation against the Vietnamese in the Paracels in 1974, rehearsed this capability again in 1980 and carried out a similar operation, again against the Vietnamese, on Fiery Cross Reef in the Spratly Islands in 1988. The East China Sea Fleet has conducted a number of large amphibious operations every year in a manner and a location plainly intended to convey messages of dissuasion to Taiwan. More recently these exercises have been conducted in the South China Sea as well – a sensitive and much disputed area in which this capability might prove almost uniquely relevant and to which the US and other states have responded accordingly.[104]

The Indian Navy has conducted a number of relatively small scale land-attack/expeditionary operations: against Goa in 1961, and in the suppression of an insurrection in the Maldives in November 1988. In the 1971 war with Pakistan, the navy intervened in operations off what was to become Bangladesh and its missile craft attacked ships and military infrastructure in Karachi. During the so-called Kargil War of 2002, the Indian Navy deployed into the Arabian Sea stripped for action; its potential capacity to repeat this performance with attacks on the shore was clearly intended as a deterrent.[105]

The Indian Navy's developing interest in littoral operations is clear from the large scale *Tropex* (Theatre Readiness Operational Exercise) series held from February 2007 in the Arabian Sea involving ships of Western and Eastern

Commands, plus specialist army units, air force fighters and coast guard ships. The aim is to ensure that the navy can significantly affect the outcome of the air-land battle. *Tropex 2009* in February of that year was then its largest ever amphibious exercise off the coast of Gujarat and included elements of the Army Air Force and coast guard, involving a sea-based assault on land defences. The trend to increasingly ambitious explorations of Indian naval power went further still in February 2012.[106]

All the same, the US Marine Corps continues to set the gold standard as an expression of the world's most powerful means of maritime power projection, but its absorption of a light infantry role in the Iraq and Afghanistan wars has worried many that it might be in danger of losing its amphibious edge. Accordingly, a series of studies and rigorous exercises have been conducted to revive and further develop this capability, in the face of expected budgetary constriction.[107] For all that there seems little prospect of the corps losing its position of global pre-eminence.

Gunboat diplomacy: competitive naval diplomacy

According to Australian naval doctrine, 'Naval diplomacy is the use of naval force in support of diplomacy to support, persuade, deter or coerce. Naval diplomacy becomes competitive rather than cooperative when it stresses combat capabilities and the ability to apply finely graduated force through the exploitation of the normally unstated, but self evident threat inherent in a warship.'[108]

Because the diplomatic utility of warships is a kind of bonus provided by their capacity to do other things, navies rarely design their forces specifically, solely or even mainly for this purpose. Certainly none of the four navies being reviewed here do.

Gunboat diplomacy thinking

Although the Japanese maintain a discreet silence on the matter, it is clear that they share with the other three major Pacific navies the belief that military power and influence derive, ultimately, from the capacity to fight and win. In testimony to the House Armed Services Committee in February 2012, the US Navy Chief of Naval Operations, Admiral Jonathan Greenert made all the usual points. The US Navy must be ready to fight and win today, while building the ability to win tomorrow. This was the navy's primary mission, and 'all our efforts from the "wardroom to the boardroom" must be grounded in this fundamental responsibility. The recent posturing and rhetoric from Iran highlight the importance of our ability to deter aggression, promptly respond to crisis, and deny any aggressors' objectives'.[109]

Naval activity is seen as a means by which India's 'Look East' and 'Look West' aspirations can be met, and frequent references are made to Indian warships visiting countries as far away as Japan and South Africa. These visits are seen as a mechanism by which India can influence perceptions abroad to national benefit. There is an element here of old-fashioned rivalry, especially perhaps with China. Admiral Mehta said in 2009: 'As the geographical competition-space between the two coincides in the Indian ocean wisdom and forbearance are going to be needed in generous measure to ensure that competition does not transform into conflict'.[110] The fleshing-out of this 'Look East' policy automatically brings maritime diplomacy to the centre of the international security stage. Indian maritime doctrine, moreover, is candid about the diplomatic value of hard military power:

> By virtue of our geography, we are ... in a position to greatly influence the movement/security of shipping

along the SLOCs in the [Indian Ocean region] provided we have the maritime power to do so. Control of the choke points could be used as a bargaining chip in the international power game, where the currency of military power remains a stark reality.[111]

Although the Chinese make much of Zheng He – the justly famous and accomplished Ming Dynasty 'eunuch admiral' – and his alleged approach to a reassuring naval diplomacy, the Chinese version of 'soft' maritime power is not necessarily as understood by Westerners following the precepts of Joseph Nye, who uses the phrase 'soft' or 'smart' power to refer to the persuasive use of the non-military dimensions of state power.[112] In the *PLA Daily*, for example, Lieutenant-General Ma Henghui remarked: 'If military hard power is a sharp sword, soft power is its awe-inspiring dream and clang' and derives from 'non-material elements such as strategic thinking, resolve and combat spirit.'[113] The 'sharp sword' element in Chinese thinking about naval diplomacy seems in part exemplified by the importance attached to the carrier programme described earlier. Thus Qi Jianguo, assistant to the chief of the PLA's General Staff, reportedly justified this programme by pointing out: 'All of the great nations in the world own aircraft carriers – they are symbols of a great nation.' In addition to their operational tasks, they are expressions of old-fashioned Chinese nationalism and considerable public pride. Thus as General Bingde Chen, told Admiral Mullen, 'China is a big country [and] we only have quite a number of ships, but small ships. And this is not commensurate with the status of the country of China.'[114] Analysts sometimes refer to this kind of thing as 'prestige racing' – potentially expensive but not necessarily destabilising provided national honour is satisfied by the mere possession, rather than the planned use, of such demonstrations of national power.

The doctrinal emphasis given to competitive diplomacy is much less evident in US and Japanese doctrinal statements – because of the new emphasis given to international collaboration in *A Cooperative Strategy* as far as the Americans are concerned, and Japan's constitutional constraints in the latter case. But by their actions, both demonstrate that the concept is familiar and considered important.

Gunboat diplomacy operations

There is clearly an element of old-fashioned display in China's expanding programme of diplomatic outreach. In July 2007, for instance, the 5,850-tonne destroyer *Ghangzhou* and the supply ship *Weishanhu* reached the Atlantic and exercised with British, Spanish and French navies, including with the Royal Navy aircraft carrier HMS *Ark Royal*. Later that year Chinese vessels also visited Australia and New Zealand. However innocent, this increased presence has caused some concern in the United States, India, Japan and indeed in Australia and New Zealand given China's increasing profile amongst the struggling island states of the South Pacific.[115] The appearance of Chinese vessels and usable facilities in the Indian Ocean, not least the new port of Gwadar in Pakistan, has also been a continuing cause for concern, especially in India – although given the distances involved and the PLAN's lack of reach, such a remote presence hardly constitutes a serious current military risk; its political significance was considerable, however.[116] China hosted a significant Naval Review in April 2009, providing another rare opportunity to display its capabilities to both domestic and the international audiences.

The most obvious manifestation of China's competitive approach to naval diplomacy has been in the South and East China seas, both towards other claimants to disputed parts of the area and to the appearance there of outside forces.[117] The

Impeccable incident, and the strident protests issued by Beijing to the projected participation of the *George Washington* in a bilateral exercise in the Yellow Sea in the wake of the sinking of the South Korean corvette, ROKS *Cheonan* in 2010 have been interpreted as the diplomatic aspect of a long-term and comprehensive strategy of sea denial.[118] The robust assertion by naval and coast guard forces of Chinese claims against Vietnam and the Philippines in the South China Sea and Japan in the East China Sea through 2011 and 2012 reinforce the point. At the day-to-day tactical level incidents of gunboat diplomacy such as Chinese harassment of the USNS *Impeccable* in March 2009 or the Japanese, Taiwanese and Chinese posturing over the Diaoyu/Senkaku Islands in September 2012 could lead to conflict.

Indian naval activities have served a number of different political purposes. One, clearly, is simply to demonstrate that India is an up-and-coming country with global aspirations. This contributed to activities as varied as the visit of an Indian warship, the destroyer INS *Tabar*, to Tonga in July 2007 (the first such visit since 1960) and the much heralded three-month cruise of a warship squadron to Singapore, Yokosuka, Qingdao, Vladivostok, Manila and Ho Chi Minh City in 2010. While fairly described as 'constructive engagement in the maritime domain', these operations bear more than a passing resemblance to the famous cruise of US President Theodore Roosevelt's 'Great White Fleet' before the First World War. To some extent they are undifferentiated exercises 'for general purposes of greatness'.[119]

Sometimes, though, they have served more specific geo-political purposes. India is keen to build its linkages with other Asia-Pacific countries. The first Japan–India exercises took place in March 2007, and India's exercises with other countries have become steadily more demanding. There is particular focus on developing closer maritime ties with the United States since 'the Indian Navy ... has come to share many of the US Navy's threat perceptions'. Combined exercises have facilitated liaison and co-operation, especially when associated with the transfer of warships like the USS *Trenton*, the signing of agreements for logistic support and so forth.[120]

Nonetheless, there are constraints, some of which have to do with domestic concerns about an over-close association with the United States. India has yet to sign up to the US-led Proliferation Security Initiative, partly for legal reasons, and retains a strong strategic relationship with Russia (if only for purposes of arms-supply) and its approach is still largely regional. The United States was not initially invited to the Indian Ocean Naval Symposium (IONS) in May 2008, although openings were left for later American participation. Nonetheless the IONS *démarche* illustrated the general convergence of thinking between the US and Indian navies which is a cause of some concern in China.

The Chinese will likewise have noted the greater presence of the Indian Navy in the Pacific. The two countries appear to be scrambling for influence around the rim of the Indian Ocean, while at the same time moderating their competition with fraternal rhetoric and the occasional bilateral exercise.[121] In contrast to its exercises with other navies, Sino-Indian exercises have so far been largely limited to search-and-rescue operations.

For all its emphasis on the kind of cooperative naval diplomacy to be discussed in the next chapter, the US Navy obviously still retains the potential for independent action of a more traditional kind, a potential perhaps best exhibited by its campaign of naval pressure on Iran.[122] The United States emphasises the symbolic importance of its forward-deployed naval forces and its home-porting policy, not least in and for

Japan, but also other countries in the Asia-Pacific, looking for a counterbalance to the rising power of China. Thus in 2010, the simultaneous surfacing of the three SSGNs *Michigan, Ohio* and *Florida* in Busan, Subic Bay and Diego Garcia respectively, was clearly intended to convey an American desire to maintain its Pacific Fleet capacities, a point given further emphasis by an energetic programme of fleet exercises with allies and partners throughout the region. It was no coincidence that Hillary Clinton chose to deliver her speech of reassurance to the Philippines in a period of rising tension with China from the deck of the destroyer USS *Fitzgerald*.[123]

For this reason, the United States attaches huge importance to the freedom of navigation, because this facilitates the forward presence that it considers a precondition for most of its traditional missions. Consequently, when these are challenged either by unwelcome interpretations of the Law of the Sea (as in the case of the USNS *Impeccable* incident) or by a pattern of shrill diplomatic protests (as in the case of the prospective passage of the USS *George Washington* into the Yellow sea after the sinking of the *Cheonan*) it is instinctively inclined to engage in freedom of navigation exercises 'with attitude'. Such traditional 'soft' uses of 'hard' power sit alongside and can be thought by sceptics sometimes to undermine the otherwise evident intention discussed in the next chapter to make such presence permanent, proactive and systemic as an intended means of preventing wars and ensuring a better peace.[124]

Conclusion

The prospects for an arms race in the sphere of nuclear deterrence are limited at present, because China and India adhere to no-first-use policies while Japan is not a nuclear-armed state. India and China are upgrading their SSBN capabilities, but neither is yet in a position to undertake continuous SSBN patrols. When they do, however, a demonstrated and secure second-strike capability may make them feel less 'threatened' and more relaxed and so may actually prove to be a stabilising rather than a destabilising development. If, on the other hand, it makes them more confident and assertive in advancing their interests the result may be the very opposite, especially if it encourages Japan to abandon its anti-nuclear stance. Exactly the same arguments may be made about the implications of BMD and here the growth of Chinese capabilities in this area may prove particularly significant. Either way, there is likely to develop a race less between countries than between competing capabilities in offence and defence in the nuclear deterrence/ BMD domain which could prove destabilising. There are, for example, signs of an asymmetric race between the US and China with regard to China's efforts to develop electromagnetic pulse and other capabilities to blunt the effectiveness of the US Navy.

In contrast to developments in the US, the traditional amphibious capabilities of China, Japan and Indian remain comparatively modest and are chiefly focused on their immediate areas. But when this capability is overtly demonstrated by exercises in the attack, and indeed the defence, of disputed island possessions in the East and South China seas it raises the diplomatic temperature, encourages the growth of nationalism in the disputing countries and sparks counter-actions.

Exactly the same may be said about an assertive naval or even coast guard presence around those islands. This kind of gunboat diplomacy (even if conducted by coast guard vessels of one sort or another) indeed has undoubtedly inflamed the situation since 2010, especially in the Philippines and Vietnam. The partial result of this has been a greater readiness to facilitate 'external' involvement in the disputes, in the shape of an increased presence in the area of the Indian, Japanese,

Australian and especially the US navies. The US Navy has, in particular, not been shy of responding in a muscular fashion when perceives a threat to its freedom of navigation, through unwelcome interpretations of the Law of the Sea. All this is most unwelcome to Beijing and may well feed the arguments of Chinese hardliners, anxious about the prospects of strategic encirclement and threats to their sovereignty. At the same time, however, the prospect of such 'interventions' may provide incentives for moderation in Chinese behaviour and so prove stabilising rather than destabilising in this complicated and difficult area.

In the fields of nuclear deterrence, BMD, amphibious and gunboat diplomacy, arms racing consequences tend to proceed less from the development of the capabilities themselves and more from the manner of their use. To some extent, though, these competitive tendencies are counterbalanced by the increased cooperativeness exhibited in the non-traditional naval missions to be discussed in the next chapter.

Notes

[1] See Toshi Yoshihara and James R Holmes, 'China's New Undersea Deterrent: Strategy, Doctrine and Capability', *Joint Forces Quarterly*, vol. 50, no. 3, Summer 2008, pp. 31–8; Srikanth Kondapalli, 'The Chinese Threat in the Indian Ocean', Rediff.com, 8 May 2008, http://www.rediff.com/news/2008/may/08guest.htm.

[2] Toshi Yoshihara and James R Holmes, *Red Star Over the Pacific: China's Rise and the Challenge to US Maritime Strategy* (Annapolis, MD: Naval Institute Press, 2010), pp. 130–6.

[3] United States Office of the Secretary of Defense Annual Report to Congress, *Military Power of the People's Republic of China*, 2006, p. 28, quotes Major-General Zhu Chenghu to this effect; *China's National Defense in 2010*, Information Office of the State Council, March 2011 at http://www.gov.cn/english/official/2011-03/31/content_1835499.htm, p. 4.

[4] Yoshihara and Holmes, *Red Star Over the Pacific: China's Rise and the Challenge to US Maritime Strategy*, pp. 146–8.

[5] This argument and its possible naval results are authoritatively explored in Toshi Yoshihara and James R. Holmes, 'Thinking About

the Unthinkable: Tokyo's Nuclear Option', *Naval War College Review*, vol. 62, no. 3, Summer 2009, pp. 59–78. The authors conclude that such an outcome is 'highly unlikely in the near future', p. 74.

6   *Ibid.*, p. 69.

7   For an account of this debate see Matake Kamiya, 'Nuclear Japan: Oxymoron or Coming Soon?', *Washington Quarterly*, vol. 26, no. 1, Winter 2002–03, pp. 63–75, and Yoshihara and Holmes, 'Thinking About the Unthinkable: Tokyo's Nuclear Option', pp. 59–78.

8   James R. Holmes, Andrew C. Winner and Toshi Yoshihara, *Indian Naval Strategy in the Twenty-first Century* (London: Routledge, 2009), pp. 96–105.

9   *Indian Maritime Doctrine 2009*, pp. 92–3.

10 *Indian Maritime Doctrine 2004*, p. 54.

11 Vijay Sakhuja, *Asian Maritime Power in the 21st Century* (Singapore: Institute of Southeast Asian Studies, 2011), pp. 95–7, 290–91.

12 Interview, 'Master and Commander' *Defense Technology International*, June 2010.

13 US Navy, *Naval Operations Concept 2010*, pp. 74–6.

14 The Nuclear Posture Review is summarised and discussed in Richard L. Kugler, *New Directions in US National Security Strategy, Defense Plans and Diplomacy – A Review of Official Strategic Documents* (Washington DC: NDU Press for Institute for National Strategic Studies, 2011), pp. 69–72; see also 'US Curbs Potential To Use Nuclear Weapons as Obama's Radical Review Reverses Bush Policies', *Guardian*, 7 April 2010.

15 Donald H. Rumsfeld, secretary of defense, *Annual Report to the President and the Congress* (Washington DC: US Department of Defense, 2002), p. 83.

16 For general background see Amy F. Woolf, *US Strategic Nuclear Forces: Background Developments and Issues* (Washington DC: Congressional Research Service Report RL 33640, 22 February 2012), especially pp. 15–22.

17 See John Wilson Lewis and Xue Litai, *China's Strategic Seapower: The Politics of Force Modernization in the Nuclear Age* (Stanford, CA: Stanford University Press, 1994); See also Lyle J. Goldstein and Andrew S. Erickson, *China's Nuclear Force Modernization* (Newport RI: Naval War College Press Newport Papers no. 22, 2005), http://www.usnwc. edu/Publications/Naval-War-College-Press/Newport-Papers/Documents/22-pdf.aspx.

18 Ronald O'Rourke, *China Naval Modernization: Implications for US Navy Capabilities – Background and Issues for Congress* (Washington DC: Congressional Research Service Report RL 33153, updated 10 July 2008), pp. 2–4. See also O'Rourke *China Naval Modernization: Implications for US Navy Capabilities – Background and Issues for Congress*, p. 9.

19 'More Details Revealed of Jin-class Submarine', *Jane's Defence Weekly*, vol. 44, no. 44, 31 October 2007.

20 Goldstein and Erickson, *China's Nuclear Force Modernisation*, pp. 13, 15, 17.

21 'US Worries over China's Underground Nuclear Network', Agence France-Presse, 14 October 2011.

22 'India Poised to Complete Russian SSN Leasing Deal', *Jane's Defence Weekly*, vol. 44, no. 46, 8 November 2007; 'India to Launch Indigenous N-Submarine by '09: Navy Chief', *Indian Express*, 4 December 2007, http://www.indianexpress.com/news/india-to-launch-indigenous-nsubmarine-by-09-navy-chief/246495/2.

23 'India set to Launch Nuclear Submarine', *Financial Times*, 9 July 2009, http://www.ft.com/cms/s/0/5e851cc0-6c20-11de-9320-00144feabdc0.html#axzz23d9PPb5z; 'India's Nuclear-Powered Submarine Ready', UPI, 13 July 2009, http://www.upi.com/Business_News/Security-Industry/2009/07/13/Indias-nuclear-powered-submarine-ready/UPI-53221247492908/.

24 'India still wants Sub', *Defence Technology International*, December 2008; 'Repairs of India-Bound Russian Sub Hit by Lack of Funds', *Daily Times*, 9 October 2009, http://www.dailytimes.com.pk/default.asp?page=2009\10\09\story_9-10-2009_pg4_7.

25 'Navy set to Complete Nuclear Triad', *The Indian Express*, 26 June 2012

26 'India to Arm Subs With Nukes in 2012' *Defense News*, 13 December 2010.

27 Ronald O'Rourke, *Navy Ohio Replacement (SSBN(X)) Ballistic Missile Submarine Program: Background and Issues for Congress* (Washington DC: Congressional Research Service, Report R41129, 18 October 2012), p. 10.

28 'Ship Shape', *Jane's Defence Weekly*, 21 April 2010; 'USN gets Green Light for SSBN-X Development Work', *Jane's Defense Weekly*, 4 February 2011; 'Generation SSBN9(X), *Defense Technology International*, March 2011.

29 US Defense Department, *Sustaining US Global Leadership: Priorities for 21st Century Defense*, 5 January 2012, at http://www.defense.gov/news/Defense_Strategic_Guidance.pdf, p. 5.

30 Yoshihara and Holmes, *Red Star Over the Pacific: China's Rise and the Challenge to US Maritime Strategy*, pp. 142–45.

31 Vijay Sakhuja, *Asian Maritime Power in the 21st Century: Strategic Transactions China, India and Southeast Asia* (Singapore: Institute of Southeast Asian Studies, 2011), pp. 290–91.

32 Melanie Kirkpatrick, 'Why We Don't Want a Nuclear-Free World', *Wall Street Journal*, 13 July 2009, http://online.wsj.com/article/SB124726489588925407.html.

33 'Navy to Toast Trident Submarines on 1,000th Patrol', *Florida Times-Union*, 15 February 2009, http://www.jacksonville.com/news/georgia/2009-02-15/story/navy_to_toast_trident_submarines_on_1_000th_patrol.

34 The Federation of American Scientists obtained these figures from the Department of the Navy using the Freedom of Information Act in March 2009. See Hans M. Kristensen, 'U.S. Strategic Submarine Patrols Continue at Near Cold War Pace', Federation of American Scientists Strategic Security Blog, 16 March 2009, at http://www.fas.org/blog/ssp/2009/03/usssbn.php.

35 Yoshihara and Holmes, *Red Star Over the Pacific: China's Rise and the Challenge to US Maritime Strategy* pp. 112–13.

36 Indian Navy, *Freedom to Use the Seas: India's Maritime Military Strategy 2007* (New Delhi: Integrated Headquarters, Ministry of Defence [Navy]), p. 76.

37 Bharath Gopalaswamy and Harsh Pant, 'Take NATO's Offer: Allies' Missile Defense Offers Benefits to India', *Defense News*, 18 September 2011, http://mobile.defensenews.com/story.php?i=7717149&c=FEA&s=COM.

38 Holmes et al., *Indian Naval Strategy in the Twenty-first Century*, p. 103; 'India "Star Wars" plan risks New Arms Race', *Guardian*, 14 December 2007, http://www.guardian.co.uk/world/2007/dec/14/india.pakistan.

39 'Japan Indicates End to Era of Declining Defence Spending', *Jane's Defence Weekly*, 3 July 2009.

40 'In Japan Trip, Gates Faces a more Independent-minded Ally', Agence France-Presse, 18 October 2009, http://www.google.com/hostednews/afp/article/ALeqM5jnHdHzur77GZiBnchXAX7f0SFQcg.

41 Euan Graham, *Japan's Sea Lane Security, 1940–2004: A Matter of Life and Death?* (London: Routledge, 2006), pp. 226–7; 'Japan Seeks Power to Strike Missile Bases', *Sydney Morning Herald*, 11 July 2006, http://www.smh.com.au/news/world/japan-seeks-power-to-strike-missile-bases/2006/07/10/1152383678544.html?from=rss; 'Japan Mulled Buying Cruise Missiles for Pre-emptive Self-defense: Ishiba', *Japan Times*, 25 January 2005, http://www.japantimes.co.jp/text/nn20050125f2.html.

42 See US Government, *Ballistic Missile Defense Review Report 2010*, summarised and discussed in Richard L. Kugler, *New Directions in US National Security Strategy, Defense Plans and Diplomacy – A Review of Official Strategic Documents* (Washington DC: NDU Press for Institute for National Strategic Studies, 2011), pp. 120–24.

43 Statement of Admiral Gary Roughead, chief of naval operations, before the Senate Armed Services Committee, 28 February 2008, available at http://www.armed-services.senate.gov/statemnt/2008/February/Roughead%2002-28-08.pdf.

44 Admiral Gary Roughhead , remarks as delivered to Fredericksburg Regional Chamber of Commerce, 4 March 4 2009; see also same remarks in highlights of the Department of Navy FY 2010 Budget, accessible at http://www.finance.hq.navy.mil/FMB/10pres/Highlights_book.pdf, pp. 1–3.

45 Adm. Gary Roughead, remarks at the Conference of Defence Associations, Ottawa Canada, 3 March 2010, at http://www.cda-cdai.ca/cdai/uploads/cdai/2009/06/roughead-cdai2010.pdf.

46 'Japan Makes First BMD Interception with US', *Jane's International Defence Review*, February 2008.

47 Scott Truver, 'Aegis Silences the Critics', *Defense News*, 2 May 2011, http://www.defensenews.com/article/20110502/DEFFEAT05/105020318/Aegis-Silences-Critics.

48 Ronald O'Rourke, *The Impact of Chinese Naval Modernization on the*

Future of the United States Navy (New York: Nova Science Publishers, 2006), p. 45.

49 Vice Adm. Barry McCullogh, Deputy CNO, testimony to House Armed Services Seapower Subcommittee, cited in 'US Navy Officials Defend Plan to Scrap Destroyer', Reuters, 31 July 2008. Vice Adm. J.D. Williams, 'Defending the Skies: US Navy Taking Lead in Missile Defense', *Defense News*, 12 July 2010.

50 Ronald O'Rourke, 'The Shape of Things to Come: CG(X) may Grow in Size and Cost to Deliver Capability', *Jane's International Defence Review*, vol. 40, no. 8, August 2007.

51 'Ship Shape', *Jane's Defence Weekly*, 21 April 2010; 'BMD to Sea', *Defense Technology International*, January 2010; but see 'U.S. Aegis Radars' Readiness Plunges', *Defense News*, 28 June 2010, http://www. defensenews.com/article/20100628/ DEFFEAT04/6280324/U-S-Aegis-Radars-Readiness-Plunges.

52 Ronald O'Rourke, *The Impact of Chinese Naval Modernization on the Future of the United States Navy*, pp. 57–8.

53 'GAO Highlights Rising Cost of Arleigh Burkes', *Jane's Defence Weekly*, February 1 2012; Ronald O'Rourke, *Navy DDG-51 and DDG-1000 Destroyer Programs: Background and Issues for Congress* (Washington DC: Congressional Research Service Report RL 32109, 18 October 2012).

54 'US Joint Staff Call for More Complete BMD Capability', *Jane's Defence Weekly*, 4 April 2012.

55 Bernard C. Cole, *The Great Wall at Sea,* 2nd ed. (Annapolis, MD: Naval Institute Press, 2010), p. 193.

56 'Anti-missile Test Heralds Advent of Chinese BMD Capability', *Jane's Defence Weekly*, 20 January 2010; 'China's Successful Anti-missile Test', *IISS Strategic Comments*, vol. 6, no. 6, February 2010.

57 'Japan Prepares to Shoot Down North Korean Missile if it Fails', *Jane's Defence Weekly*, 1 April 2009.

58 Interview with Captain Randall Hendrikson, US Navy, RUSI Defence Systems, June 2009.

59 Australia Navy, *Australian Maritime Doctrine*, http://www.navy.gov.au/ Publication:Australian_Maritime_ Doctrine, p. 75.

60 Indian Navy, *Freedom to Use the Seas: India's Maritime Military Strategy 2007* (New Delhi: Integrated Headquarters, Ministry of Defence [Navy]) pp. 111–12.

61 US Navy, *A Cooperative Strategy for 21st-Century Seapower*, October 2007, http://www.navy.mil/maritime/ Maritimestrategy.pdf, p. 14.

62 *Ibid.,* p. 10.

63 US Navy, *A Cooperative Strategy for 21st-Century Seapower*, October 2007, http://www.navy.mil/maritime/ Maritimestrategy.pdf.

64 US Navy, *Naval Operations Concept 2010*, http://www.navy.mil/maritime/ noc/NOC2010.pdf.

65 *Naval Amphibious Capability of the 21st Century: Strategic Opportunity and a Vision for Change*, Report of the Amphibious Capabilities Working Group, 27 April 2012; Marine Corps Ellis Group, 'US Amphibious Forces: Indispensible Elements of American Seapower', *Small Wars Journal*, 27 August 2012, is a convenient summary, at http://smallwarsjournal.com/ jrnl/art/us-amphibious-forces-

indispensible-elements-of-american-seapower.

66 US Navy, *A Cooperative Strategy*, p. 10.

67 *Ibid.*, pp. 6–7.

68 ACWG Report, p. S-8.

69 *Ibid.*, pp. 3, 16.

70 *Ibid.*, pp. 3, 9.

71 Capt. Gordon I. Peterson, 'The US Navy Expeditionary Combat Command: A New Focus on Green and Brown Water Missions,' *Naval Forces* IV/2006.

72 US Navy, *Naval Operations Concept 2010*, p. 61. Sea-basing is seen as a one of the benefits deriving from the sea as manoeuvre space; *ibid.*, p. 21. The issue is explored in greater depth in ACGW, 2012, pp. 21, 42, 44, 46.

73 Marine Corps Association, 'Operational Manoeuvre from the Sea: A Concept for the Projection of Power Ashore', *Marine Corps Gazette*, June 1996.

74 Vice Admiral David L Brewer, 'Strategic Deployment: A US Navy Perspective', *World Defence Systems*, April 2003. See also Douglas M. King and John C. Berry Jr, 'Seabasing: Expanding Access', *Joint Forces Quarterly*, vol. 50, no. 3, 2008. The official USMC line is available in Lt-Gen. G.J. Flynn, USMC, commanding general Marine Corps Combat Development Command, 'Amphibious Operations in the 21st Century', 18 March 2009 and 'Seabasing for the Range of Military Operations', 26 March 2009.

75 See his remarks as delivered to the Naval War College, Newport, 17 April 2009 and address to the Navy League at National Harbor, MD, 3 May 2010, commentary accessible at http://defensetech.org/2010/05/04/gates-channels-csbas-big-brains-warning-navy-ships-risk-becoming-wasting/assets/#more-6923.

76 'Ship Shape', *Jane's Defence Weekly*, 21 April 2010.

77 USMC's Commandant at a Crossroads', *Defense News*, 27 September 2010; 'US Marine Corps Urged to Refocus on Amphibious Roots', *Jane's Defence Weekly*, 7 July 2010.

78 Richard Bitzinger, 'Aircraft Carriers Back in Fashion', *Straits Times*, 26 June 2008.

79 Admiral Liu cited in Richard D. Fisher, *China's Military Modernisation: Building for Regional and Global Reach* (Stanford, CA: Stanford University Press, 2010) p. 185. See also 'China Intent on Aircraft Carrier Goal', *Washington Times*, 27 May 2007, http://www.washingtontimes.com/news/2007/may/27/20070527-115808-1213r/?page=all; Yu Chuanxi, cited in Nan Li, Reconceptualizing the PLA Navy in Post-Mao China: Functions, Warfare, Arms and Organisation, Working Paper No. 30, August 2002, Institute of Defence and Strategic Studies, available at RSISPublication@ntu.edu.sg, p. 22.

80 O'Rourke, *China Naval Modernization: Implications for US Navy Capabilities – Background and Issues for Congress*, p. 11.

81 *Ibid.*, pp. 11–12.

82 Choi Chi-yuk, 'Liaoning to Undergo Extended Sea Trials', *South China Morning Post*, 27 September 2012.

83 'China Ready to Build its First Air-craft Carrier', United Press International, 4 June 2009, http://www.

upi.com/Business_News/Security-Industry/2009/06/04/China-ready-to-build-its-first-aircraft-carrier/UPI-94321244124273; 'Watching Beijing's Air Power Grow', *New York Times*, 20 October 2009, http://www.nytimes.com/2009/10/21/world/asia/21iht-letter.html; Richard Bitzinger, 'Aircraft Carriers: China's Emerging Maritime Ambitions' RSIS Commentary 35/2009 April 2009, available at RSISPublication@ntu.edu.sg.

84 Quoted in Richard Halloran, 'China Intent on Aircraft Carrier Goal', *Washington Times*, 29 April 2007.

85 Office of the Secretary of Defense, *Military Power of the People's Republic of China, 2009* (Washington DC: Department of Defense, 2012), p. 19.

86 *Ibid.*, p. viii; see also O'Rourke, *China Naval Modernization: Implications for US Navy Capabilities – Background and Issues for Congress*, pp. 16–17.

87 Office of the Secretary of Defense, *Military Power of the People's Republic of China*, p. 39; O'Rourke, *China Naval Modernization: Implications for US Navy Capabilities – Background and Issues for Congress*, pp. 15–16.

88 Sunho Beck, 'Conflict Ready: Senkakus could be a Flashpoint for Japan and China', *Defense Technology International*, May 2009.

89 *Times of India*, 27 January 2007.

90 'India's Littoral Growth Slow but Showing', *Defense News*, 9 January 2011, http://mobile.defensenews.com/story.php?i=5414476&c=FEA&s=SPE; 'Indian Navy to Boost Amphib Fleet', *Defense News*, 14 January 2011 and 19 September 2011.

91 NewKerala.com, 26 February 2007.

92 'First Fleet Tanker for Indian Navy Launched at Muggiano', *Def Pro Daily*, 12 February 2010, http://www.defpro.com/news/details/13133; 'India Signs for Eight p-81 MRAs', *Jane's Defence Weekly*, 14 January 2009; 'India Approves Acquisitions to Boost Sealift and Surveillance' *Jane's Defence Weekly*, 13 October 2011.

93 'Changeover: US Navy Adapts SSBNs for New Mission' *Defense Technology International*, December 2008.

94 Vice Adm. Joseph A. Sestak, testimony to Seapower Subcommittee of the Senate House Armed Services Committee, 19 April 2005, p. 10; 'LPD 17 Back on Course', *Defense News*, 20 June 2011.

95 These preferences are discussed in Lt-Gen. G.J. Flynn, USMC, Commanding General Marine Corps Combat Development Command, 'Evolving the MAGTF for the 21st Century', 20 March 2009.

96 Statement of Admiral Gary D. Roughead, chief of naval operations, before the House Armed Services Committee on the FY10 Department of Defence Posture, 14 May 2009; Congressional Budget Office, 'An Analysis of the Navy's Fiscal Year 2013 Shipbuilding Plan; July 2012, http://www.cbo.gov/publication/43468, p. 5.

97 'New Horizons', *Jane's Defence Weekly*, 20 September 2010.

98 'Northrop Navy Warships "Not Survivable" in Combat, Defense Department Says', Bloomberg, 28 October 2010.

99 Andrew Koch, 'Core Seabasing Ship Concept takes Shape', *Jane's*

Defence Weekly, 19 January 2005; Robert O. Work, *The US Navy Charting a Course for Tomorrow's Fleet* (Washington DC: CSBA, 2008), p. 79.

100 The Joint High Speed Vessel (a large fast catamaran supply ship) is a good example of the effort and expense allocated to the sea-basing concept. 'Fast Forward: JHSV Speeds from the Sea Base to the Shore', *Military Logistics International*, January–February 2009.

101 Congressional Budget Office, 'An Analysis of the Navy's Amphibious Warfare Ships for Deploying Marines Overseas', November 2011, available at http://www.cbo.gov/sites/default/files/cbofiles/attachments/11-18-AmphibiousShips.pdf, p.9.

102 Work, *The US Navy: Charting a Course For Tomorrow's Fleet*, p. 77

103 'Marine Corps Operating Concepts', *Defense Tech*, June 2010, http://defensetech.org/wp-content/uploads//2010/06/usmcoperatingconcept.pdf.

104 With amongst other things a US–Philippine exercise held near a disputed shoal in the South China Sea in which a beach was stormed by marines, Evelyn Goh, 'America Faces Familiar Dilemmas in Region', *Straits Times*, 3 December 2011.

105 'Indian Warships Sail away from Pak Waters', *Reuters*, 11 June 2002.

106 'India Stages "Largest Ever" Joint Amphibious Exercise', *Jane's Defence Weekly*, 18 February 2009; for accounts of *Tropex 2012*, see http://livefist.blogspot.sg/2012/02/indian-navy-exercise-tropex-2012.html.

107 Christopher P. Cavas, 'US War Game Finds Gaps in Navy, Marine Amphibious Ops', *Defense News*, 10 September 2012; *Naval Amphibious Capability of the 21st Century: Strategic Opportunity and a Vision for Change*, Report of the Amphibious Capabilities Working Group, 27 April 2012; Marine Corps Ellis Group, 'US Amphibious Forces: Indispensible Elements of American Seapower'.

108 *Australian Maritime Doctrine*, pp. 200 and 46.

109 Adm. Greenert, statement to House Armed Services Committee, 16 February 2012.

110 Admiral Sureesh Mehta, address to the International Institute for Strategic Studies, 'India's Maritime Diplomacy and International Security', June 2007.

111 *Indian Maritime Doctrine* (New Delhi: Integrated Headquarters, Ministry of Defence [Navy] 2004, p. 64.

112 Joseph Nye, *The Future of Power* (New York: Public Affairs, 2011).

113 Ma Henghui, 'If Military Hard Power is a Sharp Sword, Soft Power is its Awe-Inspiring Gleam and Clang', *Jiefangjun Bao Online*, 25 November 2010, OSC-CPP20101125704006, quoted in James Holmes, 'China's Maritime Strategy is More than Naval Strategy', *Jamestown Foundation/China Brief*, 8 April 2011.

114 'Military Chief 'Confirms First China Aircraft Carrier', Agence France-Presse, 7 June 2011; Trefor Moss, 'Interpreting China's Carrier Ambitions', *Jane's Defence Weekly*, 14 September 2011; 'US, China Talk on Taiwan as Jet Decision Nears', Radio

Netherlands Worldwide, 30 July 2011, http://www.rnw.nl/english/bulletin/us-china-talk-taiwan-jet-decision-nears.

[115] 'US Uneasy as Beijing Develops a Strategic String of Pearls', *Guardian*, 10 November 2005, http://www.guardian.co.uk/business/2005/nov/10/china.internationalnews.

[116] Hari Sud, 'China's Strategic Role in the Persian Gulf', UPI, 26 September 2007, http://www.network54.com/Forum/242808/thread/1190860095/1218353348/Gwadar-+China%27s+strategic+post+to+the+Persian+Gulf.

[117] 'Behind Recent Gunboat Diplomacy in the South China Sea', IISS *Strategic Comments*, vol. 17, no. 28, August 2011; 'China Launches more Large-scale Military Exercises', Agence France-Presse, 3 August 2010; 'Chinese Military Holds Naval Drills in South China Sea' *Straits Times*, 4 November, 2010; 'Tensions Rise in South China Sea', *Jane's Defence Weekly*, 22 June 2011.

[118] Raul Pedrozo, 'Close Encounters at Sea: the USNS *Impeccable* Incident', *Naval War College Review*, vol. 62, no. 3, Summer 2009, pp. 101–111; Wendell Minnick Articles, 'China Condemns US Plan for Yellow Sea Exercise', http://minnickarticles.blogspot.co.uk/2010/07/china-condemns-us-plan-for-yellow-sea.html, originally published in *Defense News*; Oriana Skylar Mastro, 'Signaling and Military Provocation in Chinese National Security Strategy: A Closer Look at the *Impeccable* Incident', *Journal of Strategic Studies*, vol. 34, no. 2, April 2011, pp. 219–44.

[119] 'Indian Warship Visits Tonga', *People's Daily*, 11 July 2006, http://english.peopledaily.com.cn/200607/11/eng20060711_282054.html; Admiral Mehta address at the IISS.

[120] Mrityunjoy Mazumdar and Rupak Chattopadhyay, 'India–US Naval Exercises Bearing Fruit', *Seagull*, November 2006; 'India, US Near Agreement for Logistic Support', *Jane's Defence Weekly*, 25 July 2007.

[121] Anthony Paul, 'Asian Giants' Game of Chess in Indian Ocean', *Straits Times*, 16 May 2007, http://yaleglobal.yale.edu/content/asian-giants-game-chess-indian-ocean.

[122] 'US Considers Naval Build-up as Warning to Iran', *Guardian*, 20 December 2006, http://www.commondreams.org/headlines06/1220-04.htm; 'Bush Settling America on the Road to War with Iran', *Guardian*, 16 September 2007.

[123] 'US Joins Naval Drill in Southeast Asia', Xinhua, 17 June 2011, http://news.xinhuanet.com/english2010/video/2011-06/17/c_13935733.htm; 'Fighting Words Delivered from the Deck of a Destroyer', *Straits Times*, 16 November 2011, http://getlocalne.ws/world/singapore_singapore/straits_times_news_3517862. The text of the speech is at http://www.state.gov/r/pa/prs/ps/2011/11/177226.htm.

[124] Robert C. Rubel, 'The New Maritime Strategy: The Rest of the Story', *Naval War College Review*, vol. 61, no. 2, Spring 2008, p. 77.

CHAPTER FOUR

Non-traditional missions

The Chinese, Japanese, Indian and US navies are also involved in less traditional missions, directed not so much at the defence of narrow national interests but more at the defence of common interests and the international economic system on which their peace and prosperity is considered increasingly to depend. These missions are generally of a much more cooperative nature, the kind of activities and force structures that tend to militate against, rather than for, the development of naval arms-racing phenomena. They were notably absent from the naval thinking and policy of the early twentieth century.

The versatility of naval forces, compared to land or air forces, means that many of the characteristics associated with the performance of the competitive, traditional missions discussed in the last two chapters can be, and have been, equally well deployed for cooperative humanitarian relief and disaster response (HADR) and other cooperative tasks in defence of the global trading system. While amphibious-warfare vessels, for example, can be used to project soldiers and their equipment across a hostile shore, they are increasingly thought of as multipurpose platforms and ones which with their well-docks, flight deck and storage capacity makes them particularly suited to a range of expeditionary and humanitarian tasks. Indeed, according to one authoritative study, over half of the US military's responses to international situations since 1970 have been HADR, while combat operations made up just 3%, with 'show of force' for deterrent purposes adding another 10%.[1] In terms of actual operational activity, this is largely true of the other three navies too, most obviously India.

Expeditionary operations

Expeditionary operations, as distinct from traditional amphibious operations are nowadays usually understood to involve the use of forward deployed, or rapidly deployable, self-sustaining forces tailored to achieve a clearly stated and limited objective at a distance from the home base, often at short notice and normally in the company of allies and partners.[2] The adversary would generally be a non-state actor of some kind, unlikely to be able to contest the landing phase of any such operation at sea. Such is the inherent flexibility of the amphibious forces discussed in Chapter Three, that they will very often be the heart of such expeditionary capacities and indeed their development is increasingly tied to this mission.[3]

Expeditionary operations thinking

China is clearly developing the wider internationalist perspectives to be expected of one of the world's great trading countries. Major-General Luo Yuan of the Academy of Military Sciences has stated that 'the Chinese military now has the duty to combat numerous non-traditional threats'. This point of view was given some emphasis in the Defence White Paper of 2008, which spoke of the need to 'gradually develop ... capabilities of conducting cooperation in distant waters and countering non-traditional security threats'.[4] The *PLA Daily* of 23 September

2009 stated that expanding duties in military operations other than war – including UN peacekeeping operations, cooperation in anti-terrorist campaigns and HADR operations – and the wider range at which China may have to carry these missions out, requires greater power-projection capabilities.[5] The 2011 Defence White Paper reinforced the point that what the Chinese sometimes referred to as a 'go-out strategy' is clearly developing fast.[6]

For the Japanese, Article 9 of the constitution is a particular constraint in this area, but Japan's emerging acceptance of a wider international role in defence of the system can eventually be expected to generate more doctrinal exploration of the subject. As an indicator of this, successive Defence White Papers have recognised the need for the JMSDF to move out of its more local concerns, as part of the shift from the static deterrence of its 'basic defence force concept' into something more dynamic and flexible.[7]

There is little doctrinal discussion in Indian doctrine of expeditionary operations as such. One paragraph in *Indian Maritime Doctrine 2009* tackles the issue, following on from a conventional description of amphibious operations. It reads:

> Expeditionary Operations are another form of maritime power projection. It entails deployment of military forces overseas, and their sustenance thereupon by means of own airlift and/or sealift assets, for accomplishment of national objectives. A maritime/sea-borne expeditionary operation may also encompass amphibious operation(s), wherein land forces are inserted, supported and sustained by sea. Among the essential prerequisites for expeditionary capability are 'long-legged' and stable sealift ships equipped with integral vectors (landing craft and airlift assets) and

C4 facilities, besides logistic-lift platforms for sustaining the operation for prolonged periods.[8]

The US Navy, with its unique ability to forward deploy
combat-credible naval forces linked to the capacity to project
large-scale amphibious force ashore, is at pains to emphasise
how useful these forces are for expeditionary and humanitarian purposes as well. The *Naval Operations Concept 2010*
develops the idea of 'globally distributed, mission tailored
naval forces' which seem to be rather less powerful than
'regionally concentrated naval forces', but which should be
sufficient to deal with issues at the lower end of the spectrum
of maritime power projection.[9] Forward-deployed expeditionary capabilities are held to contribute to homeland defence 'in
depth', (where defences start further away from the homeland
being defended) to foster and sustain cooperative relationships
with other nations and 'prevent or contain local disruptions
before they impact the global system'. This is a partial reference to what the US Navy calls 'stability operations'.[10] In 2010
the requirement was summed up like this:

> We will emphasize Cooperative Security as part of a
> comprehensive government approach to mitigate the
> causes of insecurity and instability. We will operate in
> and from the maritime domain with joint and inter-
> national partners to enhance regional security and
> stability, and to dissuade, deter, and when necessary,
> defeat irregular forces.[11]

Generally, the conduct of limited, uncontested or less-
contested expeditionary operations is understood to call for
much less sophisticated and expensive maritime capabilities
than would, for example, any attempt to recreate the Iwo Jima

campaign of 1944 or Inchon landings of 1950 against serious opposition.

Capabilities for expeditionary operations

Most of the operational requirements of expeditionary operations can, as has been remarked earlier, be performed by forces designed for war-fighting, sea control and maritime force projection operations of the sort described in the last two chapters.[12] The US Marine Corps illustrates the point. It still intends to be capable of providing a two-brigade amphibious assault to ensure access for the joint force; nonetheless, the vast majority of its 107 major landings since 1991 have been focused on lower-intensity tasks such as minor interventions, disaster relief and evacuations, and this continues to be a major development priority.[13]

There are four exceptions to this general rule. Firstly, while expeditionary operations may assume rather lower levels of threat, they will often require greater sustainability a long way from home. Accordingly, all four navies are building up their logistical support and tanker fleets and developing 'sea-basing' programmes. The US Military Sealift Command and other aspects of its logistics fleet, such as its 'Afloat Forward Staging Base', however, provide the gold standard.[14] Secondly, expeditionary operations will often require particularly high levels of inter-service cooperation, and all four navies are developing joint capabilities as well, sometimes from quite a low starting point.

Thirdly, the US Navy's Littoral Combat Ship (LCS) is a rare example of a major warship specifically designed for the conduct of expeditionary operations.

> She enables our fleet to tackle head-on tough challenges like piracy, smugglers, terrorists, mines,

submarines and swarming boats that lurk in the shallow seas and in coastal waters. [USS] *Freedom* will know how to fight but she can also be a great friend.[15]

Started in 2001, the LCS grew out of Admiral Cebrowski's 'street-fighter concept' of fast, shallow-draft and smallish 3,000-tonne net-worked combatants, each separately configured to perform one of a wide variety of missions in crucial littoral waters, largely against mines, diesel submarines and small attack craft. The LCS is expected to provide much of the 30% mix of the future US fleet that is regarded as best suited for low-intensity operations and as an enabler for expeditionary operations. The LCS programme, however, has faced cost over-runs and design difficulties which are partly a consequence of its ambitious modular design and partly of deficiencies in project management.[16] For all that, an acquisition programme for 55 LCSs is proceeding, and indeed the first *Freedom*-class vessel was commissioned in early 2010, along with three partial mission packages, two years ahead of schedule in order to close what Admiral Roughead has called 'urgent war-fighting gaps'.[17] Another 20 are on order. The LCS has already proved useful in maritime security operations such as the counter-narcotics campaign in the Caribbean.[18] Nonetheless, the programme remains controversial inside and outside the US Navy.[19]

Lastly, another distinctive aspect of the capacity for expeditionary operations which has so far been illustrated only by the US Navy is the rediscovery and redevelopment of riverine operations.[20] The establishment in January 2006 of the US Navy Expeditionary Combat Command, with its strong emphasis on riverine operations, also demonstrates a clear determination to expand its expeditionary capabilities to deal with everything from traditional combat operations and special operations to HADR. Some 40,000 sailors are assigned to this command. This initiative has caused some concern in Congress that it might be at the expense of the Navy's traditional blue-water roles and in the US Marine corps that it might replicate some of their functions.

During the Vietnam War, the US Navy built up considerable expertise in riverine operations but this was later allowed to atrophy. In 1969, some 500 units were operating, but by 2005 this had dwindled to a couple of small-craft communities in the navy and the marines, whose basic aim was to keep the discipline alive. Renewing this capability is now seen as an important part of the requirement of extending the reach of expeditionary forces, part and parcel of the messy business of post-modern naval operations.[21] To some extent, the end of the Iraq campaign has also seen some consolidation and reductions of the Coastal Riverine Force but the clear intent is that, this time, it will survive.[22]

Expeditionary operations: activities and operations

Japan's Defence White Paper of 10 December 2004 increased the emphasis placed on Japan's international role.[23] Although it is still constrained by its current constitution, recent reinterpretations of that constitution have allowed the JMSDF to take on an increasingly expeditionary character with its involvement in the multilateral Afghan and Iraq operations, especially through continuing logistical support for Coalition forces engaged in *Operation Enduring Freedom* in the Indian Ocean, and indeed for its reconstruction teams in Iraq. This mission began in 2001, and was periodically renewed by the Diet Anti-Terrorism Special Measures Law. It involved the JMSDF deploying in all 44 destroyers and 27 replenishment ships at a cost of ¥71.5bn up to 2010.[24] Briefly suspended during the Hatoyama administration, the JMSDF's refuelling mission in the Indian Ocean was later reinstated.[25]

In the same way, the rules of engagement for the two JMSDF destroyers despatched to the Gulf of Aden in support of Japanese shipping interests threatened by piracy were framed by the provisions of the June 2009 Law. In order to support their engagement, Japan opened a naval base in Djibouti in April 2011,the first time since the Second World War it had set up a naval base outside the country.

The Indian Navy has also developed significant expertise in complex expeditionary operations, thanks largely to its hard-won experience in the long-drawn-out and politically complex conflict in Sri Lanka between the government and the Tamil Tigers (LTTE). This has involved the support of forces ashore for long periods, and the protection of Indian fishing boats and merchant ships from Tamil Tiger attack. The difficulties of distinguishing between innocent fishing boats and poten-tially deadly LTTE attack craft has reinforced recognition of the need for better maritime domain awareness in the Palk Strait. In similar manner, US naval operations reveal, in the wake of the attack on the USS *Cole* in Aden in 2000, an acute sensitivity to the asymmetric threats posed in littoral waters by terrorists and other irregular forces which might be encountered in the course of expeditionary operations.

The US Navy has devoted most of its higher intensity opera-tional activities since the end of the Cold War to the conduct of expeditionary operations. most obviously in the Balkans against Iraq and the Taliban and al-Qaeda in Afghanistan, all of which have proved to be at the upper end of the spectrum of expeditionary operations which shade into conventional war-fighting and seem significantly different from the British intervention in Sierra Leone or the Australian-led operation in East Timor. These experiences have refined American think-ing and capabilities. For example, Turkey's refusal to allow the passage of the 4th Infantry Division over its territory in the early stages of *Operation Iraqi Freedom* greatly reinforced earlier thinking about the need to develop sea-basing capabilities, while the 560km (350 mile) range at which conventional forces could be projected into Afghanistan from the Bay of Bengal, together with the speed, precision and persistence of its aircraft and missile strikes, amply demonstrated the way in which the concept of 'operational manoeuvre from the sea' had been translated into hard military power. At the same time, many of these capabilities have been frequently deployed in softer ways in HADR operations. The US Navy's proficiency in the conduct of operations of this sort was most recently demonstrated in the 2011 Libya operation, which was distinctive for the decisive role played by the SSGN USS *Florida* and which in some ways was an early example of the kind of 'air–sea integration' behind developing ideas of the Air–Sea battle.[26]

By contrast, the Chinese navy has not conducted any out-or-area expeditionary operations other than the counter-piracy mission in the Gulf of Aden and the non-combatant evacuation of some 30,000 Chinese workers from Libya in 2011. Nor, for all the hype about the 'String of Pearls' it is allegedly casting across the Indian Ocean is there much evidence of its laying down the base infrastructure that would allow it to do so.[27]

Stability operations/HADR

According to the *Australian Maritime Doctrine 2010:* 'Warships repeatedly demonstrate that their inherent capabilities make them uniquely valuable in providing both short notice and long term assistance in disaster relief, not only for coastal locations, but sometimes well inland.'[28] In these operations, there is no adversary as such, apart from the context of natural or man-made disaster, and typically they are conducted with a great deal of impromptu coordination between the navies present, made possible by the habits of cooperation developed earlier in exercises and visits. Warships engaged in this activity, again, rarely need to be designed specifically for the purpose. Such operations are not new, but the level of attention given to them most certainly is. Again, it is evidence of a strongly cooperative element in naval relations.

Humanitarian assistance

The armed forces of both China and Japan have been used for HADR operations, not least within their own countries, and they and other 'military operations other than war' have begun to figure prominently in doctrinal expositions.[29] Illustrating the Chinese concept of the 'harmonious ocean', the hospital ship *Peace Ark* visited five African and Asian countries in the latter part of 2010, and combined its medical tasks with a mission to let local people 'know more about China, the Chinese military and navy' and to advance the PLAN's capacity to perform its 'New Historic Missions'. The US Navy was unsettled to find the same ship operating in the Caribbean in November 2011.[30]

Indian doctrine pays even more attention to the HADR mission. HADR operations are, however, regarded by the Indian Navy as one of the most likely contingencies for which it, like other navies, needs to prepare, and one particularly relevant to the India Ocean area, given the incidence of climatic and other disasters in the region, the spread of the Indian diaspora and the particular capacity for sea-based forces, both naval and coast guard, to arrive early and usefully on the scene of disaster.

These operations are officially defined thus:

> The 'benign' role is so named because violence has no part to play in its execution, nor is the potential to apply force a necessary prerequisite for undertaking these operations. Examples of benign tasks include

humanitarian aid, disaster relief, Search and Rescue (SAR), ordnance disposal, diving assistance, salvage operations, hydrographic surveys, etc.[31]

The IN has been the preferred instrument of the state for delivering relief material and services via sea to help India's maritime neighbours in their hour of need. This has also helped project national soft power, towards improving relations and the regional maritime environment.[32]

For the Americans, HADR, part of what are sometimes called Stability, Security, Transition and Reconstruction (SSTR) operations, are said to be 'a core US military mission' that may 'involve providing humanitarian and civic assistance to the local populace ... activities may include the provision of health care, construction of surface transportation systems, well drilling, construction of basic sanitation facilities, and rudimentary construction and repair of public facilities'.[33] As the title suggests, the aim of the exercise is not only to mitigate human suffering at home and abroad, but also to buttress the stability on which the world system depends, and to prevent such crises leading to conflict. Two types of HADR operation are envisaged: the proactive and the reactive.[34]

The US Navy's particular angle on this has been the development of the notion of the 'global fleet station' (or in certain geographic locations, 'partnership stations'), a sea-based force able to respond to needs and crises in a physically appropriate and culturally sensitive manner. To make this example of 'gunboat philanthropy'[35] work, 'combatant commanders require tools that are not only instruments of war, but implements for stability, security, and reconstruction in our global neighbourhood'.[36] The emphasis here is very much on the navy working alongside other civilian aid agencies – and indeed navies – as necessary. Global Fleet Stations is about massaging the environment, but in a nice way.

This development of this notion has not been without controversy. In some parts of the US Navy there was and remains a reluctance to accept HADR as a mission equal in practical terms to other more conventional ones lest it impact badly on the resources available for the latter.[37] Such doubts were assuaged by the argument that such operations benefit the benefactor politically and strategically; also they cost little as the capacity for HADR/Stability Operations is a natural byproduct of expeditionary and conventional war-fighting capabilities that are needed anyway.

Humanitarian assistance: operations

Although all too aware of the need to respond to environmental and other disasters domestically, China has until recently played little role in sea-based HADR operations abroad and was conspicuously absent from the international tsunami-relief operation of 2004. This was politically damaging, a point that doubtless persuaded President Hu Jintao to enunciate the 'New Historic Missions' for the PLAN in his Christmas Eve speech of that year and which has since informed their carrier, amphibious-warfare vessel and acquisition and deployment programmes.[38]

Japan's activities overseas are limited, if ambiguously, by constitutional constraints on its capacity to engage in 'collective defence'. The humanitarian mission, moreover, has the advantage that it can assuage those on the pacifist left that the JMSDF is still adhering to the spirit of Article 9 of the constitution and the modernisers on the right seeking rearmament. The new *Hyuga*, for example, has large multifunctional space ideally equipping it for disaster-relief operations. The MoD has now requested the building of a 19,500-tonne amphibious warfare helicopter carrier for ¥118bn.[39] The JMSDF's power-projection capabilities have also been enhanced by the procurement of three *Osumi*-class transport ships which can operate helicopters and have a rear dock for hovercraft which are also capable of transporting tanks. Two of these were deployed to Indonesia as part of the tsunami disaster-relief operation in 2004. Grateful for the humanitarian assistance it received from the US and others during the Fukushima disaster, Japan has now made a conscious policy decision to upgrade its own capabilities in this area, both at home and abroad. This operation was one of the first in which their comparatively recent emphasis on improving cooperation with the other services was displayed.[40] Amphibious disciplines were exercised in this operation and also in the shipping of humanitarian aid after the Turkish earthquake in October 2011.[41]

The Indian Navy is likewise particularly proud of its fast and extensive reaction to the Asian tsunami of 2004, although the experience brought home just how demanding this task can be. Catering for it has assumed a greater priority ever since.[42] Twenty-two Indian naval vessels were en route, from Eastern Naval Command within hours of the disaster and were the first to arrive at some of the stricken locations. In all, 38 ships, 21 helicopters, nine fixed-wing aircraft and 5,900 sailors were involved in relief operations in Indonesia, Malaysia, Sri Lanka, the Maldives, the Nicobar and Andaman Islands and peninsular India itself. As one naval commentator put it, this disaster-relief operation by the Indian Navy 'has demonstrated its extent of strategic reach, inherent capability and reasserted India's leadership commensurate with the regional responsibilities of India.[43] But, for all that, the sheer scale of the requirement drew attention to the limits in capacity to respond, and have reinforced the navy's determination to enhance its amphibious/sea lift/ expeditionary capabilities. Likewise, at much greater range, the Indian Navy itself sent four ships to Beirut in 2006, joining in a loose and cooperative multilateral naval operation, and took in relief supplies and took out 2,280 people. One of the evident aims of the navy is to enhance its capacity to join in such collaborative operations as this.[44]

The US Navy has often engaged in HADR/stability operations in the past, as have most other navies, but at a scale no one else can yet match, and the tempo appears to be picking up, both in terms of delivering humanitarian assistance during or after conflicts, and in response to natural disasters. Examples of the former would include Yugoslavia (1992–96), East Timor (2000) and the Democratic Republic of the Congo (1996–97); in the latter, the US has carried out *Operation Sea Angel* off Bangladesh in 1991; responded to the Cuban and Haitian boat people between 1994 and 1996, the Philippines (1992), the Tsunami relief operation in 2004 and the March 2011 Fukushima disaster.

The Asian tsunami-relief operation was particularly significant, not simply because of the scale of the devastation encountered but because the *Abraham Lincoln* Carrier Strike Group and the *Bonhomme Richard* Expeditionary Strike Group delivered more than 2.7m tonnes of relief more quickly, efficiently and with much less political hassle than comparable land-based operations could have done.[45] US amphibious-warfare ships revealed their particular value for this kind of work off Pakistan in response to the catastrophic flooding in August 2010.[46] In response to the Fukushima disaster, the US provided 24,000 personnel, 190 aircraft and 24 ships to assist the Japanese.[47]

Encouraged by the international goodwill this kind of operation normally generates, and as part of its expanding interest in stability operations, the US Navy has put its 'Global Fleet Stations' into effect by sending hospital ships on cruises around Africa and South America, and in using other warships as means of offering help in the medical and civil-engineering fields. Indeed in 2010 it was claimed that, since 2004, the US Navy had conducted ten HADR missions, in which 300,000 patients had been treated and more than 3,000 medical operations had been carried out.[48]

An emphasis on HADR/stability operations of this kind, together with intensive efforts at naval engagement, has been a hallmark of the new Miami-based Southern Command. Intended as a model for the much more controversial Africa Command, this organisation was then unique in the weight it attaches to non-military 'soft' approaches to security, as evidenced, for example, in the number of its senior positions allocated to civilians.

Although it is possible for international HADR/stability operations to be misconstrued as interference in a country's internal affairs (rather as did Indonesia over American responses to the 2004 Tsunami, and Myanmar over its 2010 typhoon), these operations are in the main a kinder, more benign and cooperative aspect of naval development. Their success depends in large measure on international cooperation and the activity thus acts against arms-racing tendencies in the Asia-Pacific region.

Maritime security at home and abroad

Maritime security is now held to cover the safety of legitimate activity at sea. It is a particularly wide and potentially ambiguous concept which includes the protection of shipping, counter-terrorism and action against other forms of sea-based crime, typically with non-state actors in mind. As far as all four navies are concerned, the economic and social linkages brought about by globalisation mean that there is a 'home' and 'away' aspect to maritime security. The latter is seen as a proactive matter of extending national defences forwards as part of a cooperative global strategy in order to gain time for, or to make unnecessary, adequate defensive responses nearer to home.

Although the constabulary aspects of maritime security are frequently performed by lightly armed or even unarmed vessels of a coast guard type, higher-intensity capacities such as large ship-based patrol aircraft and ISTAR capabilities[49] often prove valuable as well. Maritime-security tasks can also be performed by forces designed for coastal defence.

There is, however, a distinctly competitive edge to the concept of maritime security, especially when it comes to the protection of one country's sovereignty and maritime resources (most notably oil, gas and fish) from others, as has been all too apparent in the East and South China seas, particularly in 2010–12.

Maritime security thinking

Public debate on the issue of maintaining good order at sea is relatively under-developed in China. Where it occurs, it is normally focused on the need to protect a national maritime estate that since the United Nations Convention on the Law of the Sea (UNCLOS) III has grown both in size and in relative commercial importance, especially given China's rapidly expanding requirements for sea-based oil, gas and fish. Wu Zuang, director of the Administration of Fishery for the South China Sea, is quoted as saying:

> Faced with a growing amount of illegal fishing and other countries' unfounded territorial claims on islands in China's exclusive economic zone, it has become necessary to step up the Fishery Administration's patrols to protect China's rights and interests.[50]

This task is often interpreted more as the business of keeping foreigners out of Chinese waters than of enforcing the rules on Chinese fishing boats. Arguably this is as much an instinctive matter of preserving Chinese sovereignty than of the oil, gas and fish stocks it covers.[51] Although as an increasingly sea-faring country, China is perfectly well aware of the more distant threats to the good order at sea on which world trade partly depends, there appears so far to be little doctrinal debate on the matter, other than an increasingly vocal call for the country to defend its maritime interests in a more integrated fashion. Thus Rear Admiral Yin Zhuo, chairman of the Expert Committee on Navy Informationalisation: 'China does not have a clearly defined ocean strategy at the national level.' Economic considerations dominate the policies of agencies within the State Oceanic Administration and 'naturally the Navy has its own ocean strategy considerations, but these are all actions by certain departments and not at the national level'. Such concerns have led in China, as elsewhere, to calls for the establishment of a 'Ministry of Oceans'.[52]

The maritime security of Japanese waters is now taken even more seriously than it was. In July 2007 the Diet passed the first Oceans Policy Basic Act which emphasises Japan's dependence on the sea for transportation and resources, while also stressing the importance of an integrated and holistic policy and the particular need to secure maritime transport through the activities of the Japan Coast Guard and where necessary the JMSDF. To that end a Basic Plan for Ocean Policy was announced in March 2008.

The Japanese share Chinese concerns about good order at sea in sensitive areas like the Malacca Strait but likewise devote their main attention to their own waters and to the defence of their disputed islands and waters, partly because of their economic potential in terms of oil, fish and gas, partly because of their historical significance and partly because this capacity to maintain Japan's maritime interests is seen as an indicator of government performance. The feeling is reinforced by the contentious and sometimes deadly nature of its maritime juris-dictional disputes with China, South Korea and Russia.[53]

The Indians, who for their part suffer from significant degrees of domestic terrorism – some of which they feel to be supported externally – see the Indian Ocean region as the 'de facto home of global terrorism' and point out that the sea is the means by which much drugs and arms trafficking is conducted:

> Most of the poppy cultivation in the region takes place in the areas that encircle the Indian Ocean. Terrorist groups operate with transnational criminal organ-isations, drug cartels and war lords. Drug money is used to procure weapons, arms and ammunition and to support terrorist activities and insurgencies. The transhipment of these tools of terror, which are used to support terrorist activities and insurgencies, often takes place in the waters of the Indian Ocean. In short, the IOR is the hotbed of narco-terrorism, smuggling, gunrunning and associated crimes.[54]

The Golden Crescent on one side of India and the Golden Triangle on the other provide financial support for al-Qaeda and Jemaah Islamiah. As Admiral Arun Prakash has observed, if one adds to this 'the freewheeling piratical activity in loca-tions like the Horn of Africa, the Bay of Bengal and the Malacca Straits, and one gets an idea of the vigil that is necessary to maintain order in these waters'.[55]

Unsurprisingly, Prakash concludes that India is the natural policeman of the Indian Ocean; 'as a major maritime power, the Indian Navy is duty-bound to work towards improving the maritime security environment in the region'. Moreover, the practical, professional advantages of performing these very post-modern low-intensity maritime tasks (LIMO) tasks in the company of other like-minded maritime powers through a deliberate policy of constructive engagement include better coordination, information sharing, and the absorption of best practice. This is clearly recognised in India.[56]

The tendency to see the sea as a security barrier against foreign threats was shattered by the Mumbai terrorist attack of 26 November 2008 in which 164 people were killed and 308 injured. Coming after earlier attacks on Mumbai in 1993 and 2006, this incident reinforced, once again, the need for a greater emphasis on coastal security.[57] The repeated failure of the security services to protect the city against attacks of this sort prompted great public anger.[58] This was reflected in the revamped Indian Maritime Doctrine of August 2009.[59] The revised IMD acknowledged the navy's need to contribute to the defence of the country's borders, citizens and property from terrorism, to control maritime crime in all its forms including piracy, and to intercept external support for internal insurgents.

Admiral Mehta argued that navies needed to adapt themselves to an era 'characterised by the rise of non-state forces ... [and the] worrying phenomenon of the occasional coalescing of the state with some non-state entities, which has created an evil hybrid'. But he also expressed his concern that 'the increasing demand on the military to assume law-and-order responsibilities is clearly an undesirable trend – this must always be a last resort. The military must never be used against our population.'[60]

All this chimes closely with American thinking. Maritime Security was one of the 'new' core capabilities in *A Cooperative Strategy for 21st Century Seapower*[61] and the focus was on mitigating the threats to good order at sea that fall short of war, 'including piracy, terrorism, weapons proliferation, drug trafficking, and other illicit activities'. Dealing with these irregular and transnational threats, the documents says, 'protects our homeland, enhances global stability, and secures freedom of navigation for the benefit of all nations' and will involve joint naval/coast guard action nationally and internationally. There is emphasis on its being a cooperative endeavour internationally since 'no one … can provide a solution to maritime security problems alone'. Instead, it requires a 'global maritime partnership'.[62]

The US Coast Guard is expected to take a leading role in translating these aspirations into reality both in home waters and more distantly. There is a recognition that the United States needs to develop a strategic approach to the problem of maritime security in the round. This in turn requires developing, not simply new tactical and operational techniques and technologies (needed to screen containers, for example), but also the institutions and procedures that will integrate the efforts of other government agencies at home and abroad. International engagement with other countries in the drive for maritime security is sometimes complicated by the American tendency to focus on counter-terrorism where other countries identify piracy, illegal fishing or people smuggling as more immediate threats.

Moreover, there remains a degree of resistance within the US Navy to the ready adoption of these softer post-modern roles, especially if they are seen as conflicting with the requirements of harder modern disciplines, or look likely to wear out ships and crews prematurely.[63]

Maritime-security capabilities

Significant numbers of new fast-attack craft began to appear in China in the 1990s, such as the 'Sea Patrol 3' and a number of catamaran missile patrol craft. These, together with the arrival of larger vessels such as the 3,000-tonne *Haixun* 31 and 5,000-tonne *Bei Hai Jiu* 111 (both operated by the Maritime Safety Agency) (MSA), demonstrate a determination to safeguard China's maritime sovereignty and interests, both at home and, interestingly, at a distance.

Until recently Chinese capabilities in maritime patrol, surveillance of a more constabulary kind were modest, and officially regarded as inadequate given the size of China's maritime domain. The State Oceanic Administration (SOA) claims its entire fleet is less than half the size of the Japan Coast Guard but has a far greater area to cover. A major expansion of the constabulary and survey fleet under the SOA and the China Marine Surveillance (CMS) Agency is now in progress, including the 1,290-tonne Maritime Surveillance Ship 75 for the South China Sea and the 3,980-tonne helicopter-carrying flag-ship, the Maritime Surveillance Ship 83.[64]

At first glance, this investment in constabulary forces intended to maintain good order at sea would seem more benign and cooperative than the PLAN's development plans. But this depends on how these paramilitary forces are used. China's critics point out that the USNS *Impeccable* was harassed by CMS ships and fishing boats rather than naval vessels and that these same ships have been used quite assert-ively in both the South and East China seas in waters claimed or indeed owned by other countries, and which tends to be regarded by them as a form of access denial.[65] To some extent this apparent assertiveness may be the product of a lack of integration between the various state and provincial agen-cies for supervision of the coastal zone, the so called 'Nine Dragons that stir the sea,' which include the CMS and the MSA referred to above but of which the largest is the PLAN itself.

Constrained both by their constitution and an implicit acceptance that defence expenditure should not rise above 1 % of GDP, the Japanese invested heavily in the separately financed Maritime Safety Agency (which became the JGCin 2006) as a means of narrowing their resources-commitments gap. The JCG maintains peace and order in Japanese waters, ensures the safety of maritime traffic, is responsible for search and rescue, helps protect the marine environment and cooperates with domestic and foreign organisations. Successive JCG Annual Reports[66] have revealed the need for an enhanced ability to react robustly to the intrusion of foreign vessels (North Korean spy boats, Chinese hydrography vessels and illegal fishermen) into Japanese waters. The JCG has expanded in recent years, in contrast with cutbacks in the JMSDF. In 2009, with 121 large patrol craft (12 of them of frigate size), 234 smaller patrol craft, 63 special guard and rescue craft, 37 other support vessels and 73 fixed-wing and rotary aircraft, and 12,500 people, the JCG ranked amongst the world's top 20 navies in tonnage terms, and according to some analysts constituted some 65% of the tonnage of the Chinese surface fleet.

Capable of providing ancillary support for the JMSDF, the JCG is, however, financed by the Ministry of Transport, with a budget in 2009 of ¥182,422m.[67] While these ships do not carry the weaponry and sensors required for standard warfare operations, they have robust rules of engagement and do constitute an effective means of handling low-intensity security threats. Rising tensions with China over the disputed islands of the South China Sea, moreover, have led to a substantial boost for the JCG budget.[68]

By contrast, the Indian Coast Guard is a much smaller, more recent and less well-endowed institution. That the recruiting slogan for the Indian Navy remains 'The Guardian of our Sea

Frontiers' shows that India shares the concerns of most maritime powers about the security of its maritime estate for its oil and gas potential, its fishery stocks and its likely growing economic importance in the future and considers this a basically naval function. The navy, the coast guard and other agencies of maritime law enforcement have to maintain law and order, environmental protection, the safety of navigation resource management and the safety of life at sea. The Indian Navy and Coast Guard have been acquiring ships and aircraft necessary for this purpose, including *Kora*-class helicopter-equipped missile corvettes and the *Tarasa*-class fast-attack craft. The latter will be used for maritime policing around the Andaman and Nicobar islands. India has just taken charge of four *Car Nicobar* 49m fast patrol craft built by Garden Reach in Kolkata, with another six to come.[69]

The failure of the Indian Navy and Coast Guard, despite an apparent advance warning by the security services, to prevent the sea-based attack on Mumbai in November 2008 prompted a re-think on the requirements of coastal defence. This led to the establishment of a new Coastal Command headed by the navy, which is intended to help integrate the contribution of the 16 government agencies involved in coastal security, and the establishment of joint operations centres in Mumbai, Vizag, Kochi and Port Blair. The Coastal Security Scheme has now allocated prime responsibility to the marine police for the territorial sea, the coast guard for the EEZ and to the navy beyond. It also led to the acquisition of more patrol craft and patrol aircraft and helicopters and aerostat radars for coastal surveillance, more shore-based infrastructure and to an expressed interest Integrated Harbour Defence Systems which electronically fence harbours and port approaches from clandestine intruders.[70] Particular attention is being paid to the need for better coordination in information-sharing and subsequent action between the various agencies involved. To improve maritime domain awareness over this vast area, the Indian Navy has also created a number of UAV squadrons starting with one focused on waters shared with Pakistan.[71]

The US Coast Guard, although neglected and under-resourced for years compared to the US Navy,[72] is still bigger and more capable than many navies and its activities span the world. Its recent partial renaissance was demonstrated by the important role in counter terrorism it was expected to play in *A Cooperative Strategy* and also by extensive fleet modernisation and replacement under the ambitious *Deepwater* programme. Inevitably, technical and construction problems have emerged, not least in the US Coast Guard's ambitious programme to procure 25 357-foot (108m) offshore patrol cutters from 2015 and larger 418-foot (127m) National Security Cutters at a cost of US$47 bn over 20 years.[73] Further, like most law enforcement agencies, it continues to face considerable budgetary challenges and its assets rarely match its commitments.[74] Even so, in the wake of 9/11 and Hurricane Katrina, the revival of American interest in the manifold requirements of maritime security can hardly be doubted.

This has affected the US Navy too. Amongst its many other roles, the Littoral Combat Ship is regarded as 'an ideal plat-form for engaging in irregular warfare and maritime-security operations, to include counter-piracy missions, and one whose reassuringly modest armament should underline its peace-ful intent'.[75] LCS-1, the USS *Freedom*, was used successfully for counter-narcotics work in the Caribbean on her maiden voyage.[76] Some would go further arguing for greater invest-ment in smaller vessels capable of performing missions such as engagement, disaster relief and constabulary duties, relieving combat-credible units from the wear and tear inevitably associ-ated with their exercise.[77]

Maritime-security operations

China

The coastal activities of the PLAN serve several purposes. Firstly, they help preserve marine resources (oil, gas and fish) which are becoming increasingly important to their burgeoning population. Accordingly, China has invested in a large number of small, modern patrol boats as a means of 'safeguarding maritime territory' by performing coast guard functions such as fisheries patrols, monitoring pollution, and search and rescue.[78] These vessels are operated by the navy, the Maritime Safety Administration and the customs. The 1999 disaster in which the Yantai–Dalian ferry sank with a loss of 291 passengers was both a tragedy and a national humiliation. It inspired the Chinese to a major overhaul of the Maritime Safety Agency, the maritime units of the Peoples Armed Police and the Chinese Coast Guard, producing much more efficient reactions when the passenger ship *Liaohai* caught fire and sank in November 2004.[79] The Chinese have also indicated a post-modern willingness to work with neighbours in campaigns against piracy and maritime terrorism.[80] They have been prepared to link up with the US Coast Guard and the North Pacific Coast Guard Forum in meetings and the occasional exercises.

Secondly, coastal activities are a way of asserting sovereignty over offshore waters, which in the East and South China seas is much contested with China's neighbours. Using naval forces adds emphasis to their views in their many disputes with neighbours over maritime borders and claims.[81] In Spring 2009, for instance the *Yuzeng* 311, China's most advanced fishery patrol vessel, was despatched to the South China Sea in response to a spate of incidents in the area, mainly with Vietnamese fishing boats. Despite the 2002 Declaration of Conduct agreement by all the claimants to the South China Sea neither to use force nor to exacerbate the situation, such clashes still occur, and in fact have shown a dismaying tendency to increase through 2010-12, Chinese 'smiling diplomacy' notwithstanding.[82]

This exclusivity is also exerted against outside powers such as Australia and the United States. The 2001 incident of the air collision near Hainan island between a US patrol aircraft and a Chinese fighter, followed shortly afterwards by a challenge to two Australian frigates and a support vessel passing through the Taiwan Strait, were other examples of a notably 'exclusive' approach to China's control of what it regards as its own waters. As a Pentagon report put it: 'China has an expansive view of it rights in the EEZ, treating the area as fully sovereign territory in a manner not consistent with international law.'[83] Again, on 8 March 2009, five Chinese vessels, including a naval intelligence collector, two civilian-agency patrol ships and two small trawlers dangerously harassed the USNS *Impeccable*, a civilian manned ship engaged in military survey work in the Chinese EEZ about 129km south of Hainan. This incident lent support to the US allegation that China was, in effect, waging a legal war to shift opinion 'away from interpretations of maritime law that favour freedom of navigation and toward interpretations of increased sovereign authority and control' over the EEZ.[84]

The Chinese are, however, also demonstrating a growing interest in the away game as well. The fact that so many of their fishing trawlers operate off East Africa and their merchant ships pass through the Gulf of Aden, for example, has drawn them into their first long-range naval deployment since Admiral Zheng He's famous voyages in the fifteenth century. Although holding themselves apart from Combined Task Force-151, the international naval counter-piracy force, Chinese warships exchange information with it by bridge-to-bridge radio, e-mail and personal visits.[85] The PLAN's original mission in the Gulf of Aden was to protect only Chinese-flagged vessels against pirate attacks but in January 2010 it announced its intention to extend this support to all merchant vessels. According to General Liang Gungli, in 2011 the PLAN had sent eight task forces of ships to the Gulf of Aden on escort missions since 2008. More than 40 % of the vessels escorted were foreign.[86] Admiral Wu, early in 2012, said the PLAN has escorted 4,411 vessels over three years, employing 8,400 men, 22 helicopters and 25 vessels in ten counter-piracy task forces.[87]

Japan

For the JCG, the main focus is on its highly-contested local waters. Chinese and Taiwanese trawlers and North Korean spy ships regularly intrude into Japanese waters. Japanese fishing vessels have frequently been detained and shot at by the Russian Border Guard in the Soya Strait and around the disputed South Kurile Islands. Maritime jurisdiction over Sakashima/Tokdo Island and its waters bitterly disputed with South Korea, is the delimitation of the East China Sea and the Senkaku/Diaoyu Islands with Taiwan and China.[88] Accordingly, the JCG needs robust rules of engagement and represents substantial capability. Significant evidence of both was demonstrated by the sinking in 2001 of a North Korean spy-ship in 2001 by gunfire from JCG vessels.[89]

Further from Japan's shores, and in response to the internationalisation of crime, the JCG participates in the activities of international agencies such as the International Maritime Organisation and takes a leading role in maritime-security issues in the Asia-Pacific. It was responsible for setting up the North Pacific Coast Guard Forum in 2000 and plays a leading role in the international campaign to combat piracy in the Malacca Strait and elsewhere. Japan was instrumental in the establishment in 2006 of the Regional Cooperation Agreement on Combating Piracy and Armed Robbery against ships in Asia (ReCAAP). The involvement of the JMSDF in this activity in Southeast Asia was contentious, but JCG and private foundation capacity and institution-building engagement here, on the other hand, was welcomed.[90]

This expanding maritime, rather than strictly naval, activity is seen as a natural Japanese contribution to the international community's response to threats to the international system, while helping to secure Japan's own SLOCs against irregular attack. The JMSDF participates in the international counter-piracy effort in the Gulf of Aden. An Anti-Piracy Law enacted on 19 June 2009 allowed JMSDF forces to protect foreign-owned ships as well as their own and in some circumstances to use their weaponry.[91]

At the same time, such activity is also seen as a means of engaging with other maritime powers (particularly the United States, China, India and the countries of Southeast Asia). Japan was one of the first countries to enter fully into the Proliferation Security Initiative (PSI) and in October 2004 hosted the *Team Samurai* multilateral training exercises involving nine navies/coast guards. The first such exercise in East Asia, this was plainly aimed at North Korea.[92] In 2007 the JMSDF hosted the PSI exercise *Pacific Shield 07*.

There are, however, limits in the extent to which Japan is able and willing to collaborate with others in the defence of maritime security outside its own waters. Most of Japan's maritime activity, as we have seen, revolves around the *local* defence of its territory and waters against air and maritime incursions, missile attack and even full-scale amphibious assault. In June 2006, the *Aegis* destroyer *Kirishima* was pulled out of an important multinational exercise off Hawaii and brought home, apparently in response to concerns over developments in North Korea.[93] Moreover, in its whaling policy Japan is willing to take a very independent and national line, and at one time there were reports that the navy rather than the coast guard might need to become involved in the conflict over whaling in the Southern Ocean.[94]

India

India has a vast EEZ of some 2.2 million square kilometres, and prospective claims to a continental shelf that perhaps doubles that area. To complicate the matter, there are outstanding jurisdictional disputes with Bangladesh and Pakistan. Faced with extensive drugs and arms smuggling, the prospect of terrorist attack, illegal fishing and environmental hazards, assuring the maritime security of its domestic waters continues to be a major preoccupation. One of the most dramatic examples of this day-to-day activity was the rescue of 361 people at night from the Bombay High North oil platform which blew up in July 2004. For the same reason India was one of the first countries in the region to sign the ISPS code on port security, and has joined the Container Security Initiative.

The Indian Navy is also concerned with the 'away' dimension of maritime security, however. It has, for example maintained anti-piracy patrols in the vicinity of the Malacca Strait. It has also gifted patrol boats to the Seychelles and the Maldives as part of a capacity-building exercise in the wider region, and its bilateral and multilateral exercise programme habitually includes counter-terrorism, anti-piracy and maritime interception operations and procedures. As already noted, the Indian Navy has also been extensively engaged in maritime-security operations against the Tamil Tigers. Finally, India is a vigorous contributor to the international counter-piracy campaign in the Gulf of Aden.

Because their cutters are seen as less threatening, provocative and politically sensitive than are conventional warships, the US Coast Guard often takes the lead role in the 'away' aspects of maritime security rather than the US Navy. This has resulted in a more equal and cooperative relationship between these two maritime services than has applied in the past, and adds further substance to the National Fleet Policy Statement signed by the navy and the coast guard back in 2006.[95] The US Coast Guard has been active in the North Pacific Coast Guard Forum established by the Japanese in 2000, and its North Atlantic equivalent set up in 2007. Inspired by the sense that it is politically and operationally best to help the locals deal with their own maritime-security issues as much as they can, a great deal of the coast guard's activity is directed towards capacity building, the provision of equipment, the establishment of an international doctrine for maritime constabulary operations and, perhaps above all, facilitating enhanced global maritime domain awareness. Then Chief of Naval Operations, Admiral Mike Mullen said:

> Technology offers us the opportunity – now – to help thwart [our enemies'] efforts by building and fielding, among other things, Web-enabled global maritime awareness. It will allow maritime forces to share knowledge in real time, without regard to geography, distance, and eventually even language. It will allow people and goods to move rapidly, efficiently and safely. For those within our maritime security network, we will maintain a high degree of confidence and trust, so that mariners won't be stopped and checked at every point along the way. And that will enable all of us to focus more of our resources and our time on those outside the network to find and fix the threats and to close the gaps where we are most vulnerable.[96]

Although content to cede a leading role in the 'away' parts of the maritime- security task to the coast guard, the navy has nonetheless been extensively involved in the business itself, particularly in the Caribbean, the Gulf of Aden and the Arabian Gulf, on a day-by-day routine basis, both on its own and, more usually, in conjunction with other naval and coast guard partners.[97]

Maritime security operations may also include counter-piracy operations at some distance from the homeland. All four navies have made significant contributions to the current and on-going counter-piracy campaign off the Horn of Africa, perhaps the most obvious example of naval togetherness against common threats. Their involvement has been differentiated, of course, by the differing extent to which they have become integrated into the broader effort, but the trend has been towards increasing levels of information-sharing and operational coordination. Illustrating the point, they all now act in defence of merchant shipping irrespective of flag, rather than simply in defence of their own shipping.[98]

Cooperative naval diplomacy

The navies of all four countries have demonstrated that there are two aspects to naval diplomacy. One is the old fashioned business of exploiting the flexibility of naval forces to deter, compel and win influence over other countries, discussed in Chapter Three. The second is the less traditional urge to construct maritime partnerships for the common good. The *Indian Maritime Doctrine* explains the divided character of naval diplomacy quite succinctly:

> Naval Diplomacy entails the use of naval forces in support of foreign policy objectives to build 'bridges of friendship' and strengthen international coopera-

tion on the one hand, and to signal capability and intent to deter potential adversaries on the other.[99]

But in this section the focus is on the first of these alternatives.

Cooperative naval diplomacy thinking

The success of China's 'smiling diplomacy' in winning support in Southeast Asia in the late 1990s and the early years of this century and apparent efforts to secure more consensual solutions to the problem of managing the dispute in the South China Sea seemed to attest to a well-thought-through conception of the value of soft power, in contrast to more traditional earlier concepts that power was simply something to be displayed. Thus Admiral Liu Huaqing, extolling the benefits of sea based defence diplomacy:

> The Chinese naval visits to other countries have given foreign countries a better idea of the Chinese navy, expanded our military's influence in the world and exalted our navy's image ... These visits have also tempered the officers and men of the navy, broadened their thinking and contributed to the navy's modernisation drive.[100]

Thinking about the need for, and the techniques of, naval diplomacy was another novel aspect of the upsurge in professional strategic thinking in the Chinese navy from the mid-1980s. It was considered to involve 'altering the deployment of the maritime military force, or developing such force and facilities to express our political and diplomatic intentions'. Ship visits and participation in scientific exploration and surveys, 'serve to promote mutual understanding, and to propagate China's independent foreign policy and the accomplishments of construction and reform'.[101]

In the media and in China's communications strategy, much use is made of the experience of its greatest sailor, Admiral Zheng He, 'Ambassador of Peace', whose remarkable fifteenth-century voyages around the Indian Ocean are cited as a typical example of non-exploitative naval diplomacy in pursuit of the general aim of 'harmonious oceans'. [102] Thus Guo Chongli, China's Ambassador to Kenya in 2005, argued that 'Zheng He's fleet [was] large … But his voyages were not for looting resources but for friendship. In trade with foreign countries he gave much more than he took.'[103] Making extensive if sometimes over-blown use of this historical example of Chinese naval diplomacy, scholars and officials repeatedly argue that China, unlike its Western predecessors, is a non-predatory power whose rise threatens no-one's interests or territory.

Japan flirted with a similar declaratory line during the brief premiership of Yukio Hatoyama (October 2009–June 2010), giving some emphasis to the idea that the country's naval forces should be used proactively in international peace cooperation activities. The timing of this idea was unfortunate, however, in that it coincided with the sinking of the ROKS *Cheonan* by the North Koreans and the passage through Japan's island chain of one of the biggest Chinese task forces for years. Since then Japan has shown rather more interest in the traditional variant of naval cooperation with the United States, India, Japan and Australia, which actually helps serve as a counter to the growing naval power of China.[104]

Significantly, the very first topic to be explored in India's naval diplomacy doctrine is also a concern to 'strengthen political relations and goodwill' through 'constructive engagement in the maritime domain':

India advocates the need to evolve a new paradigm of cooperation, relevant to the contemporary world, in which global threats are addressed by global responses, and multilateralism becomes the preferred norm for addressing global challenges.

Building partnerships and enabling all forms of maritime cooperation is therefore seen as an important part of the navy's business in time of peace and the principal weapon against all manner of threats to maritime security.[105] Consolidating the pioneering approach of former Chief of the Naval Staff Admiral L. Ramdass, multinational naval cooperation of this sort is seen as an accelerating and necessary development for the twenty-first century.[106]

At the 2009 Shangri-La Dialogue, Admiral Mehta, then chief of staff, made the point that building these kinds of naval relationships would benefit the whole world in stabilising an area of extreme economic and strategic importance. He said:

We see the Indian navy as a significant stabilising force in the Indian ocean region, which safeguards traffic bound not only for our own ports, but also the flow of hydrocarbons and strategically important cargo to and from the rest of the world across the strategic waterways close to our shores ... And so, the safety of SLOCS will always remain a priority for India in the foreseeable future.[107]

Beneath this, though, there seem (certainly in the eyes of some of India's neighbours) to remain hegemonic aspects to India's peacetime attitudes towards the Indian Ocean.

Finally, India, like Japan, is broadly sympathetic to the US notion of the Global Maritime Partnership. The development of this notion in *A Cooperative Straegy* and the *Naval Operations Concept 2010* exemplified a major shift in American collaborative thinking. Admiral Mike Mullen had described it back in 2005:

> Today's reality is that the security arrangements and paradigms of the past are no longer enough for the future. And today's challenges are too diverse to tackle alone; they require more capability and more resources than any single nation can deliver.[108]

'Trust and cooperation', says *A Cooperative Strategy*, 'cannot be surged'. They have to be built and sustained over time, though the development of increased understanding amongst maritime forces and the forging of international partnerships. The document's discussion of naval diplomacy accordingly focuses on coalition-building, with the Global Maritime Partnership initiative being its most significant expression.[109] This became one of the navy's six strategic imperatives, and was clearly crucial to two of its six core capabilities, namely maritime security and humanitarian assistance and disaster response. Since the concept grew out of Admiral Mullen's earlier concept of a 'Thousand Ship Navy',[110] this emphasis was not entirely new. But the retitling of the concept was more than merely cosmetic. It suggests a significant move away from the traditional 'modern' thinking that probably explained the 'Thousand Ship Navy' label originally given to the concept. Striking though it was, this title was profoundly misleading since it seemed to exclude coast guard forces, had clear hierarchical connotations that inevitably sparked the unwelcome question of 'Who's in charge?' and raised equally unfortunate suspicions that the navy's hidden aspirations were to recreate a grander vision of the '600-ship navy' of the Reagan years.

Hence, in Admiral John Morgan's words: 'We are beginning to distance ourselves from that moniker.'[111] It is noticeable, also, that the Global Maritime Partnership would benefit significantly from all three of the document's Implementation Priorities. All of this presaged a clear move away from the technocentric thinking that characterised US defence policy earlier in the G.W. Bush administration.

However, the continuing debate on whether the United States should ratify UNCLOS provides significant contrary evidence of a readiness to cooperate with the wider international community. Many in Congress are resistant to the loss of sovereignty and independence of action they consider implied by collective action of this sort, and are likely to be thoroughly sceptical of the advantages of the much heralded Global Maritime Partnership.[112] This has encouraged a certain scepticism in some countries about the extent to which the US Navy is really prepared to turn theory into practice. For evidence, countries such as China point to the continued US emphasis on the advantages of 'Forward Presence' as means of diplomatic and strategic advantage, apparently considering the Global Maritime Partnership as a covert way of facilitating this, a point to be discussed further in the next chapter.[113]

Certainly in *A Cooperative Strategy*, and indeed in the public statements of regional commanders around the world, there is at least declaratory acceptance of the need to respond to such differences of view. As Admiral Mullen said,

> The changed strategic landscape offers new opportunities for maritime forces to work together – sometimes with the U.S. Navy, but oftentimes without. In fact, a greater number of today's emerging missions won't involve the U.S. Navy. And that's fine with me.[114]

The essential point that the US Navy does not *necessarily* seek to lead this development, has also been made by his successors and chimes exactly with the Indian navy's position on Indian Ocean Naval Symposium. [115] In sum, the US Navy aims to be 'the security partner of choice'.[116]

Cooperative naval diplomacy operations

The Chinese seem to be making increasing use of their naval forces to reach out to other countries and areas in a policy of constructive engagement.[117] One early indication of a change in this direction was the presence of observers at the inaugural *Pacific Reach 2000* combined submarine rescue exercise in October held that year in Singapore, and attended by Japan, South Korea and the US. The Chinese have participated in a variety of multilateral meetings such as the Western Pacific Naval Symposium, though often at a relatively low or observer-status level. In March 2006, Chinese frigates participated in a large-scale multinational exercise off Pakistan in 'a display of international unity in the fight against terrorism and human, drugs and weapons trafficking'. All exercises were conducted in English, an important part of the drive to 'improve communications skills, procedures and international cooperation'.[118]

The Chinese have made efforts to improve particular relationships with the US Navy by a sequence of port visits and exchanges. Operational cooperation between the two navies remain rudimentary, being largely restricted to search and rescue missions, but they at least resulted in the signing of a Sino-American Maritime–Military Consultation Agreement (MMCA) in 1998 and both have apparently communicated using the Code for Unalerted Encounters at Sea regime, developed by the Western Pacific Naval Symposium. These confidence-building measures are seen as an important means of conflict avoidance in the Asia-Pacific region. One problem with this, however, is that the withdrawal from such amicable exchanges may send quite hostile messages. The episodes in November 2007 in which China denied entry to Hong Kong to two small US minesweepers seeking shelter from an approaching cyclone and later temporarily excluded the USS *Kitty Hawk* on a good will visit undoubtedly caused great offence.[119] American commentators, moreover, make the point that varying degrees of Chinese cooperativeness in advancing the aims of the MMCA suggest that they see it more as a means of rewarding or punishing the US Navy than of substantially improving relations with it.[120]

This episode reinforce the cynical view that these cooperative activities are little more than covert struggles for power and influence. China's attempts to engage in bilateral and multilateral exercises with the countries of Southeast Asia, for example, has been seen as likely to heighten the political competition for influence in the area with the US, India and Japan.[121]

The Japanese constitution, paradoxically, is a constraint on Japan's ability to engage in cooperative naval diplomacy. The ostensible ban on collective defence, for example, complicates the aspiration for interoperability. In 2002 Japanese *Aegis* destroyers were unable to exchange battle theatre imagery with their US counterparts for this reason.[122] For the same reason, the Japanese are anxious not to let their PSI role attract too much attention, lest it spark unhelpful domestic debate.

The close historic relationship of the JMSDF with the US Navy and the constitutional restraints under which it has operated has meant that while 'we have a very rich and complex training and operations experience with the USN – probably the best in the world ... our experience of working with other navies still remains too short'.[123] Much Japanese naval activity is still directed at strengthening its relationship with the United States, but with an increasing focus on Australia, Singapore and

India as an additional balance against the burgeoning power of China.

Tensions between China and Japan, however, have waxed and waned, and exchanges of good will, such as port visits involving the Japanese destroyer *Sazanami* and the Chinese *Shenzhen* with *Sazanami* calling at Zhanjinag in June 2008, were the first such visits in 60 years and proved a useful means of signalling improved relations.[124] More recently, tensions in the East China Sea have made relations between the two navies, and associated coast guards distinctly cooler.

India's major effort in constructive engagement for the greater good was the creation of the IONS in May 2008. This has turned out to be a major exercise in constructive engagement, with 26 of the 31 Indian Ocean region heads of navies attending and with the remainder, including Pakistan, being represented by ambassadors and the like. IONS was modelled on the US-led Western Pacific Naval Symposium and focuses on cooperative endeavour against common threats, such as natural disasters, terrorism and piracy. That the second, bigger, IONS meeting was held in March 2011 in the UAE shows that India does not claim ownership of this process of multinational naval cooperation.

India's 'soft' maritime power has frequently been deployed around the region, not least through the provision of staff, training, equipment, refit facilities and hydrographic support for Oman and island nations such as Mauritius and the Seychelles.[125] The diplomatic value of such activities is clear. According to the Indian Defence Ministry:

> The regular presence of Indian naval survey ships in Mauritius has generated a swell of goodwill and further reinforced the strong links between the two countries. The crew of the survey ships have not only

been involved in surveying uncharted waters but have also endeared themselves to the local populace by participating in community-building exercise during their short visits to the harbour, providing assistance in reaching supplies to far-flung islands and acting as goodwill ambassadors.[126]

A final 'soft' use of India's maritime power *Indian Maritime Doctrine* thought worth noting was the departure of Indian warships from the Pakistani theatre in *Operation Parakram* in 2002, a move intended to signal a major lowering of tension to Islamabad.[127] China's increasing reach into the Indian Ocean may worry the Indian Navy, but this tends to be overshadowed by wider concerns about Pakistan and the northern land border. In this instance, naval relations between the two countries are largely set by continental concerns.[128] Closer naval relations with the PLAN, therefore, still tend to dominate India's strategic attitudes towards China, rather than the other way around.

Putting its ideas of naval collaboration in general and the global maritime partnership in particular into effect has become a major focus of the current operations of the US Navy. It is putting a huge stress on a heavy programme of focused naval engagement as part of what Hillary Clinton has called 'forward deployed diplomacy'[129] with prospective maritime partners all around the world, but perhaps especially in and around the Persian Gulf and the Asia-Pacific. This is intended to serve two complementary purposes. Firstly, it facilitates the kind of multilateral naval cooperation required to defend the system against non-traditional threats such as terrorism and piracy. Secondly, it offers a medium by which the relationship between the naval powers, both with each other and with the United States itself, can be improved. The biennial

RIMPAC (Rim of the Pacific) exercises off Hawaii, which started in 1971, are a good example of that. In 2010, the exercises focused on 'maritime domain awareness dealing with expanded military operations across the complete spectrum if warfare'. It involved 13 navies. By contrast the exercises of 2012 involved 22 different navies, nearly 50 ships and submarines, 200 aircraft and 25,000 personnel, and the Chinese are to be invited for RIMPAC 2013.[130] The US Navy has been particularly active in Southeast Asia with the strengthening of its Cooperation Afloat Readiness and Training (CARAT), *Cobra Gold* and Southeast Asia Cooperation and Training (SEACAT) exercise programmes.[131]

In this, the US Navy also recognises that the range of requirements also calls for the strongest possible integration of the naval effort with other forces of maritime order, particularly the US Coast Guard. Often, indeed, as both the Japanese and the Americans discovered in the Malacca Straits, coastguard forces will provide a far more appropriate response to developing situations, that may well be able to head off the need for more forceful interventions later on. The US Coast Guard is a unique organisation unlikely to be replicated anywhere else; nonetheless it has much to offer in advice on many aspects of maritime security that can be adopted or adapted by anyone else – and it can make that advice available in a manner that represents little threat to the sovereignty of others.[132] By doing so, it indirectly defends the system, whilst at the same time serving US national interests and contributing to the United States' maritime outreach.

The US Navy recognises that the positive encouragement of allied participation in all manner of maritime operations calls for a focused, deliberate and intelligent maritime assault on all the things that make this difficult at the moment. Interoperability is key. This is a partly a matter of shared technical proficiency, which is ultimately 'fixable', and also of protocols and standard operating procedures,[133] matters in which the American tendency to over-classify everything does not help.[134] Policy divergences with coalition partners may be rather more intractable, especially if the United States is thought to be pursuing a unilateralist and nationalist agenda.

Putting the concept of partnership into effect, however, will require practical steps. These include a concerted effort to make maritime domain awareness work, by moving from an information culture based on 'the need to know' to one based on 'the need to share' and by the open-handed provision of skills and equipment in a sophisticated capability-building campaign for those countries that need it. Sophisticated, in this case, means two things. Firstly, a practical appreciation of the need fully to integrate naval efforts with coast guards, both foreign and domestic, in a manner which gives the latter full credit for their particular strengths in this area. Secondly, it will require particular awareness of the political and cultural sensitivities of the region in question. The emphasis on language training and cultural awareness and the creation of the Maritime Civil Affairs and Security Training Command (MCAST) is a step in this direction, although it may prove susceptible to future budget cuts.

But against all this, sceptics point to the strategic utility that the United States itself may derive from this kind of focused engagement. Regional allies, once trained up through collaborative exercises, the International Military Education and Training program (IMET) and so forth, may act as force multipliers, perhaps especially in an era of relative naval decline, by eventually providing additional resources, skill sets and basing facilities of various kinds. The basing of US Marines in Australia and the LCS in Singapore for example, adds significantly to the on-station deployment time of the US Navy, for whatever may eventuate. The apparently very collaborative concept of a Global Maritime Partnership may therefore also serve quite traditional purposes as well.

This mixture of motives is also evident in the slowly developing instruments of rapprochement between the US and Chinese navies, the establishment of a 'hot line' and the holding or regular talks through the Military Maritime Consultative Agreement and the Defence Consultative Talks. On the one hand the intention suggests an urge to cooperate; on the other progress is limited since the hot line often appears unimplemented and talks on vexed issues such as the freedom of navigation of warships in the EEZ have not as yet made significant progress.[135]

Conclusion

Reaching conclusions about the implications of all this for future naval relationships in the Asia-Pacific region is complicated by the fuzziness of some of the missions, firstly in the difficulty of distinguishing between traditional amphibious warfare and non-traditional expeditionary operations and secondly in shifting and diverse interpretations of what stability, humanitarian and maritime-security operations actually mean. For all that these non-traditional missions have a strong collaborative element to them since they involve common action against common threats such as instability, catastrophic weather events, maritime crime and terrorism. The need for collaboration is reinforced, paradoxically, by the fact that for all four countries, traditional state-centred missions tend to take top priority. This means that non-traditional roles can only be serviced through the allocation of resources that remain after the traditional ones have been satisfied – and there are always significantly less of these than are needed given the scale and complexity of the varying challenges offered by non-traditional threats. Hence the need for collaboration between different navies and coast guards.

Once again, it is a question less of the nature of the resources devoted to such tasks that will determine future relations, but the spirit in which those tasks are performed. It is likely that China, for example, will expand its capacity to engage in out-of-area expeditionary operations in the performance of the 'New Historic Missions' enumerated by President Hu Jintao back in 2004.[136] But there is as yet little evidence that will be unduly competitive in tone.

When considering the beneficial consequences of such collaborative behaviour, however, some issues need to be born in mind. Firstly, the jurisdictional disputes over the South and East China seas severely limits prospects for the four navies concerned to collaborate *with each other* in the Western Pacific. Secondly, there are clear national advantages, both political and strategic, to be derived from being seen to participate fully and effectively in collaborative activity not least the capacity to watch and observe other units and develop best practice militarily. For all that, though, all four navies recognise the fact that maritime crime in its various forms, the sustainability of fishing stocks and the like are problems common to all which simply cannot be handled at the national level alone and which consequently require coordination and cooperation between them. There is also a general recognition that the habits of cooperation which develop when they perform these tasks, increase transparency between them and so act in effect as confidence building measures. Notably absent in the Europe of the early twentieth century, such cooperative activities act as a very real restraint on arms-racing behaviour and provide some support for notion that there is, instead, some kind of meaningful fellowship of the sea.

Notes

1   Figures from Eugene Cobble, Hank Gaffney and Dimitri Gorenburg, *For the Record: All U.S. Forces Responses to Situations, 1970–2000* (Alexandria, VA: Center for Naval Analyses, 2003), http://www.cna.org/sites/default/files/research/D0008414.A3.pdf, with additions covering 2000–2003, as cited in Larissa Forster, 'Trust cannot be Surged: Challenges to Naval Forward Presence', *Military PowerRevue*, no. 2, 2011.

2   This definition owes something to *Australian Maritime Doctrine*, p. 193, but see also Geoff Till, *Seapower: A Guide for the 21st Century*, 2nd ed. (London: Routledge, 2009), pp. 221–52.

3   See, for example, *Naval Amphibious Capability of the 21st Century: Strategic Opportunity and a Vision for Change'*, Report of the Amphibious Capabilities Working Group, 27 April 2012.

4   Quoted in *East Asia Strategic Review* 2009, p. 139; See 'China's National Defence in 2009: Part V – The Navy', available at www.china.org.cn/government/whitepaper/2009-01/21/content_17162859.htm.

5   Office of the Secretary of Defense, *Military Power of the People's Republic of China, 2009* (Washington DC: Department of Defense, 2009), p. 39; Ronald O'Rourke, *China Naval Modernization: Implications for US Navy Capabilities – Background and Issues for Congress* (Washington DC: Congressional Research Service, 23 November 2009), pp. 15–16.

6   *China's National Defense in 2010*, Information Office of the State Council, March 2011, at http://www.gov.cn/english/official/2011-03/31/content_1835499.htm, pp. 1–6 et seq.

7   'Mid-term Defense Program FY2011–FY2015', summary at mid_FY2011-15.pdf.; 'Japan Adopts Proactive Defence Policy to Counter China, N Korea' and 'JMSDF: The Role of Our Defense Capabilities: Effective Response to New Threats and Diverse Situations', Ministry of Defense, Japan, at http://www.mod.go.jp/msdf/formal/english/defense/index.html.

8   *Indian Maritime Doctrine 2009*, pp. 83–4.

9   US Navy, *Naval Operations Concept 2010*, http://www.navy.mil/maritime/noc/NOC2010.pdf, p. 70. Interestingly, the word 'expeditionary' hardly appears in this document, the older and more traditional phrase 'power projection' being used instead.

10 US Navy, *A Cooperative Strategy for 21st Century Seapower*, http://www.navy.mil/maritime/Maritimestrategy.pdf.

11 Department of the Navy, Chief of Naval Operations, *The U.S. Navy's Vision for Confronting Irregular Challenges*, January 2010, p. 3.

12 Ronald O'Rourke, *Navy Irregular Warfare and Counter-terrorism Operations: Background and Issues for Congress* (Washington DC: Congressional Research Service Report, RS 22373, 18 October 2012). For an overview of relevant Indian and Chinese expeditionary capabilities that illustrate this point, see Vijay, Sakhuja, *Asian Maritime*

Power in the 21st Century (Singapore: Institute of Southeast Asian Studies, 2011), pp. 79–81, 104–5.

13 Interview, General James Amos, commandant, US Marine Corps, *Jane's Defence Weekly*, 21 September 2011.

14 'US Army to Navy: Take Our Boats', *Defense News*, 8 November 2010; 'US Buys 2 High-Speed Vessels, Orders More', *Defense News*, 18 October 2010; 'Floating US Mobile Base Heads for Development', *Defense News*, 30 January 2012.

15 'The US Navy's Riverine Revival', *Jane's Defence Weekly*, 14 February 2007.

16 Government Accountability Office, 'Navy's Ability to Overcome Challenges Facing the Littoral Combat Ship Will Determine Eventual Capabilities', Report GAO-10-523, August 2010.

17 Stephen Trimble, 'Treading Water', *Jane's Defence Weekly*, 28 March 2007; 'Lockheed Martin Secures Deal to Continue International Littoral Combat Ship Design', *Jane's International Defence Review*, January 2008; 'Littoral Comeback Ship' and 'Fast Mover', *Defense Technology International*, December 2009 and May 2010.

18 'US Navy: LCS Beating Initial Cost Projections', *Defense News*, 11 April 2011; 'LCS Shakedown', *Defense News*, 8 August 2011.

19 'US Navy's LCS Yet to Fulfill its Promise', *Defense News*, 23 April 2012; 'LCS: Quick Swap Concept Dead', *Defense News*, 16 July 2012.

20 'USN's Newest Pirate Hunters?', *Defense News*, 13 June 2011.

21 Robert C. Benbow et al, *Renewal of the Navy's Riverine Capability:* *A Preliminary Examination of Past, Current and Future Capabilities* (Alexandria, VA: Center for Naval Analyses, March 2006).

22 'US Navy Reorganises Post-War Riverine Forces', *Defense News*, 7 May 2012.

23 'Japan to Join Cobra Gold 2005 Exercise', *Jane's Defence Weekly*, 9 March 2005.

24 Robert Karniol, 'Japan Shifts from Symbolism to Substance', *Straits Times*, 1 February 2010.

25 'Japan to End Afghan Refuelling Mission', *Asian Defence Journal*, November 2009.

26 Rear Admiral James Foggo, 'A Promise Kept', *Proceedings of the US Naval Institute*, June 2012.

27 Bernard C. Cole, *The Great Wall at Sea: China's Navy in the Twenty-First Century*, 2nd ed. (Annapolis, MD: Naval Institute Press, 2010), p. 191.

28 *Australian Maritime Doctrine 2010*, p. 110.

29 *China's National Defense in 2010*, Information Office of the State Council, March 2011, at http://www.gov.cn/english/official/2011-03/31/content_1835499.htm, p. 6.

30 'Chinese Hospital Ship Back after Treating Thousands', *China Daily*, 27 November 2010, quoted in Leah Averitt, *Chinese Hospital Ships and Soft Power* (Canberra: Seapower Centre, Semaphore, April 2011); Peter W. Mackenzie, *Red Crosses, Blue Water: Hospital Ships and China's Expanding Naval Presence* (Washington DC: CNA China Studies, September 2011); *Military and Security Developments in the People's Republic of China, 2012*, pp. 3–4.

31 *Indian Maritime Doctrine 2009*, p. 119.

[32] *Ibid.*, p. 120.

[33] *Military Support to Stabilization, Security, Transition and Reconstruction Operations,* Directive 3000.5, 28 November 2005; *Naval Operations Concept,* p. 19.

[34] *Naval Operations Concept 2010,* p. 47.

[35] Alex de Waal, 'Against Gunboat Philanthropy', *Prospect,* 29 June 2008, http://www.prospectmagazine.co.uk/magazine/againstgunboatphilanthropy/.

[36] Adm. Mike Mullen, 'What I Believe', *Proceedings of the USNI,* vol. 132, no. 1, January 2006. See also O'Rourke, *Navy Irregular Warfare and Counterterrorism Operations: Background and Issues for Congress.*

[37] 'Global Fleet Stations' may be another term that needs further examination. To some observers it implies something more akin to a floating naval base for possibly offensive action than a means of alleviating local distress. For a review of the background to and purposes of the Global Fleet Station see Kathi A. Sohn, 'The Global Fleet Station: A Powerful Tool for Preventing Conflict', *Naval War College Review,* Winter 2009.

[38] *Military and Security Developments in the People's Republic of China, 2012,* p. 3.

[39] Kosuke Takahashi, 'Japan's New Dawn', *Janes Defence Weekly,* 18 November 2009.

[40] Interview with General Hajima Massaki, Joint Staff Council Chairman, Japan Defence Agency, *Jane's Defence Weekly,* 16 February 2005.

[41] 'Ground-breaking Relief Effort in Aceh Under Way', *Japan Times,* 28 January 2005.

[42] Indian Navy, 'Humanitarian Activities and Disaster Relief by Indian Navy', at http://indiannavy.nic.in/hadr-jul10.pdf.

[43] Cdr Sunil Srivastava, 'Post-tsunami Relief Operations by the Indian Navy', *Seagull,* May 2005.

[44] 'IN Fleet Leaves for Historic Exercise', *Daily News and Analysis India,* 25 March 2007; James R. Holmes and Andrew C. Winner, 'A New Naval Diplomacy', *Proceedings of the United States Naval Institute,* July 2007, pp. 35–8.

[45] Statement of John R. Young, Vice Adm. Joseph A. Sestak and Brigadier General Martin Post before the Senate Armed Services Committee Airland Subcommittee, 6 April 2005.

[46] 'US Amphibs Bringing Relief to Pakistan', *Defense News,* 16 August 2010.

[47] Robert Gates, address at IISS Shangri-La Dialogue, 4 June 2011, available at http://www.iiss.org/conferences/the-shangri-la-dialogue/shangri-la-dialogue-2011/speeches/first-plenary-session/dr-robert-gates/.

[48] For a useful summary of such activity in the Asia-Pacific see 'Pacific Partnership Mission' in *Asia-Pacific Defense Forum,* first quarter 2008, available at http://forum.apan-info.net; highlights of the Department of Navy FY2010 Budget, accessible at http://www.finance.hq.navy.mil/FMB/10pres/Highlights_book.pdf, p. 1–5.

[49] Intelligence, Surveillance, Target Acquisition and Reconnaissance.

[50] 'China Displays Naval Might in Fleet Review', *Asian Defence Journal,* May 2009.

51 Philip Andrews-Speed, Xuanli Liao and Roland Danreuther, *The Strategic Implications of China's Energy Needs*, Adelphi Paper 346, (Oxford: Oxford University Press for the IISS, 2002), pp. 78, 81

52 Quoted in James Holmes, *China's Maritime Strategy is more than Naval Strategy*, China Brief, Jamestown Foundation, April 2011; 'General Calls for New Coastguard to Patrol South China Sea', *Wall Street Journal*, 7 March 2012; 'Calls for Establishment of Ministry of Oceans', Xinhua, 5 March 2012.

53 Justin McCurry, 'Russian Coastguards kill Japanese Fisherman in Disputed Waters', *Guardian*, 17 August 2006.

54 *Indian Maritime Doctrine 2009*, p. 60.

55 Admiral Arun Prakash (former chief of the Naval Staff), 'A Vision of Maritime India: 2020', *Seagull*, August 2007; *India's Maritime Military Strategy 2007*.

56 *Ibid.*, pp. 89–94.

57 Admiral Sushil Kumar, 'We need to Secure our Own Base', *Seagull*, May–July 2009; Vice Adm. R.N. Ganesh, 'Evolving Maritime Challenges', *Indian Defence Review*, July/September 2009; P.K. Ghosh, 'India's Coastal Security: Challenges and Policy Recommendations', Observer Research Foundation Issue Brief no. 22, August 2010, accessible from http://www.orfonline.org.

58 Adm. Arun Prakash, 'India's vulnerable maritime flanks', *Seagull*, February –April 2009.

59 'Navy Factors in Terrorism, Coastal Security in Revamped Maritime Doctrine', *Times of India*, 30 August 2009.

60 Quoted in Meelam Mathews, 'Futures Market: India makes Big Investment in Homeland Security', *Defence Technology International*, December 2009.

61 US Navy, *A Cooperative Strategy for 21st Century Seapower*, http://www.navy.mil/maritime/Maritimestrategy.pdf.

62 *Ibid.*, p. 5, and the more expansive account in *Naval Operations Concept*, 2010, pp. 35–44; highlights of the Department of Navy FY2010 Budget, accessible at http://www.finance.hq.navy.mil/FMB/10pres/Highlights_book.pdf, pp. 1–4. There now appears to be rather less emphasis on the 'Global Maritime Partnership' but the concept still appears. Thus Ronald O'Rourke, *Navy Irregular Warfare and Counterterrorism Operations: Background and Issues for Congress*.

63 'US Navy Prepares to Say No', *Defense News*, 27 September 2010.

64 'China Expands Fleet to Protect its Sea Rights', *Straits Times*, 29 October 2010.

65 'China to Bolster Paramilitary Fleet', *Jane's Defence Weekly*, 11 May 2011.

66 Kaijo Hoan Report (Maritime Safety Report by the Japanese Coast Guard). For a review of these see Tetsuo Kotani, 'Japan's Maritime Challenges and Priorities', unpublished paper presented at RSIS Conference 'Maritime Challenges and Priorities in Asia', 20–21 January 2010.

67 The organisation changed its name from the Japanese Maritime Safety Agency in April 2000. For details see *Japan Coast Guard* issued by the JCG Agency Public Relations Office, http://www.kaiho.mmlit.go.jp/e/pamphlet.pdf.

68 Yoko Masuda, 'The Race to Beef Up Japan's Coast Guard', *Wall Street Journal*, 27 October 2012.

69 Vijay Sakhuja, *Asian Maritime Power in the 21st Century* (Singapore: Institute of Southeast Asian Studies, 2011), pp. 81, 105–8.

70 Rahul Bedi, 'Homeland Defence', *Jane's Defence Weekly*, 21 January 2009; 'India to Fence "Naval" Harbours', BBC Online, http://news.bbc.co.uk/1/hi/world/south_asai/8402973.stm. But see also 'After 26/11, Nothing Changed in Mumbai', *New Straits Times*, 28 November 2009. See also P.K. Ghosh, *India's Coastal Security: Challenges and Policy Recommendations* (New Delhi: Observer Research Foundation, 2010); Government of India, *Ministry of Defence Annual Report 2008–9*, para 1.26.

71 'Guarding Access: India Strengthens Coastal and Border Security', *Defense Technology International*, January 2011. 'Forging Ahead', *Defense Technology International*, September 2011.

72 See Congressional Research Reports of 28 May 2012 and 25 June 2012.

73 'No Benefit in Linking Ship Programs', UPI Staff Writers, Washington, 20 July 2009.

74 Jaqueline Klimas, 'USCG Vice Commandant's Top Priority: Ship Acquisition', *Defense News*, 30 July 2012.

75 Statement of Adm. Gary D Roughead, chief of naval operations, before the House Armed Services Committee on the FY10 Department of Defence Posture, 14 May 2009, p. 6; James Holmes, 'LCS Diplomacy: A New Old Option When Facing China', *Defense News*, 13 February 2012.

76 'On the Job: US Navy takes its Littoral Combat Ships to Sea', *Jane's International Defence Review*, May 2010.

77 I am grateful to Capt. Robert Rubel, US Navy [Retd] for an elegant exposition of these views.

78 'China's Most Advanced Maritime Patrol Boat Hits the Water', *People's Daily*, 23 February 2005.

79 Lyle J. Goldstein, 'China: A New Maritime Partner.' *Proceedings of the USNI*, August 2007, pp. 26–31.

80 Qian Xiaohu, 'China's Navy Engaging in Unprecedented Coordination with India, Japan on Anti-piracy Patrols', Xinhua/Assocated Press, 5 April 2012.

81 'Taiwanese White Paper Records Chinese Incursions Reaching All-time High', *Jane's Defence Weekly*, 6 September 2006.

82 Carlyle A. Thayer, *China's New Wave of Aggressive Assertiveness in the South China Sea*, paper to Conference on Maritime Security in the South China Sea, Center for Strategic and International Studies, Washington DC, 20–21 June 2011.

83 Cited in You Ji, *The Evolution of China's Maritime Combat Doctrines and Models*, Working paper no. 22 (Singapore: IDSS, May 2002), p. 15.

84 *Military Power of the People's Republic of China 2006*. The Chinese position in this incident is unclear. They could either claim that the *Impeccable's* activities constituted a threat to China's security, or that it was actually engaged in marine scientific research for commercial purposes. China's failure to clarify its position and the dangerous manner in which the action was conducted weakens the Chinese

case. Sam Bateman, 'Clashes at Sea: When Chinese Vessels Harass US Ships', RSIS Commentary 27/2009, http://dr.ntu.edu.sg/handle/10220/6093.

85 Rear Adm. Michael McDevitt (retd), Testimony to the US–China Economic and Security Review Commission, US Senate, 11 June 2009, available at http://insidedefense.com/secure/display.asp?docnum=dplus2009_1565&f=defense_2002.ask.

86 Ker Xu, 'Review of China's Counter-Piracy Operations and Problems', Peace and Development [heping yu fazhen], no.3, June 2011, p. 51.

87 General Liang Guanglie, Minister of National Defense China, address at the 10th IISS Asian Security Summit, 5 June 2011.

88 'Coast Guard Sent to Disputed Waters', Taipei Times, 15 September 2009.

89 Marcus Warren, 'Japan Sinks "North Korean Spying Ship"', Daily Telegraph, 24 December 2001.

90 Tetsuo Kotani, 'Japan's Maritime Challenges and Priorities', unpublished paper presented at RSIS Conference 'Maritime Challenges and Priorities in Asia', 20–21 January 2010 and Nazery Khalid, 'Burden Sharing, Security and Equity in the Straits of Malacca', Japan Focus, ID: 2277, http://www.japanfocus.org/-Nazery-Khalid/2777.

91 Japan Defence White Paper 2009, Section 4, pp. 123–8. Accessible at http://www.mod.go.jp/publ/w_paper/pdf/2009.html. The text of the Basic Law is to be found in http://www.kantei.go.jp/singi/konkyo6.pdf. The text of the Piracy Law is available at http://www.sof.or.jp/en/topics/pdf/09.

92 'No Place to Hide – Maybe' Economist, 30 October 2004.

93 'Japan Orders Destroyer Home Amid North Korean Concerns', International Herald Tribune, 29 June 2006.

94 'A Firm line on Whaling in Japan', International Herald Tribune, 14 March 2007. Interestingly, the paper quotes Ayako Okubo of the Oceans Policy Research Foundation: 'It's not because Japanese want to eat whale meat. It's because they don't like being told not to eat it by foreigners.' For possible naval involvement see 'Military May Defend Japanese Whalers', New Zealand Herald, 11 January 2006.

95 National Fleet: A Joint Navy/ Coast-guard Policy Statement, 3 March 2006, at 2006_national_fleet_policy.pdf.

96 Adm. Mike Mullen at the Regional Sea Power Symposium in Venice, 12 October 2006, text available at http://www.navy.mil/navydata/people/cno/mullen/Regional_Sea_Power_Symposium_Venice.pdf.

97 See also Ronald O'Rourke, Navy Irregular Warfare and Counter-terrorism Operations: Background and Issues for Congress.

98 See, for example, http://indiannavy.nic.in/AntiPiracy.htm.

99 Indian Maritime Doctrine 2009, p. 105.

100 Liu Jixian, as cited in Nan Li, 'Reconceptualizing the PLA Navy in Post-Mao China: Functions, Warfare, Arms and Organisation', Working Paper No. 30 of August 2002, Institute of Defence and Strategic Studies, available at RSISPublication@ntu.edu.sg, p. 7.

101 *Ibid.*

102 *The Great Explorer Cheng Ho: Ambassador of Peace,* with a preface by Johannes Widodo (Singapore: Asiapac Books, 2005) is a spectacular example of this. For a more sceptical account see Geoff Wade, *The Zheng He Voyages: A Reassessment* (Singapore: NUS Asia Research Institute Working Paper no. 31, October 2004). Wade argues that Zheng He's force was militarily so overwhelming that it did not need to use force, and that most local authorities obligingly did what was asked, with the exception of Ceylon where Chinese forces intervened in a civil war and proclaimed suzerainty over the island. See also Toshi Yoshihara and James R. Holmes, *Red Star Over the Pacific: China's Rise and the Challenge to US Maritime Strategy* (Annapolis, MD: Naval Institute Press, 2010), pp. 158–68.

103 Quoted in James R. Holmes and Toshi Yoshihara, 'China's Naval Ambitions in the Indian Ocean', *Journal of Strategic Studies,* vol. 31, no. 3, June 2008, p. 375.

104 'Japan Protests over China Ships in Disputed Waters', Reuters, 24 August 2011; 'Keen Sword 2011 Brings US and Japanese Sailors Together', 12 June 2010. Story NNS101206-01 at http://www.navy. mil.; 'India–Japan Defence Talks Signal Closer Ties', *Straits Times,* 2 November 2011.

105 Vijay Sakhuja, *Asian Maritime Power in the 21st Century* (Singapore: Institute of Southeast Asian Studies, 2011), pp. 197–202.

106 Adm. L. Ramdas, 'Dismantling Prejudice: the Road to a People Based Peace Strategy', *Seagull,* May 2005; *India's Maritime Military Strategy,* p. 29; *Indian Maritime Doctrine 2004,* p. 51.

107 Adm. Sureesh Mehta's address at the IISS Shangri-La Dialogue, 30 May 2009, available at http://www. iiss.org/conferences/the-shangri-la-dialogue/shangri-la-dialogue-2009/ plenary-session-speeches-2009/ second-plenary-session/ admiral-sureesh-mehta/.

108 Adm. Mike Mullen, in John B. Hattendorf, *Seventeenth Annual Seapower Symposium: Report of Proceedings* (Newport, RI: Naval War College Press, 2005), p. 5.

109 Christopher J. Castelli, 'New Maritime Strategy would Emphasize Soft and Hard Power', *Inside the Navy,* 18 June 2007; Vice Adm. John G. Morgan and Rear Adm. Charles W. Martoglio, 'The 1,000-ship Navy Global Maritime Network', *Proceedings of the US Naval Institute,* November 2005.

110 Adm. Mike Mullen formally launched this concept at the 17th International Seapower Symposium in September 2005. See John Hattendorf (ed.), *Report of the Proceedings 19–23 September 2005* (Newport RI: US Naval War College, 2006), pp. 3–8.

111 Vice Adm. John G. Morgan, quoted in 'Maritime Strategy to be Unveiled Next Month', *Navy Times,* 26 September 2007.

112 'UN's Sea Law Treaty Pushed', *Washington Times,* 27 September 2007.

113 *Naval Operations Concept 2010,* pp. 25–6.

114 Adm. Mullen at the 17th International Seapower Symposium, in Hattendorf, *Report of Proceedings,* p. 6.

115 Chief of Naval Operations Adm. Gary Roughead, remarks at MAST Americas, Washington DC, 22 June 2010.

116 *Sustaining US Global Leadership: Priorities for 21st Century Defense*, 5 January 2012, p. 3 accessible at www.defense.gov/news/Defense_ Strategic_guidance.pdf.

117 'China puts on a Friendly Face in PR drive', *Straits Times*, 17 May 2007. Vijay Sakhuja, *Asian Maritime Power in the 21st Century* (Singapore: Institute of Southeast Asian studies, 2011) pp. 186–92.

118 'Chinese Navy on Target in Joint Drills', *The People Daily Online*, 10 March 2007, http://english. peopledaily.com.cn/200703/10/ eng20070310_356268.html.

119 *Annual Report to Congress: Military Power of the People's Republic of China 2008*, p. 6.

120 Discussions with China Special Focus Group, Pacific Command, Hawaii, November 2012.

121 'China sees Joint Exercises with ASEAN Countries', *Jane's Defence Weekly*, 25 May 2007.

122 Yokio Okamote, 'Japan and the US – the Essential Alliance', *Washington Quarterly*, Spring 2002, p. 66.

123 Vice Adm. Yoji Koda, 'Maritime Powers and National Security in an Interdependent World', in Alessio Patalano ed., *Maritime Strategy and National Security in Japan and Britain from the Alliance to Post 9/11* (Dorset: Global Oriental, 2010).

124 'First Japan Warship in China in 60 Years', *Straits Times*, 25 June 2008; *East Asian Strategic Review 2009*, pp. 118–19.

125 'India to Supply Patrol Ship to Mauritius', *New kerala.com*, 5 July 2010; 'India to Help Seychelles Boost Sea Surveillance', *Defense News*, 19 July 2010; 'India, Oman Launch First Exercise', *Defence News*, 14 October 2009.

126 'Indian Navy to Survey Islands of Mauritius', *Defense News*, 18 March 2010.

127 *India Maritime Doctrine 2009*, p. 27.

128 Vivek Raghuvaneshi, 'China, India To Resume Joint Military Exercises', *Defense News*, 10 September 2012.

129 Hillary Clinton, 'America's Pacific Century', *Foreign Policy*, November 2011.

130 Vice Adm. Richard Hunt, Cmdr 3rd Fleet, quoted in 'Ships, Marines begin RIMPAC Exercises', *Navy Times*, 7 July 2010; See Rear Adm. Michael Smith, director of OpNav, Strategy and Policy Division (N51) posting on US Navy blog, http:// navylive.didlive.mil/author/sburns, posted 22 October 2012.

131 John Bradford, 'The Maritime Strategy of the United States: Implications for Indo-Pacific Sea Lanes', *Contemporary Southeast Asia*, August 2011, pp. 200–03. Discussions with Rear Adm. Thomas Carney, USN Cdr Logistics Group Western Pacific, Singapore, November 2011.

132 The Model Maritime Service Code issued by the US Coast Guard in 1995 and now being reworked is a good example of this since it is intended to 'assist other nations in developing a Maritime Force to help them meet the changing needs of the twenty-first century'.

133 See Paul T Mitchell, *Network Centric Warfare: Coalition Operations in the Age of US Military Primacy*, Adelphi Paper 385 (London: IISS, 2006)

134 This was even a problem in the tsunami relief operation; Bruce A. Elleman, *Waves of Hope* (Newport, RI: Naval War College Press, 2007), p. 72.

135 Discussions with Admiral Patrick Walsh and his PACFLT Staff, Honolulu, September 2011. The freedom of navigation issue is a particularly difficult one. For a vigorous statement of the US position on this in regard to the *USNS Impeccable* see James Kraska, 'Sovereignty at Sea', *Survival*, vol. 51, no. 3, June–July 2009, pp. 13–18. See my forthcoming paper *Close Encounters of the Maritime Kind: Freedom of Navigation and its Impact on the South China Sea Problem*, Taipei, September 2011.

136 Cortez A. Cooper, 'The PLA Navy's "New Historic Missions"', RAND Corporation report, June 2009, http://www.rand.org/pubs/testimonies/2009/RAND_CT332.pdf.

CONCLUSION

All four countries, in their public discourse, their fleet programmes and their operational activities, emphasise the need for a balanced portfolio of tasks and capabilities that have little to do with immediate bilateral rivalries. India, for example, has specifically rejected the notion of a trilateral line-up with Japan and the United States and wants to go its own way.[1] The United States for its part appears perfectly aware of the new complexities of a multimodal world:

> This changing distribution of power indicates evolution to a 'multi-nodal' world characterized more by shifting, interest-driven coalitions based on diplomatic, military, and economic power, than by rigid security competition between opposing blocs.[2]

Navies these days have evidently to cater for all contingencies and can no longer plan, as in 1909, for a simpler world of identified adversaries. Battleships had little function other than to deal with other battleships, preferably by blowing them out of the water or threatening to do so. Much of the effort in the Asia-Pacific, and certainly a high proportion of the money expended on naval development, likewise centres on the acquisition of equivalent high-intensity capabilities, such as ballistic-missile defence, nuclear deterrence systems, sophisticated submarines and ASW capabilities, long-range missile capabilities, 'electromagnetic dominance and informa-tionisation' (to use Chinese terminology) aimed at peer or near peer competitors. Around the Asia-Pacific region, navies are acquiring ever more technologically sophisticated platforms, weapons and sensors, many of which seem justified primar-ily by their utility against other navies rather than against commonplace threats such as pirates or drug smugglers. Moreover many of them seem essentially more offensive than defensive, insofar as weapon systems can be said intrinsically to have these characteristics (rather than be conferred by the manner of their use). While the general quality of a particular weapon system does not of course necessarily imply offensive characteristics, the techniques may in some cases do so. For example, electronic warfare (EW) capabilities are being widely developed in the region and, for these to be effective, have to be both intrusive and specifically targeted at the particular characteristics of an adversary's EW systems and techniques.[3] Even here, peering into a neighbour's forces, may or may not be offensive depending on one's wider purposes, but the general balance between EW capabilities and the other side's electronic counter-measures is, for all that, a good example of the action-reaction dynamics of a true arms race.

Turning to how these burgeoning capabilities are being employed, the relative lethality of their use is apparent. With such episodes as the forcible Chinese seizure of various features in the South China Sea, the extent to which fishermen both here and elsewhere are subjected to sometimes lethal physical force, as well as the sinking of the South Korean *Cheonan*, naval relations sometimes actually seem significantly worse than they did in Europe before the First World War.

Malign geography requires prospective competitors to focus attention on the same sections of the world ocean, and this simple fact confers a potentially dangerous level of specificity to their priorities. Japan sits squarely across China's access route to the broader Pacific. Much of the South China Sea is directly contested by Vietnam, the Philippines and China. Already difficult relations between South Korea and Japan are bedevilled by the Tokdo/Takeshima island dispute.[4] The US and China are both preoccupied with the security of what the China calls the 'near seas' within the first island chain. Indeed, the most obvious and worrying example of a potentially dangerous operational specificity has to be the emerging competition between Chinese Anti-Access/Area Denial concepts on the one hand and American responses in the shape of the Air–Sea Battle on the other. Both concepts only really make sense, and justify their enormous budgets, when pitted against each other – just as did the German and British concepts of battlefleet operation of 1914.

This challenge has contributed to a striking increase in the US priority given to the Pacific, in both political and military terms. The 7th Fleet has been strengthened by the new carrier USS *George Washington* replacing the old *Kitty Hawk*, the upgrading of Destroyer Squadron 15 at Yokosuka into an all *Aegis* force, increased ASW training for Pacific Fleet forces, the strengthening of its mine warfare capabilities and the deployment of three *Global Hawk* aircraft to the region for surveillance purposes, a noticeable switching of US submarine forces to the Pacific, including all three *Seawolf* SSN-21 submarines and three *Los Angeles*-class SSN-688s to Guam, plus two of the Navy's four converted Trident boats to Bangor. The decision to switch back from the DDG-1000 *Zumwalt*-class to renewed production of the *Arleigh Burke* DDG class of *Aegis* destroyers is attributed to the rise of Chinese anti-access capabilities as well.[5] Both the Quadrennial Defense Review 2010 and the Independent Panel's report on it called for the overall posture and capabilities of the US to be enhanced in the Asia-Pacific region, especially in the maritime sphere.[6] Obama's announcement of the deployment of US Marines to Darwin and the prospective basing of Littoral Combat Ships in Singapore have carried this priority switch still further.

Given this possible range of US responses, the PLAN could not hope to overwhelm the US Navy for the foreseeable future provided the US were able to concentrate sufficient assets in the area of concern. But the PLAN would nevertheless seem able to hold the US Pacific Fleet at increasing risk. At the very least, the US Navy's capacity to provide 'dominance on demand' in the waters of Northeast Asia is going to be significantly harder to achieve in the future than it has proved in the past.[7] The need for the US Navy to concentrate its forces is suggested in *A Cooperative Strategy*, where 'combat credible forces' will be provided for the Gulf and Northeast Asia, but only 'globally distributed, mission-tailored forces' elsewhere.[8]

Certainly, China's conscious pursuit of such capabilities and the US Navy's response to it indicates the state-centred competitive approach to force planning, most characteristic of arms races. But in declaratory terms, both sides continue to acknowledge that a hedging strategy, if overdone, could be counterproductive, precipitating the very situation it was designed to deter. This is likely to be particularly true for China, facing three potential adversaries as it does.

There are other examples of the same operational specificity as well, not least the line up between the two Koreas, Taiwan and the mainland, and India and Pakistan. Sometimes these specific rivalries can take a symmetrical form – such as the competition in the deployment of long-range precision strike apparently developing between China and the US. Sometimes it is asymmetric, for instance the Japanese stress on BMD aimed against North Korea and probably China or the Vietnamese and Taiwanese bids to develop sea-denial capabilities against China, strategies that might be thought to make sense on the assumption that in any such confrontation the bulk of China's strategic focus would still have to be on the US.

In Japan, as we have seen, a government panel has suggested something of a switch in defence priority away from the Korean peninsula, despite the deterioration of north–south relations after the sinking of the corvette *ROKS Cheonan*, and towards Japan's southwest, the scene of recent worries with China.[9] Thus Jun Azumi, vice-minister for defence, said in December 2010:

> Our attention was on the north during the Cold war. But we have to shift our focus to the defence of the south-west … The most important step to strengthen our defence over the next ten years is to secure the mobility (of our forces).[10]

The announcement both of an expansion of Japan's submarine arm and the strengthening of Japan's island garrisons, referred to in Chapter Two, need to be seen in this context. The turning point for the Japanese was the passage of a large PLAN force through the Japanese island chain in 2010, a very public event which brought home to many the simple consequences of their geo-strategic position, a point repeated in the passage of another six ship task force in November 2011. While the continuing problems of the Japanese economy[11] and Japan's constitutional limitations on defence developments are likely to impede any dramatic naval expansion, the JMSDF remains arguably the most advanced of all the navies of Asia (except the US Navy). For all its wider concerns, the JSMDF is still largely focused on the defence of its own immediate area, the so-called Tokyo-Guam-Taiwan triangle, and this inevitably means it sits geographically firmly across much of China's access to the wider world ocean. Given this and their troubled history, there are bound to remain significant strategic tensions in the relationship between the two countries, despite their economic inter-dependence. One other consequence of this has been a noticeable coming together between Japan and the United States, Australia and to an extent India.[12]

Against all this, however, may be set the many other operational preoccupations that the great majority of the navies of the Asia-Pacific region also have and which do not pit them against each other as specific competitors. These mitigate what might otherwise be seen as a primary focus on a putative adversary, plainly a leading characteristic of arms racing behaviour.

Thus, the US Navy's *A Cooperative Strategy for the 21st Century* and its focus on expeditionary operations, HADR, and the global maritime partnership and constructive engagement are demanding aspirations that have little to do with China. Both India and Japan exhibit the same characteristics, the first perhaps rather more than the second. The Indian Navy's Indian Ocean Naval Symposium (IONS) *démarche* and its avowed sense of responsibility for helping to stabilise the Indian Ocean against regional conflict and irregular threats such as drugs smuggling and piracy provide good examples of this. Left-wing and Ghandian elements in India are clearly reluctant for the country to be seen to dominate the region or to get involved with any kind of naval arms race with China or any other external power.[13] China has growing concerns around the world and many of these are only indirectly related to its rivalry with the US, Japan, India or anyone else for that matter.

Constrained by their constitution, experience and circumstances, the Japanese have been somewhat more circumspect
in their military engagement, but they did organise the Pacific
Coastguard Forum, supported *Operation Enduring Freedom*,
and hosted the Pacific Security Initiative Maritime Interdiction
Exercise (*Pacific Shield 07*) and have been both active and sensitive in helping secure shipping safety in the Straits of Malacca.
Encouraged by the success of their 'smiling diplomacy,' even
the Chinese have shown a greater willingness to participate
in cooperative measures of maritime security, but markedly
less so than the other three. Chinese suspicion of multilateralism, especially when it involves the Americans, runs deep.
Nonetheless, the Chinese have recently developed the notion
of the 'harmonious ocean' and argue it to be one of the guides
of their acquisition policies.

The expansion of the PLAN also needs to be seen against
a broader aspirational maritime context than simply a
competitive relationship with the US; its national economic
development has been prioritised in its recent Five-Year Plans,
alongside the build-up of the its non-military agencies of maritime security, the support of all its maritime industries not just
the defence-related ones, (and especially those devoted to the
exploitation of marine energy resources)[14] and the country's
remarkable interest in the Arctic. Its putative strategic rivalry
with the United States, and with Japan and India is therefore
far from being Beijing's sole maritime preoccupation. If it was,
we could expect much more focus on outmatching the US Navy
and rather less on its general maritime development.

Within China there is widespread debate amongst the military and attendant academics about PLAN priorities. Some
want to concentrate efforts on 'fighting informatised local
wars' and others are interested in power-projection capabilities to defend China's wider interests.[15] The latter tends to be

associated with the navy more than the army. One can clearly see the concern for power-projection at work in a speech given by Kang Geng, the political commissar of the South Fleet, at the 2009 National People's Congress: 'China has thousands of enterprises spreading over the globe. We must seriously consider how to effectively protect [them].'[16] But the PLAN still faces choices. In 2009, the Minister of Defence, General Liang Guanglie remarked: 'The navy will be capable of both a strong coastal defence and certain measures for blue water combat.'[17] This ambivalence in priority was reflected in subsequent defence white papers. The 'New Historic Missions' of 2004 dealt with the safeguarding national development and the protection of world peace and prosperity. The 2006 equivalent focused on local wars under conditions of informatisation, while the 2008 paper left room for wider Maritime Operations Other Than War and non-military assignments such as 'disaster relief, maintaining social stability and conducting military diplomacy'.[18]

Another high-profile contributor to military policy debates, Chen Zhou from the Academy of Military Sciences, outlined the dilemma facing Beijing: 'The PLA must respond to traditional security (threats), and at the same time, to non-traditional security (threats)'.[19] For this reason, China has increasingly had to develop a balanced portfolio of capabilities, not just one narrower set aimed principally at the United States.

The acquisition programmes of other countries in the Asia-Pacific region are similarly broad. Indeed, the recent pattern of naval acquisitions can be read as an attempt to develop a portfolio of general all-round naval capabilities rather than a set narrowly aimed at another state. The ROK Navy's bid to develop capabilities tailored to meet its global interests, rather than simply focusing on the threat from the north can be seen as particularly interesting example of this.

There may sometimes be an element of 'prestige racing' involved in this as well. Countries in the region have certainly bowed to the pressure to acquire showy platforms largely on the basis that neighbouring countries have them (for what was in 1912 famously called 'general purposes of greatness'),[20] even when those countries have a notably limited capacity to maintain and operate them properly. In China, for example, appealing to national pride supports the Communist Party's imperatives for survival, as Robert S. Ross has observed: 'Military nationalism has become increasingly important to the Chinese Communist party's domestic prestige.'[21] Deng Xiaoping apparently agreed: 'It has always been, and always will be , necessary for China to develop its own high technology [...] If it were not for the atomic bomb, the hydrogen bomb and the satellites [...] China would not have its present international standing as a great influential country.'[22] This interest in the acquisition of impressive naval platforms for the sake of national pride is by no means confined to China, or indeed simply to the major naval powers of the region – as submarine development in Southeast Asia would seem to suggest. To the extent it operates in the region, this kind of competitive arms acquisition may be economically wasteful, but it also seems relatively unfocused and harmless, if not taken too seriously.

Remaking the regional order

The seriousness of the naval competition between these four naval powers of the Asia-Pacific, and the likelihood that it will degenerate into an arms race is in large measure a function of what is considered to be at stake. In the competition between China's 'counter-intervention capabilities' and the United States' Air Sea Battle concept for example, three issues stand out.

Firstly, there is the military strategic issue of forward presence and continued access. As Admiral Greenert has testified:

> We provide the nation offshore options to deter, influence and win in an era of uncertainty. Our Navy is at its best when it is forward, assuring allies and building partnerships, deterring aggression without escalation, defusing threats without fanfare, and containing conflict without regional disruption. We keep the Fleet forward through a combination of rotational deployments from the United States, Forward Deployed Naval Forces (FDNF) in Japan, Guam and Italy, and forward stationing ships in places such as Bahrain or Diego Garcia. Our ability to operate forward depends on our U.S. bases and strategic partnerships overseas that provide 'places' where the Navy-Marine Corps team can rest, repair, refuel and resupply.[23]

Second, there is the grand strategic issue of the relative position of the two countries in the present and particularly the future world order. Especially in an age of perceived declinism and reduced public support for 'heavy' US involvement in world affairs according to the latest Gallup surveys,[24] the US feels its global leadership and indeed the whole international order to be at risk.[25] For their part, the Chinese are plainly aware that the first two decades of this century present an opportunity to remake the world order to some degree in a manner that would provide China with greater status, relative to the US.[26] Against this background the relative naval balance between the two navies assumes tremendous symbolic value, not least in the eye of local beholders.

Third, there is the complex but related issue of what the balance between the two navies actually is and will be. The significance of this in the essentially maritime Asia-Pacific Region warrants more substantial discussion. Here, for the time being the situation seems fairly stable. Although the gap between the US Navy, China and indeed the rest of the world may be narrowing (in terms of the total number of platform), it remains considerable when one considers capability. For all the caveats and nuances, the United States *is* still the world's main military power and seems likely to remain so for the foreseeable future. In some sense, the figures speak for themselves. At some US$ 687 billion in 2010, the United States spends nearly as much on defence as the rest of the world put together. This amounts to 4.7% of GDP, a proportion that is unmatched by most countries; in strictly economic terms, it appears to be affordable.[27] Even now, the United States is nowhere near the level of defence spending that contributed to the fall of the Soviet Union. Moreover, the West, if construed as the United States and its NATO allies, still accounts for about 70% of the world's global defence spending, and if allies such as Japan, South Korea and Singapore are factored in as well the total goes higher still. China's level of defence spending is notoriously hard to measure, but almost any calculation suggests that while China is catching up there remains a huge gap in military spending between the two.[28]

While the US Navy's planned expansion to a future fleet of 313 ships may seem unaffordable, its *current* level of 280 ships far exceeds the naval strength of any possible competitors. In the hey-day of its global power, the Royal Navy could sometimes achieve a two-power standard, that is, its forces were equivalent to the fleets of its next two rivals combined. In terms of the total numbers of major combatants, the US Navy also has a two-power standard over the Chinese and Russian fleets: 203 ships to their 205.[29] But in themselves, numbers count for little. The Royal Navy was rarely able to achieve a two-power standard and for much of its period of dominance, it actually operated fewer ships than its immediate adversaries.

Tonnage is a better indication of strength since the offensive and defensive power of an individual unit is usually a function of its size and moreover is one of the main means by which ship categories are classified. In aggregate tonnage, the US Navy has a 13 power standard, with a 263:1 advantage over a combined Russian–Chinese fleet, which in any case includes many ships and submarines that are not in fact combat-ready. Its eleven fleet carriers and ten light carriers provide a nine power standard, and they operate 980 aircraft, twice as many as those carried on all sixteen carriers of the next nine countries, put together. In major surface combatants, factoring in the advantage that the US Navy possesses through its below deck Vertical Launch Missile Systems, its 105 warships transforms a comfortable numerical two-power standard into an effective 20 power standard. Its 56 SSN/SSGN nuclear powered submarine fleet might on the face of it seem overpowered by the world's other 220 SSNs and SSKs but the qualitative advantages of the US submarine force are huge. It is much the same story in regard to the US Navy's amphibious and crucial support fleets, in its capacity to support special forces operations, in its broad area maritime surveillance capabilities, in its US Coast Guard (the equivalent of many of the world's navies) and in the enormous advantages conferred by the experience of many decades of 24/7 oceanic operations.[30] It will be many years before this commanding global lead in deployable naval power is seriously compromised:

> The consensus of sources is that the size and level of operational experience of the US Navy and Air Force makes it nearly impossible for potential opponents to mount a serious challenge in the waters and air space

over the world's oceans. This is likely to continue until 2035.[31]

Another factor often forgotten is that of the world's next 20 fleets in aggregate tonnage terms, no less than 18 are either formal allies of the United States (13, nine of these coming from NATO Europe) or friendly towards it (five). NATO Europe's fleets already reach high levels of cooperation with the US Navy and the ideas expressed in *A Cooperative Strategy for 21st Century Seapower*[32] are expressly designed to spread such levels of cooperation still further. Moreover the American lead in new as well as established naval technologies is at least as great. For instance, the development of unmanned systems and the introduction of high-energy ship-board military lasers are potential 'game-changers' as dramatic and far-reaching as the development of the aircraft carrier at the beginning of the twentieth century;[33] in technological transformation as in so much else , the United States is far ahead of any competitor.

The disturbing thing from the American point of view is less the situation now than its trajectory for the future. Here expectations are central. In his 2009 Annual Threat Assessment, the US Director of National Intelligence concluded: 'We judge that China over the past several years has begun a substantially new phase in its military development by beginning to articulate roles and missions for the PLA that go well beyond China's immediate territorial interests.'[34] As a result, current margins of superiority are likely to be reduced in the future by declining naval appropriations in the United States over the next few years. The navy currently has some 280 ships and submarines; as many commentators have pointed out this is the smallest American 'battleforce' since 1916. The navy's 2005 target over a 30 year period was a 313 strong battleforce, approximately to meet the future operational requirements of a two medium wars against regional adversaries plus the permanent presence levels of readiness recommended by the Bottom-up Review of 1993 and the Quadrennial Defense Reviews of 1997 and 2001. Estimates of the numbers of ships needed for this target have varied between 300 and 346.[35] The Independent Panel on the Quadrennial Defense Review of 2010 indeed recommended that 346 should once more become the target. This advice was rejected by Secretary Gates in August 2010, who argued that the target should remain 313–323 ships, and that any greater number was at once unnecessary and unaffordable within the constraints of his future spending plans.[36]

The United States' current economic travails seem likely to reinforce this point, because the scale of cuts envisaged on current estimates, will on best estimates produce a battle-force level of 304 ships in FY 2028, dropping to 301 in FY 2040. The current budgetary imbroglio between the Obama administration and Congress has already delayed the start of a number of new submarine and surface ship builds which will now have to be re-assigned to the end of their respective queues, together with a number of early decommissioning of existing ships seem likely to widen the difference between current and ideal ship numbers.[37] Closing the gap between the ideal fleet and the resources likely to be available may require further radical re-thinks of the composition of the fleet, and of a reduction in the current 'torrid' and in fact unsustainably worsening US fleet operational tempo of 40–50 per cent sea time.[38] There is talk of reducing carrier numbers and, more significantly, readiness states from the current level of 3 (deployed) + 2 (at 30 days) + 1 (at 90 days) – with some even suggesting that 2+0+0 might prove necessary. As the former Secretary of Defense Robert Gates, has pointed out, 'A smaller military, no matter how superb, will be able to go fewer places, and be able to do fewer things.'[39]

Moreover, most of the US Navy's present and future difficulties stem not from the naval policies of China but from the country's own intrinsic economic difficulties. Objectively, this seems likely to make it increasingly difficult for the US to produce half the world's defence spending on the basis of less than a quarter of its economy, especially as Gates has said when this seems to require $3–6 billion destroyers, $7bn submarines and $11bn carriers.[40]

Finally, the United States' capacity to stay in the maritime lead is conditioned by its industrial capacity to produce the necessary materiel, but '[F]or the first time since 1890 ... the US Navy is faced with the prospect of competing against a potentially hostile naval power possessing a ship-building capacity that is equal to if not superior, to its own'[41] – in volume respects at least. As Admiral Roughead pointed out, whereas in previous down-turns there were six major shipbuilding corporations in the United States, today there are but two. The average age of a naval shipyard worker in the United States is now 45.[42] Admiral Roughead's worry was that the general ship-building decline in the United States could well imperil the navy's future plans and undermine its current strategic supremacy.

Other factors have also to be entered into the calculation of the relative future standing of the American and Chinese navies, most particularly a sense of what both navies have to do with what they have. The real strength of a navy is not the number of units that it has, or their relative sophistication, but how these compare to the requirements of the tasks that it needs to perform. In this more nuanced mode of assessment the sheer diversity of the US Navy's capabilities will reflect the extraordinarily varied scenarios (in terms of both geography and type) for which it feels it has to prepare. All these considerations seem likely to increase the prospects for China's naval power to grow, relative to that of the US, firstly within the region itself and secondly more globally. Such a view would be consistent with the PLAN's apparent ambitions at some future date of extending an effective reach beyond the first and even the second island chain. Hence the interest in Admiral Keating's testimony that recently 'one of their senior admirals said "We're going to start building aircraft carriers. You guys can have the east part of the Pacific, Hawaii to the States. We'll take the west part of the Pacific, from Hawaii to China." I was allowed to say we probably would not accept that bargain.'[43]

To summarise, China's rise, not just as a continental power with a huge population, a vast geographic area and with nuclear weapons and relative impermeability to large-scale overland attack, but as a developing naval and maritime power too, fundamentally changes things. Because of its growing and absolute dependence on overseas commodities, energy and markets, China, like the rest of the Asia-Pacific region has little choice but to become more maritime in its orientation. Almost inevitably, it is developing more ambitious naval forces, and even more significantly, the maritime industries that historically tend to go with it. Almost equally inevitably, these will challenge the strategic primacy of the United States in a geographic area hitherto dominated by American naval power; as such this momentous development could easily degenerate into the levels of competition and conflict that have until now often characterised great changes in the relative power of great states.[44]

Many in Beijing arrive at the same conclusion, if from a radically different direction. Here there has been much discussion of the new vulnerability of the United States as a world leader at a time of financial crisis, economic weakness, and growing economic dependence on a more confident China. As a report delivered to Fourth Plenary Session of the 17th Congress of the Communist Party of China stated in 2009: 'the competition among major powers for a position of overall, comprehensive strength is becoming an important feature of changes in the global situation.'[45] Thus what is at stake could be seen as success in a competition for strategic dominance either at the global or 'merely' the regional level, though given the future importance of the Indo-Pacific Region there is not likely to be much difference between the two.

These three aspects of the stake in the competition between A2/AD and ASB, when taken together, could indeed lead to more intense arms-racing behaviour and strategic distrust between China and the US reaching 'dangerous levels.'[46] The fact that, as Henry Kissinger has pointed out, neither the US nor China, have much experience in sharing power[47] can only increase the sense in both countries that there is a very great at stake in the uneasy relationship between them.

In this changing and challenging situation the current level of naval modernisation particularly between these two countries could indeed approximate a naval arms race. The markedly maritime nature of the Asia-Pacific Region in general and of the US approach to the area in particular makes the naval rivalry between the two countries seem particularly intense, for rather the same set of reasons that determined the British to secure their crucial maritime interests if necessary by winning their construction competition against the Germans before the First World War. One way or another, the conclusion might run, Washington has to preserve its naval dominance in the area, and Beijing has to challenge it.

But a number of factors need to be set against such alarming prognostications. The stakes may in fact be nothing like neither as high nor the outcome so momentous as they might appear at first glance. Firstly, there is a good deal of deterrent shadow-boxing in the apparent contest between A2/AD and Air–Sea Battle, which is quite different from, and less dangerous than, the prospective battleship line-up between Britain and Germany in 1909–14. The land-attack element implicit in both strategies (if fully carried out) means that any naval conflict between the US and China would rapidly escalate to full-scale war, an outcome acceptable to very few in either country. It is hard to imagine a scenario in which translating these generic concepts fully into actual operations would make strategic sense, although hard-liners could well argue for deterrent strategies of risk based on these concepts and even for their limited application in some extreme circumstances. The naval planners of 1914, by contrast, had few such qualms about imagining a full-scale naval conflict.

Secondly, there is very little prospect of the Chinese being able seriously to challenge American maritime leadership for the next decade or so. The extent of the threat the PLAN poses towards the currently commanding position of the US Navy should not be exaggerated, particularly outside China's immediate maritime neighbourhood. The Chinese themselves appear to be under no illusions in the matter. Although the technological development of the Chinese defence economy since the major sector reforms of the 1990s has indeed been impressive, it is still far behind that of the United States. According to General Liang Guanglie, Defence Minister and member of the Central Military Commission, when Kissinger has claimed that Chinese equipment was 20 years behind America's, he was basically right: 'I am afraid that the level of our military hardware is exactly as Mr Kissinger said.' China's military developments 'do not cause any major threat to any country and we have never attempted to pose any threat to any country.'[48] Nor is it clear that publicly displayed platforms necessarily work in the sense of being fully equipped and conceptually and logistically supported. Many are sceptical for example of the true capabilities of the much hyped DF-21D carrier-killer ASBM and the new 'fifth generation' *Chenghu* J-20 'Black Eagle', which dramatically appeared in January 2011 for example.[49] Essentially, the Chinese are still 'late innovators', duplicating and refining Western or Russian equipment of a decade or two before, although doing rather better than many analysts expected.[50]

There is therefore little talk, even amongst the strongest advocates of the Chinese navy, of its achieving dominance over the US Navy. Thus when discussing the Chinese carrier programme, the State Oceanic Administration in its report for 2010 stated: 'Building China as a maritime power is the mission of China in the whole 21st Century, and 2010 to 2020 is the critical period for accomplishing this strategic mission, *with the goal to place China among mid-tier maritime powers.*'[51] General Luo Yuan, senior researcher with the Academy of Military Sciences reinforced the point in July 2011. The aim of the exercise was to match the developing efforts of India and Japan, not the United States. Both countries would have three carriers by 2014, and so should China, 'so we can defend our rights and our maritime interests effectively.'[52] Thus when President Hu urges his navy to 'make extended preparations for military combat,' the justification adduced is to make 'greater contributions to safeguard national security and world peace.'[53] This is a far cry from the language of the arms race of the early twentieth century, and suggests a much lower degree of challenge (if challenge there is) than that posed by Germany to Britain during that time.

Thirdly, the extent of the challenge within China's immediate neighbourhood has been answered by the much-discussed 'American pivot to Asia' after the distractions of Iraq and Afghanistan. This policy was revealed by President Obama's speech to the Australian parliament in November 2011, and exemplified by a comprehensive and impressively integrated strategy of political engagement with countries all around the region, together with a marked strengthening of its forces in Guam and new agreements to establish the US Marines in Darwin and deploy Littoral Combat Ships to Singapore. The rationale was again made clear in February 2012 in *Sustaining US Global Leadership: Priorities for 21st Century Defense*:

> The United States will continue to lead global efforts with capable allies and partners to assure access to and use of the global commons, both by strengthening international norms of responsible behavior and by maintaining relevant and interoperable military capabilities.[54]

This all may well have reignited fears in Beijing that the United States, whatever it might say, is seeking to preserve its leadership by encircling and containing China.[55] But in truth there are many caveats and limitations in the readiness of the US's local partners to enter into any such arrangement, even were Washington to have any serious intentions to create one. There is within the region more generally considerable resistance to the notion that by improving relationships with the US they may in effect be participating in an anti-China coalition.[56] The political and strategic reality is much more complicated than this. The mere prospect of a 'recessed' maritime alliance of this sort appearing, possibly in response to increasingly assertive Chinese foreign-policy behaviour, however, could help preserve peace and stability in the region.

Fourthly, China's maritime rise may not necessarily mean America's demise; the 'competition' between the two may not need to be seen as a zero-sum game. Thus the Obama administration accepts that while the US will need to remain strong in Asia, 'a successful China can make our country more prosperous not less.'[57] Accordingly, the argument goes, the rise of China as an emerging superpower need not be seen as conforming to the general historic pattern of association with conflict between the existing great power(s) of the time.[58] Said Robert Gates in June 2011: 'We are not trying to hold China down. China has been a Great power for thousands of years. It is a global power and will be a global power.'[59]

Fifthly, while accepting that there are elements of confrontation in their relationship with the US, many in China also nonetheless believe the cooperative tendency to be much stronger than the competitive tendency. As Rear-Admiral Yang Yi has argued:

> China is different from the Soviet Union, and China's strategic path and (the) means it adopts are not as overbearing as those of the Soviet Union. Moreover, the overall international strategic background is now different from the Cold war era.'[60]

Their case is strengthened by reference to the growing economic inter-dependence of the two countries and the harm to both that would result from excessive levels of competition.

China's military policy is represented by the Chinese as conforming to the general approach of a non-confrontational strengthening of the country's defences. Echoing the sentiments in the 2010 Defence White Paper, General Zhang Qinsheng, Deputy Chief of the General Staff told the Royal United Services Institute in May 2011: 'China does not pursue hegemony. We will not do it even when we grow stronger. This is not only the basic state policy, but also a solemn commitment to the people of the world'.[61] This non-confrontational approach is reflected in declaratory statements by the Chinese military too: 'I can tell you,' said General Chen Bingde, Chief of the General staff, 'China does not have the capability to challenge the United States.'[62]

Of course, the naval relationship between China and the United States is far from being the only potentially destabilising naval relationship in the Indo-Pacific region, but it is fundamental to the strategic calculations of all the other navies and the consequent sub-balances to be found there. The fact that the centre of gravity for the US Navy lies off northeast Asia, and that this area will become more challenging for it, has implications for other areas even within the Asia-Pacific region. As one Australian expert has commented:

> Perhaps this explains why the [Australian] government's 2009 Defence White Paper put so much emphasis on boosting the strategic weight of our defence forces – not just as an encouragement for the United States to remain involved in our region, but as hedge in case it decides not to.[63]

The same kind of thinking can be seen in, and about, India. Its wariness about a Chinese presence in the Indian Ocean seems to have reinforced its 'Look East' policy[64] and its developing engagement with Japan, Australia, Vietnam and above all the United States.[65] All this suggests a lively local appreciation that there is a 'discretionary' element to the United States' forward presence in the Western Pacific that does not apply, say, to Vietnam, Japan or the Philippines, who geographically have no choice about their forward positions in the area. And this again might be thought to reduce the prospect for serious arms racing behaviour.

Conclusions

The evidence that naval modernisation in the Asia-Pacific approximates to a naval arms race, then, seems mixed. There are certainly elements of arms racing at play in the developing relationship of the American, Japanese, Indian and Chinese navies, particularly the first and the last. There remains accordingly the possibility of future miscalculation and future deterioration. But there is also a great deal of evidence against the proposition, not least in the region's high levels of sea-based economic inter-dependence and declaratory and operational stress on naval cooperation against common threats such as natural disasters, piracy, terrorism and other forms of maritime crime.

Colin Gray argues that acutely competitive forms of naval modernization are best seen as symptoms, rather than causes, of international tension. It is certainly true that they can only be ended through political accord.[66] Here the proposition is that the propensity for arms-racing lies less in the mere acquisition of armaments and more in how they are used, and how they are perceived to be used. Accordingly, breathless accounts of a build-up in those armaments may well give a more alarming impression of the situation than it warrants. The extent, in particular, of China's naval build-up poses a strategic challenge to the US and its allies and partners and so warrants a robust response could, however, easily be exaggerated; the nature of that response could in fact prove more destabilising than the original stimulus for it, given China's neuralgic fear of strategic encirclement.

Accordingly, the real issue is how China and other countries actually use their enhanced capabilities, especially in the highly sensitive areas of the Western Pacific, but out of area too, not least in the Indian ocean, because this provides strong indicators of the regional and global position they wish to take and therefore will tend to explain the responses they elicit.

Finally, one might argue that, even if Asia is in the midst of an arms race, its consequences would not necessarily be as bad as its critics assert. After all, although the naval preparations of Germany and Britain did certainly cost a great deal of money that could profitably have been spent on other things (social welfare, submarines or the army according to taste) and at times poisoned the international atmosphere, they had precious little to do with the actual outbreak of war in 1914, which was far more to do with the more general foreign policies of the powers, the limitations of contemporary diplomatic procedure and the constraining effect of army deployment plans. The Germans had in effect resigned themselves to losing the naval race. In the UK, Sir Edward Goschen, Ambassador to Berlin and many others were convinced that Britain's determination to outbuild Germany was actually good for sustained Anglo-German relations. It showed that liberal Britain had not become effete and soft; it deserved respect and its strength provided incentives for friendship.

Moreover, there is something to be said for the notion that in the 1930s the reluctance of Britain, France and the United States to respond appropriately to the military preparations of Japan and Germany and their preference instead for a strategy of relying on the beneficial effect of a series of arms-control treaties that Bernard Brodie described as 'faith, hope and parity'[67] was much more to blame for failing to prevent the outbreak of war in 1939 than was the Anglo-German naval arms race for the coming of war in 1914. From this point of view the eventual deployment of Chinese SSBNs to Ya Long in Hainan province might be considered a good thing in that it would provide China with a secure second strike capability likely actually to improve strategic stability in the area, and so becomes a contemporary example of the beneficial consequences of competitive naval modernisation.

Crucially, and despite the breathlessness of media coverage, the pace of apparent transformational change nowadays is much slower, and therefore more controllable, than it was in the Europe of the early twentieth century. HMS *Invincible*, the Royal Navy battlecruiser, commissioned in 1909 but was obsolescent by 1916 when it was sunk in the battle of Jutland. By contrast the carrier USS *Enterprise* that deployed for the Afghanistan campaign at the start of 2011 first saw active service in the Cuban missile crisis of 1962.[68] From this perspective, the naval arms race of the Pacific, if there is one, seems decidedly 'slow-motion' in comparison with the *Dreadnought* race of the early twentieth century. This reduces the prospect of naval arms development in the region encouraging inter-state conflict, although some aspects of that development, (most obviously submarine acquisition and development, the ongoing competition between the offensive and the defensive characteristics of naval missiles and cyberwar developments) clearly have the potential to increase it.

Looking to the future

There are some obvious indicators of how the maritime future of the Asia-Pacific region will unfold and what the consequences of naval modernisation in the area are likely to be. Expanding collaborative activities in defence of the sea-based trading system, and their institutionalisation in the holding of more exercises, naval visits and information sharing would suggest a trend away from the prospect of destabilising naval competition, especially if these were extended back from the Gulf of Aden and into the vexed shared areas of the South and East China Seas. An improved capacity to manage, if not resolve, these disputes would be also indicate the same kind of benign trajectory. On the other hand, continuing reluctance to participate in such collaborative activities, emerging evidence of a capacity to attack SLOCs rather than defend them along the lines of the 'Offshore Control' strategy discussed in Chapter Two,[69] the technological and strategic instabilities in the tension between the offensive and defensive characteristics of strategic deterrence and BMD, the overt deployment of assertive maritime power projection capabilities and acts of overt gunboat diplomacy in and around the islands of the Western Pacific would all do the reverse. The disproportionate development of anti-submarine or anti-air capabilities (which can only really be aimed at serious state adversaries) would also suggest a worrying trend if it led to a significant reduction in their capacity to collaborate.

Any sense that the world can therefore afford to be reasonably relaxed about naval developments in the Asia-Pacific region, would be going too far, for three separate reasons. The first is that at the moment there are few if any of the specific constraints on competitive naval development that emerged for example during the Cold War, and before, in the shape of arms control or incidents at sea agreements. For a variety of reasons, the US and Chinese navies have been unable to conclude any 'Incidents at Sea agreement' such as those negotiated with the Soviet Union during the Cold War, for example. Levels of transparency about naval intentions remain low, especially in China and Southeast Asia. Instead there is a wealth of neighbourly rhetoric and, to be fair, reasonable levels of cooperative endeavour against common threats such as piracy in the Straits of Malacca and so forth. It is debatable whether this provides sufficient defence against naval modernisation turning into destabilising competition at some future date.

Secondly, although the current state of naval modernisation in the region has not yet become a fully-fledged naval arms race, it clearly has the potential to do so and such a development were it to happen would at the very least not improve future prospects for cooperation, and would almost certainly worsen them. An important element here is that the public mood in all four of the countries is exhibiting an enthusiasm for active naval development and use not entirely dissimilar to the nationalistic *Dreadnought* fever of Britain and Germany before the First World War. Were this, aided by social networking sites, to become still stronger it might, in a crisis, force governments into more robust policies than they might otherwise wish.[70]

Lastly, the maritime nature of the Asia-Pacific region through its absolute dependence on sea-based trade, energy security and access to marine resources means that the answer to the question of whether a naval arms race is in prospect is fundamental to the future maritime security of the Asia-Pacific region and, because of the region's increasing economic weight to the rest of the world as well. If only because of the United States' consequently growing preoccupations with the Asia-Pacific and with the variety of strategic challenges that it faces there, the resultant naval balance in the region is likely to be a, possibly even the, major determinant of the world's strategic future. For that reason alone, naval developments in the Asia-Pacific region require the closest attention.

Notes

1. 'India Snubs Australia, US Move to Check China', *Times of India*, 2 December 2011.

2. *The National Military Strategy of the United States of America*, 8 February 2011, http://www.jcs.mil//content/files/2011-02/020811084800_2011_NMS_-_08_FEB_2011.pdf, p. 2.

3. An excellent point made by Desmond Ball, in 'Naval Acquisitions in Northeast Asia: Modernization or Arms Racing ?', unpublished notes for seminar on Enhancing Asia Maritime Security and Confidence Building Measures, Singapore, 26 January 2010.

4. Lee Seok-woo, 'Dokdo symbolizes Korea's Sovereignty', *Korea Times*, 3–4 November 2012.

5. Testimony of Ronald O'Rourke, Congressional Budget Service, before US-China Economic and Security Review Commission; 'Implications of China's Naval Modernization for the United States', 11 June 2009. The DDG-1000 was primarily seen as a land-attack ship, the *Arleigh Burkes* as a cheaper, much more versatile

and upgradable platform with considerable Air Defence utility.

6   The Independent Panel's report of 2010 report is accessible at http://www.usip.org/files/qdr/qdrreport.pdf. See pp. xiii, 58–60, 66.

7   Daniel Whiteneck et al., *The Navy at a Tipping Point: Maritime Dominance at Stake?* (Washington DC: Center for Naval Analyses, March 2010), p. 16.

8   I am indebted to Captain Barney Rubel of the US Naval War College, Newport for this insight.

9   'Japan Panel Moots Major Defence Policy Shift: Reports' Agence France-Presse, 27 July 2010; 'Japan's islet Defence Splits Residents', *Straits Times* 12 February 2011; Jonathan Holslag, *Trapped Giant: China's Military Rise*, Adelphi Paper 416(Abingdon: Routledge for the IISS, 2011), p. 80.

10 'Japan to Update its Defence Guidelines', *Straits Times*, 9 December 2010; Japan to Deploy Troops Near Disputed islands', *Straits Times*, 22 November 2010.

11 'Japan Struggling With Debt, Approves a $1 Trillion Budget', *New York Times*, 24 March 2010.

12 'China "Driving Japan Closer to US"', *Straits Times*, 10 March 2011.

13 Joshy M. Paul, Cooperative Security in the Indian Ocean Region', *RSIS Commentary* 55/27 May 2010.

14 'China "Water Dragon" to Explore Deepest Seas', *Daily Telegraph*, 16 July 2011.

15 Huiang Ruixin and Zhang Xibin, 'Understand Anew the Nature of Growth of China's Military Spending', *Jiefangjun Bao*, 2 February 2008, WNC 200802281477.1_bd770a06d055b297.

16 Kang Geng, 'Contribute to the Stability of China's Reform and Development: Military NPC Representatives Actively Discuss the Years' Government Work Report', *Jiefangjun Bao*, 6 April 2009, WNC 200904061477.1f70103a02cf7271b.

17 'PRC Defence minister Touts PLA's Achievements Under CPC in Past 60 years', Xinhua, 21 September 2009, WNC 2009090211477.1_860b00adef 8d198b.

18 Andrew Scobell, 'Discourse in 3-D: The PLA's Evolving Doctrine, Circa 2009', in Roy Kamphausen, David Lai and Andrew Scobell eds., *The PLA at Home and Abroad: Assessing the Operational Capabilities of China's Military* (Carlisle: Strategic Studies Institute, US Army War College, 2010), pp. 104–5, 110–17.

19 Chen Hui and Wang Jingguo, 'Promoting an Active Defense Military Strategy', *Liaowang*, 19 August 2008, WNC 200808191477.1_b310069f0d41f768.

20 A phrase used by the German Chancellor Bethman-Holweg to Lord Granville in October 1912 as quoted in Sir Edward Llewellyn Woodward, *Great Britain and the War of 1914–1918* (London: Methuen, 1967), p. 167.

21 Robert S Ross 'China's Naval Nationalism: Sources, Prospects, and the US Response', *International Security*, vol. 34, no. 20, Fall 2009, p. 64.

22 Deng Xiaoping, 'China Must take its Place in the Field of High Technology', in *Selected Works of Deng Xiaoping 1982–1992*, (Beijing: Foreign Languages Press, 1994), p. 273.

23 Statement of Adm. Jonathan Greenert to House Armed Services Committee, 16 February 2012, p. 7.

24 Most Americans today want the United States to be highly engaged in world affairs, while those favouring a constrained role remain in the minority. However, the percentage of Americans preferring a more limited U.S. role has grown over the past two years, rising to the highest level since 2001. This has occurred at the same time that the United States has ceased combat operations in Iraq and experienced a prolonged period of economic difficulty, events that might be expected to shift Americans' focus from global concerns to the home front. See Gallup Report, 'US Role in the World' at http://www.gallup.com/poll/116350/position-world.aspx.

25 For evidence see 'Mr Y', *A National Strategic Narrative*,(Washington DC: Brookings Institution, 2012 and Seth Crospey 'Anchors Away: Sea Power in Dry Dock', *World Affairs*, March/April 2012.

26 Timothy R. Heath, 'What Does China Want? Discerning the PRC's National Strategy', *Asian Security*, vol. 8, no. 1, 2012.

27 SIPRI Yearbook for 2010, p. 8, and SIPRI Military Expenditure Database. The domestic and political costs of these levels of defence spending, on the other hand are more difficult to calculate and may prove significantly less easy to bear.

28 Eberhard Sandschneider, Is China's Military Modernization a Concern for the EU ?' in Marcin Zaborowski, ed., *Facing China's Rise: Guidelines for an EU Strategy* (Paris: Institute for Security Studies, Chaillot Paper no. 94, 2006), pp.

40–41; Kishore Mahbubani, *The New Asian Hemisphere* (New York: Public Affairs, 2008), p. 105.

29 These figures and the comparisons that follow are from Robert Work [Now Assistant Secretary of the US Navy]: Robert Work, *The US Navy: Charting a Course for Tomorrow's Fleet* (Washington: CSBA, 2008)

30 Work, *The US Navy: Charting a Course for Tomorrow's Fleet*, pp. 7–12.

31 Sam J. Tangredi, *The Futures of War* (Bloomington, IN: Xlibris, 2008), p. 103

32 General James T. Conway, Admiral Gary Roughead, and Admiral Thad W. Allen, *A Cooperative Strategy for 21st Century Seapower* (Washington DC: Department of the Navy, 2007), October 2007.

33 Department of the Navy, 'The Navy Unmanned Surface Vehicle (USV) Master Plan', 23 July 2007; Ronald O'Rourke, *Navy Shipboard Lasers for Surface, Air and Missile Defense; Background and Issues for Congress*, Congressional Research Service Report, R41526, 19 October 2012.

34 Dennis Blair, *Annual Threat Assessment of the Intelligence Community for the Senate Select Committee on Intelligence*, 12 February 2009, SSCI ATA FEB 2009-IC Statement for the Record. (Washington: US Congress, 2009), p. 23.

35 Work, *The US Navy: Charting a Course for Tomorrow's Fleet*, p. 14

36 The Independent Panel's report of 2010 report is accessible at http://www.usip.org/files/qdr/qdrreport.pdf. See Secretary Gates, letter of 11 August 2010 to the Honorable Ike Skelton, Chairman House Armed Services Committee. 'Gates seeks

Pentagon Overhaul' *Defense News*, 8 May 2010; Michael J Mazarr, the Folly of 'Asymmetric War' *The Washington Quarterly*, Summer 2008.

37 Director, Warfare Integration (OPNAV N8F), Office of the Chief of Naval Operations, Report to Congress, February 2010, 'Annual Long-range Plan for the Construction of Naval Vessels for FY 2011', and Ronald O'Rourke, 'Navy Force Structure and Shipbuilding Plans: Background and Issues for Congress, 7-5700, April 6 2011; 'Budget Uncertainty Multiplies US Navy's Stress', *Defense News*, 11 April 2011; 'Twelve Ships Face Axe in US Budget Cuts.'

38 Joshua Stewart, 'Mideast crises Force US Navy To Keep Carriers at Sea Longer', *Defense News*, 30 July 2012; Sam Fellman, 'World Crises Challenge US Navy Deoployments', *Defense News*, 1 October 2012.

39 'Torrid Operational Pace Taxes US Navy' *Defense News*, 11 April 2011; 'Gates, Mullen Warn Cuts may Hollow US Military', *Defense News*, 20 June 2011; 'DoD Braces for $30B cut in '12', *Defence News*, 5 September 2011; SECNAV to SECDEF Memo on 'overhead efficiencies', November 2010

40 'Gates Questions USN's Future Structure', *Jane's Defence Weekly*, 12 May 2010. The extent of the likely relative US naval decline is explored in 'Conclusions: Transitions and Futures', in Geoffrey Till and Patrick C. Bratton, *Sea Power and the Asia-Pacific: The Triumph of Neptune?* (London: Routledge, 2011), pp. 237–68.

41 Work, *The US Navy: Charting a Course for Tomorrow's Fleet*, p. 71.

See also Chief of Naval Operations, Adm Gary Roughead, Remarks at the Navy League of Denver, 24 August 2010.

42 *Ibid.*, p. 4.

43 Testimony of Admiral Timothy J. Keating, Commander, US Pacific Command, before the House Armed Services Committee on the Posture of the Pacific Command, 12 March 2008.

44 For the dangers of such 'power transition' see Steve Chan, 'Exploring Puzzles in Power-transition Theory: Implications for Sino-American Relations', *Security Studies*, vol. 13, no. 3, pp. 103–41. This was also the thinking behind such books as Richard Bernstein and Ross H. Munro, *The Coming Conflict with China* (New York: Vintage, 1998) and Robert D. Kaplan, 'How we would fight China', *The Atlantic*, June 2005, pp. 49–64.

45 Wei Zhong and Fu Yu, 'China's Foreign Strategy: Constantly Deepening and Broadening', *Contemporary International Relations*, vol. 20, no. 2, March/April 2010, pp. 80–1.

46 Kenneth G. Lieberthal Wang Jsi, *Addressing US-China Strategic Distrust* (Washington: Brookings Institution, 2012); 'Rising U.S.-China Mistrust has Dangerous Long-term Implications, Brookings Study says', *Washington Post*, 3 April 2012.

47 Dr Henry A Kissinger, Keynote Address, 8th IISS Global Strategic Review, Geneva, 10 September 2010.

48 Speaking at Shangri-La Dialogue, 2011. *IISS News*, July 2011, p. 5. See also Bernard C. Cole, *The Great*

Wall at Sea (Annapolis, MD: Naval Institute Press, 2010, 2nd ed.), pp. 199–200.

49 The fact that China has still to purchase large numbers of aero-engines from Russia rather than make them domestically exemplifies the point; 'Russian Experts Skeptical About China's New J-20, *Jane's Defence Review*, 12 January 2011. General Gary North, Commander US Pacific Forces, has argued that the US has been flying the fifth generation F-22 *Raptor* for 15 years, and that three of its six squadrons are based in the Asia Pacific region. Interview, *Jane's Defence Weekly*, 20 July 2011.

50 Richard A. Bitzinger, 'China's Defense Technology and Industrial base in a Regional Context: Arms manufacturing in Asia', *Journal of Strategic Studies*, vol. 34, no. 3, June 2011, pp. 425–50.

51 Quoted in 'China Reveals Aircraft Carrier Ambitions', *Jane's Defence Review*, 5 January 2011.

52 Quoted in 'China Needs at Least Three Aircraft Carriers: General', Agence France-Presse, 30 July 2011.

53 'Be Ready to Fight, Hu Tells His Navy', *Straits Times*, 7 December 2011.

54 US Department of Defense, *Sustaining US Global leadership: Priorities for 21st Century Defense*, 5 January 2012, p. 3.

55 'Full text of Barack Obama's speech to Australian Parliament' at http://www.smh.com.au/national/text-of-obamas-speech-to-parliament-20111117-1nkcw.html;___see also Hillary Clinton, 'America's Pacific Century' *Foreign Policy*, November 2011. Ching Cheong, 'Beijing Wary

of Overseas Uncertainty', *Straits Times*, 22 November 2011. Xue Litai, 'The Role That US Plays in Asia', *China Times*, 24 November 2011.

56 A point well made by Ambassador Tommy Koh, key-note address, RSIS, Conference on Engaging the US: Asia-Pacific Responses' Singapore, 2 December 2011.

57 'Biden Says China Rise Not America's Demise', Agence France-Presse, 8 September 2011.

58 Michael S. Chase, 'Chinese Suspicion and US Intentions', *Survival*, vol. 51, no. 3, June–July 2011.

59 'Gates Denies US Wants to 'Hold China Down', Agence France-Presse, 2 June 2011.

60 Cited in Chase, 'Chinese Suspicion and US Intentions', p. 145.

61 'China Military Build-up No Threat: Senior Army Official', Agence France-Presse, 1 June 2011. See also General Liang Guanglie, Minister of National Defense China at the 10th IISS Asian Security Summit, 5 June 2011.

62 'China Will Not Challenge US militarily', *Straits Times*, 20 May 2011; 'General says US Inflates China Threat', *Wall Street Journal*, 20 May 2011.

63 Mark Thomson, 'Trends in US Defence Spending: Implications for Australia', Paper 56, Australian Strategic Policy Institute, 16 March 2010.

64 S.D. Muni, 'India's Look-East Policy: the Strategic Dimension' ISAS Working Paper No.121, 1 February 2011.

65 See President Obama's speech to the Indian parliament of November 2010 at http://ibnlive.in.com/news/

full-text-of-obamas-parliament-address/134649-3.html.

66 Thus Germany would only agree to respond to Churchill's offer of a building holiday on condition that some of its political objectives were met; Colin Gray, *Weapons Don't Make War* (Lawrence, KS: University of Kansas Press, 1993), cited in John H. Maurer, 'Churchill's Naval Holiday', *Journal of Strategic Studies*, vol. 5, no.1, January 1992, pp. 119–25.

67 Bernard Brodie, *Sea Power in the Machine Age* (Princeton, NJ: Princeton University Press, 1941), p. 336.

68 Adm. Gary Roughead, then Chief of Naval operations, remarks at the Hudson Institute, Washington DC, November 16 2010.

69 J. Noel Williams, 'Air–Sea Battle: An Operational Concept Looking For a Strategy,' *Armed Forces Journal*, September 2011; T.X. Hammes, 'Offshore Control: A Proposed Strategy for an Unlikely Conflict', INSS Strategic Forum, National Defense University, June 2012.

70 'Tokyo's Foreign Policies Under Fire in Latest Polls', *Straits Times*, 8 November 2010; 'Coastguard Video Riles Japanese Lawmakers' *Straits Times*, 2 November 2010; Kan Government Rapped As 'Weak-Kneed', *Straits Times*, 4 November 2010.

Fig 1 **Top ten defence budgets**

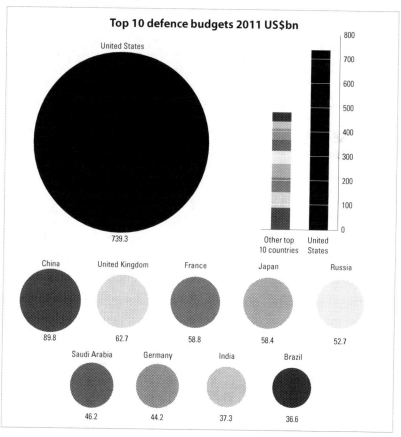

Top 10 defence budgets 2011 US$bn

United States
739.3

Other top 10 countries | United States

China
89.8

United Kingdom
62.7

France
58.8

Japan
58.4

Russia
52.7

Saudi Arabia
46.2

Germany
44.2

India
37.3

Brazil
36.6

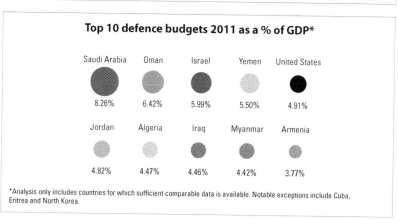

Top 10 defence budgets 2011 as a % of GDP*

Saudi Arabia
8.26%

Oman
6.42%

Israel
5.99%

Yemen
5.50%

United States
4.91%

Jordan
4.82%

Algeria
4.47%

Iraq
4.46%

Myanmar
4.42%

Armenia
3.77%

*Analysis only includes countries for which sufficient comparable data is available. Notable exceptions include Cuba, Eritrea and North Korea.

Source: *The Military Balance 2012*

Fig 2 **Naval fleets**

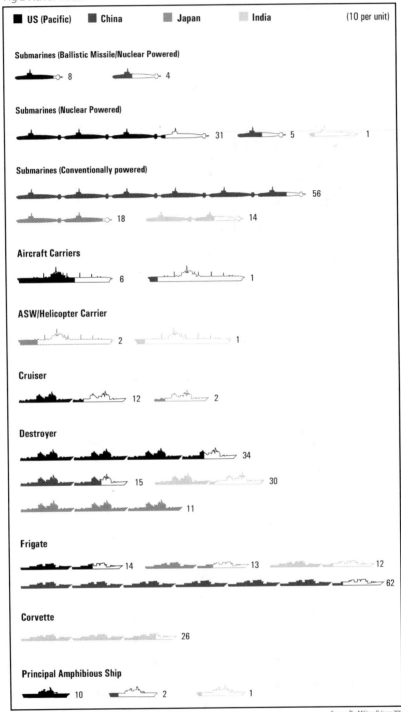

Source: *The Military Balance 2012*

Table 1 **Defence budget as % of GDP: India, US, China, Japan** US dollars, 2011

	% of GDP	Budget
US	4.91%	(793.bn of 15.1tr)
China	1.26%	(89.9 bn of 7.06 tr)
Japan	0.99%	(58.4bn of 5.89 tr)
India	1.68%	(31.9bn of tr 1.89)

Source: *The Military Balance 2012*

Adelphi books are published eight times a year by Routledge Journals, an imprint of Taylor & Francis, 4 Park Square, Milton Park, Abingdon, Oxfordshire OX14 4RN, UK.

A subscription to the institution print edition, ISSN 1944-5571, includes free access for any number of concurrent users across a local area network to the online edition, ISSN 1944-558X. Taylor & Francis has a flexible approach to subscriptions enabling us to match individual libraries' requirements. This journal is available via a traditional institutional subscription (either print with free online access, or online-only at a discount) or as part of the Strategic, Defence and Security Studies subject package or Strategic, Defence and Security Studies full text package. For more information on our sales packages please visit www.tandfonline.com/librarians_pricinginfo_journals.

2013 Annual Adelphi Subscription Rates			
Institution	£557	$979 USD	€824
Individual	£199	$338 USD	€270
Online only	£487	$857 USD	€721

Dollar rates apply to subscribers outside Europe. Euro rates apply to all subscribers in Europe except the UK and the Republic of Ireland where the pound sterling price applies. All subscriptions are payable in advance and all rates include postage. Journals are sent by air to the USA, Canada, Mexico, India, Japan and Australasia. Subscriptions are entered on an annual basis, i.e. January to December. Payment may be made by sterling cheque, dollar cheque, international money order, National Giro, or credit card (Amex, Visa, Mastercard).

For a complete and up-to-date guide to Taylor & Francis journals and books publishing programmes, and details of advertising in our journals, visit our website: http://www.tandfonline.com.

Ordering information:
USA/Canada: Taylor & Francis Inc., Journals Department, 325 Chestnut Street, 8th Floor, Philadelphia, PA 19106, USA. **UK/Europe/Rest of World:** Routledge Journals, T&F Customer Services, T&F Informa UK Ltd., Sheepen Place, Colchester, Essex, CO3 3LP, UK.

Advertising enquiries to:
USA/Canada: The Advertising Manager, Taylor & Francis Inc., 325 Chestnut Street, 8th Floor, Philadelphia, PA 19106, USA. Tel: +1 (800) 354 1420. Fax: +1 (215) 625 2940. **UK/Europe/Rest of World**: The Advertising Manager, Routledge Journals, Taylor & Francis, 4 Park Square, Milton Park, Abingdon, Oxfordshire OX14 4RN, UK. Tel: +44 (0) 20 7017 6000. Fax: +44 (0) 20 7017 6336.

Printed in the United States
by Baker & Taylor Publisher Services